TWENTIETH CENTURY VIEWS

The aim of this series is to present the best in
contemporary critical opinion on major authors,
providing a twentieth century perspective on
their changing status in an era of profound
revaluation.

Maynard Mack, *Series Editor*
Yale University

O'NEILL

A COLLECTION OF CRITICAL ESSAYS

Edited by

John Gassner

A SPECTRUM BOOK

Prentice-Hall, Inc. *Englewood Cliffs, N.J.*

Current printing (last digit):

11

© 1964 BY PRENTICE-HALL, INC.

ENGLEWOOD CLIFFS, N.J.

LIBRARY OF CONGRESS CATALOG CARD NO.: 64-19679

Printed in the United States of America—C

P 63426
C 63427

Table of Contents

vii

O'NEILL

Introduction

by John Gassner

The stature of Eugene O'Neill casts a long shadow on the American theater. Whether it stretches or contracts in the critical estimates of a particular period or critic, this much is certain: the height and breadth of the American theater is measured by it. Find fault with O'Neill and you find fault with the entire American stage; find merit in him and you find worth in its striving, or straining, toward significant drama. It is possible to single out American playwrights endowed with greater refinement and facility than can be attributed to him but none who made a comparable impression on the twentieth century. Chiefly as a result of his persistent efforts after 1915, the American drama actually *entered* the century and made contributions to world theater that could be considered significantly modern.

Like other pioneers he had the proper temperament for adventure. He was too restive to be content with the familiar terrain, which in his case was the commercial American theater of private management and production for profit. Its literary pretensions were, in the main, Victorian and genteel; their effeteness deserved his scorn. Its popular offerings consisted chiefly of roughhouse farces and prefabricated melodramas; their assumptions of mindless joviality and one-sided moralism on the part of the public earned his contempt. Its few and tentative displays of serious drama could not satisfy or conciliate him; they offered one-dimensional glimpses of character that could but appear laughable to so complex and driven a man as the young O'Neill. The small number of plays which indicted political corruption and capitalistic greed could not greatly impress him (despite his early socialistic leanings) because they were reformatory while he was rebellious; they were committed to temporizing optimism while he devoted himself to uncompromising pessimism. It was to the Greek tragic poets and to the sultry Strindberg, rather than to any American predecessors, that O'Neill had to turn for company during his convalescence from tuberculosis and for example in the pursuit of his emphatically elected career as a modern dramatist.

1

It is no exaggeration to say that he had to leave the American theater in order to reorient and invigorate it.

Significantly, he had such venturesome associates in this enterprise as the visionary scenic artist Robert Edmond Jones, the critic Kenneth Macgowan, the playwright Susan Glaspell, and George Cram Cook, the founder of the Provincetown Players. In collaboration with them in 1915, O'Neill established the Provincetown Players—one of the two important experimental groups located in Greenwich Village that revolutionized the American theater. He wrote most of his early plays for that group, and fortunately when its always precarious existence came to an end after a decade, he could bring his exacting dramatic experiments to the flourishing Theatre Guild, an offshoot of the Washington Square Players, the other important little Greenwich Village theater, which went "uptown" in 1919 and became the country's leading professional producing company. In this way O'Neill's highly individual strivings gained organizational support strong enough to establish him as the foremost American playwright, and to facilitate his acquiring the international reputation that brought him the Nobel Prize and numerous stage productions abroad.

Several factors operated in favor of O'Neill's career. One of these was the fact that as the son of the successful actor-manager James O'Neill and an occasional actor and stage manager in his father's productions, he directed his energies into playwriting after some early endeavors in journalism and poetry. He acquired a strong aptitude for dramatic writing and theatrical effect. He was able to compensate for his defects as a writer with the power of his stage action; had he elected to write novels and been forced to rely on description and narration rather than dramatization and visualization, he might have proved a second-rate author. And had he been constrained to express his restiveness and disorientation in lyric terms his romantic emotionalism and infelicitous phrasing might have made an awkward minor poet of him. His penchant for the sentimental poetry of the eighteen-nineties would have dated him by 1920, if not even earlier. Dramatic action, pictorial composition, and sound-effects such as the beating of the tom-toms in *The Emperor Jones* concealed or minimized his literary infelicities, and sustained his intense—often, indeed, over-intense—dramatic intentions.

His chosen medium, the theater, was, moreover, open to him in America and sorely needed him. It had gone as far as it could in drawing on its old resources and was, in fact, falling behind its cosmopolitan public in intellectual substance and behavioral sophistication. That public had had enough of Victorian conformity and Main Street complacency; it was ready for the social and esthetic rebel. Out of intellectual curiosity made exigent by private tensions he brought to the American stage forceful exhibitions and analyses of character that modernized its content. The growing vogue in America of Freudian views on sex, Jungian concepts of racial memory, anti-Puritanism in morals and mores, reactions against middle-class materialism, and postwar disillusion with received values and factitious liberal promises—all these and related factors needed to be expressed in the theater. O'Neill represented them on the stage, and so introduced a modern and timely content into the American drama.

He was able to do so, however, not merely because he had a general talent for dramatization, but because he employed the resources of the modern theater as developed abroad. Along with his associates of the Provincetown and Washington Square companies he made use of the two overlapping developments in dramatic art without which modernism in the Western theater is inconceivable. The first of these was subsumed under realism in general and naturalism—the naturalism of Strindberg —particularly. A development already overfamiliar to Europeans when O'Neill started to write, naturalism was relatively new to the American public. Flavoring it with the colloquial speech of the sea and the land, and thus paralleling the use of regional dialect by Synge and other leaders of the Abbey Theatre in Dublin, O'Neill brought to a head a belated naturalistic trend in the American drama. Early in his career, and considerably before the Depression drama of the 1930s, he introduced an anti-genteel and seemingly authentic reality to the American stage with *Beyond the Horizon, Anna Christie,* and *Desire Under the Elms,* as well as a number of effective one-act plays.

But O'Neill, discontented with realism as a routine style, and as aware as his associates Macgowan and Jones that it had been supplanted in the advanced European theaters by the more imaginative styles of symbolism and expressionism, carried out a second revolution in the American theater almost simultaneously with the first. By 1920 he had begun the experimental phase of his work. Successive productions of *The Emperor Jones, The Hairy Ape,* and *The Great God Brown* led to his being identified with the avant-garde "Art Theater" movement initiated earlier in Europe by the latter-day Strindberg of *The Dream Play* and *The Ghost Sonata,* Gordon Craig, Max Reinhardt, and other proponents of symbolist and expressionist stylization. Unwilling to remain the captive of any single style and undaunted by practical considerations, moreover, he pressed on to fulfill the cyclopean intentions he entertained in *Lazarus Laughed, Strange Interlude,* and *Mourning Becomes Electra,* composing huge plays and recovering in modernized form the chorus, the aside, and the trilogy for the stage before going into well-earned retirement in

1935. When he began to return to the stage a decade later it became evident moreover that he had renounced none of his ambitions for the drama during his isolation. And in the two major surviving plays, *The Iceman Cometh* and *A Long Day's Journey into Night,* as well as a number of minor ones, it was evident that, like the twentieth century theater as a whole, he had not forsaken modern realism once and for all. Instead, his return to this still viable style of drama, deepened by his introspective and ruminative temperament, accounted for two of his least vulnerable plays.

O'Neill's experiments, which sometimes ended in disaster, and his waverings between one style and another proved unsettling to critics. His work has posed a problem of some difficulty to criticism—that of arriving at a just estimate of a writer who has been disproportionately effective on the stage and disappointing in print. It has also been necessary to determine the degree to which his achievements matched his often egregious intentions, and ultimately to establish his place in the theater, whether in the company of the world's major dramatists or in that of the less fortunate playwrights who fell short of their ambitions and frustrated the hopes reposed in them by contemporary partisans. The present collection of analysis and opinion presents the reader with some of the points of the discussion which has already engendered heat as well as light and is not likely to be concluded within the foreseeable future.

Although O'Neill had immense integrity as an artist, he cannot be considered an integrated writer. It is therefore hardly surprising that there should have been fluctuations in his reputation and that critics should have been divided in their estimates of his work. For some of his critics, the playwrights Virgil Geddes and St. John Ervine among others, he was too melodramatic (this may have been the brunt of Shaw's reference to him as "a banshee Shakespeare"), whereas Broadway reviewers, notably Robert Benchley, were impressed with the strong pulse of his plots and playwriting. Some of his critics considered his want of distinguished language a fault beyond repair (Mary McCarthy, who denied that he possessed "the slightest ear for the word, the sentence, the speech . . . ," exclaimed "How is one to judge the great logical symphony of a tone-deaf musician?") while others were troubled by the defect, as Joseph Wood Krutch was, only to the extent that it prevented them from assigning to O'Neill a position in world drama comparable to that of the theater's greatest masters. And here it should be noted that the lines of defense have ranged all the way from those who, like Lionel Abel, commend O'Neill's command of convincing dialogue to those who hold with Krutch that he had a writer's "one indispensable gift" of being able to convey "the situation, the characters, and above all the depth of his concern with them," [1] and those who took proper cognizance of his ability to achieve a "poetry of the theater" without verbal virtuosity. This subject is given detailed treatment here in Robert F. Whitman's essay, "O'Neill's Search for a 'Language of the Theater.' " Alan Downer also advanced an argument on O'Neill's behalf when he wrote in *Theatre Arts* magazine (February 1951) that "If to judge an artist is to evaluate his use of his medium, we must observe not so much the dramatist's words as his characters-in-action and, in the modern theater, his handling of the more mechanical resources of the stage."

Some critics found his artistic ambitions extravagant while others considered them laudable and at least moderately fulfilled. His probing into the murky depths of character, into the strained and divided psyche, failed to impress some commentators (Eric Bentley, the most penetrative of them, ranked him well below Strindberg and Wedekind in this respect) while overawing others. And although the Freudian and Jungian elements in his work seemed too arbitrary or schematic (a fault no doubt in *Strange Interlude* and *Mourning Becomes Electra*), the defense could contend, as W. David Sievers did in *Freud on Broadway,* that O'Neill enriched the drama with his insights and with the techniques of projecting them.

O'Neill's outlook on life was no less subject to praise and blame. He was insufficiently spiritual for religious critics and too metaphysical and passive for Marxists; and while both could deplore his pessimism, others had no difficulty in approving his huge despair as salutary defiance of facile American optimism or as existentialist truth. For Joseph Wood Krutch, in his *Modernism in the Modern Drama,* O'Neill's distinction derived chiefly from his "determination to confer upon man a tragic dignity."

At the same time, friends of the playwright denied that he was consistently morose and depressing. Insofar as a critic found tragedy in O'Neill's work he could not but find exhilaration in it as well. Even in conceding that O'Neill seemed to have succumbed completely to nihilism in *The Iceman Cometh,* Krutch went out of his way to contend that "No spectator who has followed his work one after another . . . is likely to suppose that such pessimistic views are a constant, or in my opinion the most striking aspect of his work." George Jean Nathan maintained that O'Neill was well supplied with a sense of humor and a zest for life in spite of his tragic outlook and posture. In the present collec-

[1] Review of O'Neill's *A Touch of the Poet* in the *New York Times* Book Review of September 22, 1957.

tion, Travis Bogard makes an excellent argument for a comic impulse in *Anna Christie,* and there is further evidence of humor, ranging from the finely comedic to the grotesquely raffish, in *Ah, Wilderness!, The Iceman Cometh,* and *A Moon for the Misbegotten.*

O'Neill's dividedness and the dividedness of his critics have afforded occasions for lively comment and for considerable illumination of his work. It is necessary only to warn those who intend to make a thorough study of the subject that there is much more material available in a large number of sources (the bibliography should be of some help here), and that since O'Neill's work was written for the stage rather than for the study it is essential for the student to consult reviews of the original productions of the plays and the important revivals, and above all, to attend or perform in the plays themselves.

Eugene O'Neill and the Escape
from the Château d'If

by John Henry Raleigh

Two of Eugene O'Neill's boyish acts of aggression against his father were peculiarly symbolic. On the base of the handsome, polished balustrade of the family summer home in New London, Connecticut, he carved a large and disfiguring "M. C." (standing for "Monte Cristo"), and he poured a can of green paint into a box containing some metal statuettes depicting James O'Neill in his role of Edmund Dantes in *The Count of Monte Cristo*.[1] If the boy believed in witchcraft, and he probably did, he was destroying or mutilating his father by these acts of vandalism, for James O'Neill's entire life, and the life of his family, was dominated by his role in *The Count of Monte Cristo*. He had already been playing it for five years when Eugene O'Neill was born, and Doris Alexander in her biography of the playwright speculates that the words "Monte Cristo" must have been among the first words that Eugene O'Neill ever heard. We know that he grew up hearing about the play, watching it being rehearsed, and seeing it performed. Later on he was to play a small part in it himself. James O'Neill played the role more than six thousand times; it earned him some $800,000, but it used up an acting talent that at one time anyway was thought to be of the first order. He began playing Dantes in 1883; by 1908 he declared that he was as much a prisoner of the Château d'If as Dantes ever was.

James O'Neill was the fourth of six children in an Irish family that had immigrated to America in 1856. His early life was one of grinding poverty, the father having deserted the family and gone back to Ireland

"Eugene O'Neill and the Escape from the Château d'If" by John Henry Raleigh. A paper presented at the English Institute, Columbia University, September 1963. Copyright © 1964 by John Henry Raleigh. Printed by permission of the author.
[1] Barbara and Arthur Gelb, *O'Neill* (New York, 1962), p. 84. Another version of the "M. C." on the balustrade was that it was done by boyish vandals, after the O'Neills had departed the premises.

to die. The essential story is told, quite movingly, by James Tyrone in Act IV of *Long Day's Journey into Night*. James O'Neill drifted casually into acting but soon realized it was his destiny. In an age of such great actors as Forrest, Jefferson, and Booth—all of whom O'Neill played with and held his own with—he promised to become one of the most eminent. He knew Shakespeare by heart; he had overcome his brogue; he had good looks, personal charm, a regal bearing, great ambitions, and a splendid voice—"my organ," he called it jokingly. But, like the characters in his son's plays, he was finally balked—by fate, by circumstance, and by himself. The tragedies of James O'Neill's private life have been stressed by his son in *Long Day's Journey into Night*. But, his professional life was, if possible, an even greater tragedy. One of the many reasons that James O'Neill admired Booth was precisely because Booth had managed to surmount private disasters enough to pursue his professional career, always with an admirable reticence about his personal life. But James O'Neill had to add, to his wife's narcotic addiction and to the monumental dissipations and failures of his two sons, the knowledge that his great dramatic gifts had never been fully realized.

On his death bed, agonized by a lingering cancer to which his superb physique long refused to yield, he mumbled to his son: "Eugene—I'm going to a better sort of life—this sort of life—here—all froth—no good —rottenness!" (Gelbs, p. 431) For he had been trapped, as surely as Eugene O'Neill's tragic protagonists are trapped in their respective ways, by the stage version of the Dumas novel. The money he could never resist, and anyway when he tried other roles, serious ones, his audience disappeared. He was finally forced to drain the cup to the last dregs. In 1911, when he was sixty-five years old, he took Dantes on his last tour. The play was by now a tabloid version, condensed below the level of lucidity and merely one of the "acts" in a vaudeville show. It invoked only nostalgia in the audience. Both of his sons, for whom the tour was a prolonged alcoholic binge, were playing parts—no other manager would have hired them—and were given to crude jokes on the stage at their father's expense. He brought his wife, usually in a morphine stupor, to the theater every day because he was afraid to leave her alone in the hotel room. Sometimes she waited in the wings and would become rapt at one of the climactic moments of the play—at the end of Act IV when Mercedes reveals to Dantes, by now the Count, that Albert is their son. At this point Ella O'Neill would begin to move toward the stage like a sleepwalker. She never actually arrived on the stage, but the threat always added to her husband's sense of harassment. In February 1912 *Variety* carried the news that the tour was ended. The Count was finally dead and a splendid acting talent with it.

It is clear, then, that *The Count of Monte Cristo* was not only the millstone around the neck of James O'Neill; it was also all tied up with the life of his family and with its various tragedies: the drunken, irresponsible, vengeful sons misplaying their roles while the stupefied mother haunted the wings like a ghost and the old man, past his prime, tried to hold together a mutilated version of what had been at best only a good melodrama.

That Eugene O'Neill as a playwright was in rebellion against all that *The Count of Monte Cristo* stood for—melodrama, sentiment, easy popularity, stage tricks, cardboard characters, stale rhetoric—is all too obvious. What is not so apparent is how deeply *The Count* was stamped on his creative imagination. His father always obsessed him, and it was impossible to conceive of his father without his father's alter ego, Edmund Dantes. Like his own carving on the balustrade in the house in New London, like the green paint on the statuettes, it was all there, inescapably and almost inexpugnably. If consciously he thought his inspiration derived from Nietzsche, Dostoevski, and Strindberg, which to a considerable degree it did, unconsciously he was often projecting variations on *The Count of Monte Cristo* throughout the whole first part of his creative life.

As a playwright O'Neill had at least two careers. The first career, by which he gained his fame, was played under the shadow of the Château d'If; the second—the one that incorporates *The Iceman Cometh, Long Day's Journey,* and the other late masterpieces—represents, among other things, *his* final escape from the dungeon in which his father lay. I shall confine myself here to the first phase or career, where the imprint of *Monte Cristo* can be most clearly seen. Further, it should be emphasized that what are being discussed here are not the good plays—and there are many in O'Neill's first career—nor the bad parts of the good ones, nor the good parts of the bad ones, but, by and large, the bad parts of the bad ones. The point, of course, is that O'Neill was at his worst when closest to *The Count of Monte Cristo.* A corollary point, often overlooked, is that O'Neill, reader of Strindberg and student of Nietzsche, also had strong roots in the popular stage tradition of the nineteenth century.[2]

James O'Neill's *The Count of Monte Cristo,* which he purchased in

---

[2] Doris Alexander observes that O'Neill learned much from his father's career: "From watching rehearsals, Eugene learned the value of 'strong situations,' as his father called them: Father and son about to fight, not knowing their relationship *(Monte Cristo);* brother against brother *(The Two Orphans, When Greek Meets Greek);* the husband whose child has been begotten by a trusted friend *(The Manxman).* He would use such situations in his own plays—more meaningfully perhaps, but just as surely for their dramatic value." *The Tempering of Eugene O'Neill* (New York, 1962), p. 84.

1885 and hence earned exclusive rights to, was adapted by Charles Fechter and was known as the "Fechter version." Fechter's *Monte Cristo* is a model nineteenth century melodrama, and because it was so deeply interwoven into Eugene O'Neill's life, it serves as a kind of implausible bridge between the popular culture of nineteenth century middle-class America and the art of America's greatest and most original playwright. Fechter's play has five acts and six scenes; and one is immediately reminded of the great numbers of acts and scenes of many of O'Neill's plays in the Twenties and Thirties.[3] Act I begins in 1815 and takes three scenes to describe how Dantes is sent to the Château d'If, torn from the arms of Mercedes just after their marriage and with her already pregnant with his child. Guilty in one way or another in the plot against Dantes are the three villains: Fernand, Danglars, and de Villefort. Eighteen years pass between Acts I and II, during which Albert, the son of Dantes and Mercedes, is born and grows up, unaware of who his father is, and Dantes lies in prison. Acts II, III, IV, and V describe Dantes' escape from the Château d'If, his assumption of the wealth and title of Monte Cristo, his revenge on Fernand, Danglars, and de Villefort, his discovery of his son, and his reunion with Mercedes.

The high points of the play as a melodrama were two theatrical flourishes, to which, presumably, James O'Neill gave his all. The first, and most celebrated, occurred in the miniscule scene 3 of Act II when Dantes makes his escape. The scene is a platform of the Château d'If at night. Two jailers appear carrying a sack, which they think contains the body of a dead man but which actually holds Dantes. The jailers remark on the bad weather, swing the sack into the ocean, and disappear inside the prison. The moon breaks out, lighting up a projecting rock, and Dantes rises from the sea. He is dripping (with salt and sawdust), has a knife in his hand, and, on the rock (a stool), exclaims: "Saved! Mine, the treasures of Monte Cristo! The world is mine!" (One theatergoer interviewed by the Gelbs for their biography of O'Neill professed to have seen this scene forty or fifty times over a twenty-five year period, and always to have found a fresh joy in it.) Years later Eugene O'Neill was to say:

---

[3] Dumas himself "O'Neilled" O'Neill in his own dramatization of his novel. The Dumas version, presented in London in 1848, had twenty acts, thirty-seven tableaus, 221 scenes, and fifty-nine characters. It took two evenings to perform. The opening night audience rioted. J. B. Rusak, ed., *America's Lost Plays* (Princeton, 1941), XVI, 3. There are other incidental ironies in the relationship between *Monte Cristo* and Eugene O'Neill. For example, when Charles Fechter played the role in October 1868, the first name of the actress who portrayed Mercedes was "Carlotta." *Ibid.*

I can still see my father dripping with salt and sawdust, climbing on a stool behind the swinging profile of dashing waves. It was then the calcium lights in the gallery played on his long beard and tattered clothes, as with arms outstretched he declared the world was his.[4]

The other flourish was James O'Neill's equally celebrated "One! Two! Three!" uttered at the ends of Acts III ("One!") and V ("Two! Three!"), as each of his enemies falls dead. Each act ended in a thunderclap: Dantes sent to prison (Act I); "The world is mine!" (Act II); "One!" (Act III); Mercedes' revelation to Dantes that Albert is their son (Act IV); "Two!" "Three!" and the revelation to Albert that Dantes is his father (Act V). The ending of the play in particular was meant to be a series of melodramatic hammer-strokes. Only Danglars, the deepest dyed villain, is still alive, and although Dantes knows that Albert is his son Albert does not know that Dantes is his father:

Dang. Have at thee! [*lunging at him*]
Edmund. Die! [*runs him through*]
Dang. Ha! [*dies and rolls at his feet*]
Edmund. "Three!"
Merc. Your prayers have saved your father's life, Albert—you are his son!

CURTAIN

This likable, implausible old pot-boiler meant almost as much to Eugene O'Neill as Nietzsche, although he would have been the last to admit it. Occasionally, however, O'Neill's preoccupation with *The Count of Monte Cristo* became explicit. Once he declared, "I know more about a trap door than any son of a bitch in the theatre." (Gelbs, p. 568) Again, William Zorach, the sculptor and painter, who designed some of the settings for the Provincetown Players when O'Neill was getting his start, remembered that O'Neill's concept for staging *Thirst,* a one-act play of the sea, by using a sea cloth with someone wriggling around underneath it, was suspiciously and uncomfortably like the Château d'If scene in *Monte Cristo.* (Gelbs, p. 313) Occasionally reviewers picked up echoes. Heywood Broun described *Desire Under the Elms* as a piece of "theatricality" eminently worthy of the son of the man who played *The Count of Monte Cristo* so many times, and noting

---

[4] Alexander, p. 184. John V. A. Weaver spoke of "how Gene's earliest delight was to make the canvas waves into which his father, the unforgettable Count of Monte Cristo, dived. . . ." "I Knew Him When," *O'Neill and His Plays,* ed. Oscar Cargill, N. Bryllion Fagin, and William J. Fisher (New York, 1961), pp. 26-29.

that *Desire* was a revenge-play like *Monte Cristo,* said that it would have been possible to count " 'one, two, three' as this new tale of vengeance clicked into certain old and well worn grooves." (Gelbs, p. 570) And Robert Benchley's review of *Mourning Becomes Electra* conjured up an old actor with a white wig and drawn sword standing in the wings and exhorting: "That's good, son! Give 'em the old Theatre!" (Gelbs, p. 753) although, unlike Broun, Benchley meant it as a compliment. In his review of *Dynamo* Benchley remarked that, "the royal blood of the *Count of Monte Cristo,* which is always with Mr. O'Neill . . . gives him the power to throw a dramatic spot-light on all his works so that the lurid glow of the theatre lies over his dullest passages." [5]

More specifically, the "Fechter version" affected the content, the technique, the rhetoric, and the rhythm of many of the plays of O'Neill's first career. It likewise affected the content of the projected and unfinished cycle plays. O'Neill was once asked to do a modern version of *Monte Cristo* and seriously considered doing it, but this most interesting of dramatic possibilities remained only that.

The links in content between *Monte Cristo* and O'Neill's plays are so obvious that they can be easily overlooked. In the first place, as a revenge play, *Monte Cristo* was the prototype for *Abortion, The Sniper, The Rope, The Emperor Jones, Desire Under the Elms, The Great God Brown,* and *Mourning Becomes Electra.* This is not to mention so many other plays where revenge appears but is not the main-spring of the plot; or plays in which revenge is frustrated, as it is for Con Melody in *A Touch of the Poet* or for Yank in *The Hairy Ape;* or those in which revenge is contemplated but not pursued, as in the case of Mat Burke in *Anna Christie.* Indeed the whole relationship between the sexes in O'Neill's world is pervaded by the idea of revenge, as is the psychology of so many of the major characters—for example, the impossible Nina in *Strange Interlude.* The revenge motif, of course, is one of the most basic, elemental, and satisfying of dramatic devices; it is at the heart of Greek and Elizabethan tragedy. But it is doubtful if it plays such a seminal role in any other modern playwright as it does in O'Neill, and certainly *The Count* is at least in part responsible for this preoccupation.

Secondly, *Monte Cristo* was an historical play. The first act explains that Dantes, who is a ship captain, had stopped at Elba on his way back to France and received a secret missive from Napoleon, and it is Dantes'

---

[5] Robert Benchley, "Dynamo," *O'Neill and His Plays,* p. 188. There have been many other instances of this kind of observation about O'Neill. For example, Bernard De Voto, in an attack on O'Neill: "(With an overtone from many generations of sure-fire stuff, and the ghost of Monte Cristo raising a finger aloft and intoning 'One'!)" *ibid.,* p. 306.

involvement with this high-level skullduggery that gets him into trouble. So too O'Neill, while we think of him as a playwright of the contemporary American scene, was actually as much or more, and increasingly so during the latter part of his career, an historical dramatist. In fact it could be argued that his best plays are the historical ones. Nearly all his early plays dealt with contemporary life although usually in an unusual or exotic setting: an open boat, the bowels of a tramp steamer, and so on. His first full-length produced play, *Beyond the Horizon* (1918), is not precisely dated but could well take place in nineteenth century or, at the latest, early twentieth century rural America. Of all the plays he wrote after this, only a few can be described as contemporary, i.e., as dealing with the life of the period during which they were written. The principal ones in this category are *The Straw* (1918-19); *Anna Christie* (1920); *The First Man* (1921); *The Hairy Ape* (1921); *Welded* (1922-23); *Strange Interlude* (1926-27); *Dynamo* (1929); and *Days Without End* (1932-33). *All God's Chillun Got Wings* (1923) and *The Great God Brown* (1925) also deal with modernity, but have their beginnings and roots set back in the late nineteenth or early twentieth century. All the other plays take place in history, near or distant (the first dates for each play indicate the year or years when O'Neill was writing it, and the second dates indicate the time of the action itself): *Diff'rent* (1920; 1890-1920); *The Fountain* (1921-22; late fifteenth and early sixteenth century); *Desire Under the Elms* (1924; 1850); *Marco Millions* (1923-25; late thirteenth and early fourteenth century); *Lazarus Laughed* (1925-26; c. A.D. 37); *Mourning Becomes Electra* 1929-31; 1865-66); *Ah, Wilderness!* (1932; 1906); *A Touch of the Poet* (1935-42; 1828); even the last masterpieces are really historical: *The Iceman Cometh* (1939; 1912); *Long Day's Journey into Night* (1939-41; 1912); *Hughie* (1941-42; 1928); and *A Moon for the Misbegotten* (1943; 1923).

O'Neill's "histories" actually fall into four categories: the historical exotics about the distant past like *Lazarus Laughed, The Fountain,* or *Marco Millions;* those about the American nineteenth century like *Desire under the Elms* or *Mourning Becomes Electra;* those about the "remembered" past like *The Iceman Cometh* or *Long Day's Journey;* and finally the contemplated cycle plays about the fate and fortunes of a Yankee-Irish family in America from the eighteenth century to the twentieth century, of which only *A Touch of the Poet* survives.

For this retreat into the past O'Neill had all kinds of reasons, the most clear-cut of which was the conviction that you could not write about the present. When the first production of *The Iceman Cometh* opened he told an interviewer:

I do not think that you can write anything of value or understanding about the present. You can only write about life if it is far enough in the past. [Gelbs, p. 873]

In this retreat into the past one can see, once more, the shadow of *The Count*, especially in the cycle plays. As *Monte Cristo* was fake history attached to real history, through the evocation of Napoleon, O'Neill's cycle was intended to be imaginary (but "real," psychologically considered) history, once more attached to real history through the re-creation of the American past. And Napoleon was to come in too. The projected cycle not only kept growing in the number of separate plays that would compose it, it kept extending itself further back in time beyond 1828, the date of the only finished play of the series, *A Touch of the Poet*.

In *A Touch of the Poet* O'Neill introduced briefly Mrs. Deborah Harford, a quite believable, for O'Neill, and rare picture of a New England aristocratic matron. This character fascinated him, and he planned to give it a play, *And Give Me Death*, which was to take place in Rhode Island and Paris from 1783-1805 and was to have one scene set in Paris on the day of Napoleon's coronation in Paris. In fact it would seem that Napoleon, as he was a tutelary figure in the early part of *Monte Cristo*, was also to be a tutelary figure in the early plays of O'Neill's cycle. The Harford family on the male side are described in *A Touch of the Poet* by Mrs. Harford as extravagant admirers of Bonaparte. The whole family, she tells Sara Melody, Con's daughter, had accompanied her and her husband to Paris on their honeymoon—"to Paris to witness the Emperor's coronation." Con Melody himself had fought in the Napoleonic Wars; and Sara tells Mrs. Harford that she has always admired Napoleon and that one of the things she has held against her father was that he fought against Napoleon.

It is impossible to know how many times Eugene O'Neill witnessed, or played in, *The Count of Monte Cristo*, but that invocation of the great Emperor in the first act, with its resultant sense of attaching the imaginary event—the play—to a potent historical figure—Napoleon—and to tumultuous and stirring historical times—the Napoleonic era—certainly remained with him, to emerge and become explicit in his mightiest projected imaginative effort.

Allied to the historic interest and setting of *The Count of Monte Cristo* was the motif of the buried treasure (which in *Monte Cristo* was also historical since Monte Cristo's treasure supposedly derived originally from the Borgias). Again in O'Neill's plays the incidence of buried or hidden treasure is extraordinarily high for a modern and a "serious" playwright. Twice, in *Where the Cross is Made* (1918), a one-acter, and in *Gold* (1920), a four-acter—actually Act IV of *Gold* is a re-write of *Where the Cross is Made*—O'Neill employed all the characteristic paraphernalia of the classic treasure hunt as in Stevenson's *Treasure Island*: the map, the desert island, the obsessed seekers, the plots and counterplots, the voyage, and so on, all with the significant difference that the treasure itself is illusory and hence a phantom in the minds of the characters rather than an objective fact. Similarly, in *The Fountain* Ponce de Leon pursues an illusory "treasure" through southern America. A hidden treasure, a secret horde, also plays a role in *The Hope, The Emperor Jones,* and *Desire Under the Elms*.

O'Neill's life-long preoccupation with the mystery of the family and the ambiguities of paternity, maternity, and son-ship likewise may have had its roots in *Monte Cristo*. Until the last line of the play Albert never does know who his father is, and throughout most of the last part of the play Dantes does not know that Albert is his son. And to the ambiguity of familial relationship is added also its mystique, the supra-rational feeling that the biological link between father and son is a reality that cuts across space or time or separation, and is always recognizable in a flash of intuition. Thus when Albert meets the disguised Dantes, he exclaims:

> I experience when near you, feelings akin to those their souls must experience. I love you! Yes, from the moment I met you on the way, I felt the necessity of hastening to your aid, of being some service to you. [III]

Similarly, in *Strange Interlude* young Gordon Evans feels some kind of intuitive, almost mystical, affinity for Darrell whom he consciously hates but who is, unbeknownst to the boy, his biological father. In Scene 7 when Darrell, whom the boy never calls by his name, is about to leave, Gordon blurts out, "Good-bye—Uncle Ned," and then, in his interior monologue, asks ". . . why did I like him then? . . . it was only for a second. . . ." And he never does find out who his real father is, as Albert finally does, although only in the last lines of the play.

Or one is reminded of O'Neill's much more somber broodings on the paternal relationship, at once so palpable and so obscure. In *The Great God Brown,* in one of those flashes of wisdom and power that crop up in what is otherwise a totally confusing play, he has Dion Anthony exclaim about his parents:

> What aliens we were to each other! When he lay dead, his face looked so familiar that I wondered where I had met that man before. Only at the second of my conception. After that, we grew hostile, with concealed shame.

And my mother? I remember a sweet, strange girl, with affectionate and bewildered eyes as if God had locked her in a dark closet without any explanation. I was the sole doll our ogre, her husband, allowed her and she
played mother and child with me for many years in that house. . . . [I, 3]

This, of course, is a precise description of the life of Albert Dantes and
of his relationship to his mother, except that the father became a
stranger not because of his presence but because of his absence. And like
so many children in O'Neill's plays, as in *Desire Under the Elms, Strange
Interlude,* and *A Touch of the Poet,* Albert had been conceived out of
passion and out of wedlock, a genuine "love-child." The familiar O'Neill
preoccupation that the family is a millstone around the neck of the
individual likewise received expression, if on the side of villainy, in
Monte Cristo. One of the villains, de Villefort, has a brother, Noirtier,
who is a "good guy." For de Villefort, Noirtier is a nemesis who keeps
turning up to balk him. To de Villefort is given a cry that O'Neill was
to give to his protagonists—and himself—over and over again: "Great
heavens, is the hateful past of my family to haunt me ever on my aspir-
ing path?"

The Count of Monte Cristo begins in a tavern, by a harbor, with the
characters waiting for a ship to return. Two scenes occur in inns. Thus
it suggests two of the four principal places that O'Neill chose so many
times for his plays: the barroom and the ship (the other two places being
the house, with either the columns or the piazzas, and the farm). There is
a stage "drunk" in *The Count of Monte Cristo* who gives what is
meant to be a comic expression of the philosophy of the "happy drunk"
and is thus a prototype for O'Neill's "happy" drunks. He is Caderouse,
another "good guy," who voices one of the philosophies that underlie
The Iceman Cometh.

I drink so much as ever I like—as much as I can—and then I open the
floodgates of truth and avow I love wine, hate work, and pray for widow-
hood! Come on, have a glass. You won't? Well, give me your arm. You see,
my head is light, but my legs are like pillars of lead. You never feel that
way, for you drink water like a shark. [*Sings*] "The bottle for me, the pump
for thee!"

Later he says, prophesying scene after scene in O'Neill's plays, "nothin'
like love of the bottle!" On the serious side, it is Caderouse's being
drunk at a crucial moment which allows Danglars to weave his nefarious
plot against Dantes. Thus one of the key events in the chain of circumstances that leads to Dantes' eighteen-year incarceration is a surfeit of
spirits.

As important as the content of *Monte Cristo* for O'Neill's plays was the form; perhaps the form is more so, since some of the content-links are surely coincidental, but in the form there seem to be no accidents. O'Neill was regarded as a great innovator, or a renovator of Elizabethan stage devices, when he introduced asides and soliloquies, but, of course, these devices were integral to the structure of *Monte Cristo,* and in trying to account for O'Neill's use of them for psychological information rather than for melodramatic effects, there is no need to look any further than the Fechter play. O'Neill's various experiments with disguises, usually in the forms of masks and once again to convey the effect of psychological complexity, also have their genesis in the old melodrama in which disguises play a key role in the plot. Noirtier's existence is only possible because of various disguises, and the intricate plans of Dantes for his revenge depend upon disguises too.

These matters, however, are mechanical. Much more profound and subtle was the effect of the rhythm of *Monte Cristo* on some of O'Neill's earlier work. "Rhythm" was one of the key words in O'Neill's technical vocabulary. Under it he seems to have included almost everything: words and rhetoric, the staging, and the dramatic action of the play. By "rhythm" generally he meant verbal repetition, alternation of scene and mood, transition from one emotional climate to another, and differing modes of temporal duration. As for the verbal repetition, first, that "One, Two, Three" of Dantes seems to have sounded deep in O'Neill's memory, as with all the other devices of *Monte Cristo,* and reiteration of a key word or phase was one of the basic devices of his own rhetoric, even in his late plays. When *The Iceman Cometh* was being rehearsed, someone pointed out to O'Neill that one assertion by Parritt was repeated eighteen times. O'Neill replied that he had *intended* it to be repeated eighteen times.[6] Moreover, his real wish was that these repetitions would be highlighted, in the same fashion that Dantes' "One, Two, Three" was highlighted, by having the actors call attention to the reiteration. In *Diff'rent,* an early play, the key word is the title itself. The word "diff'rent" is repeated, in various and differing contexts, more than twenty times in Act I, and O'Neill actually wanted the actors to "freeze" every time they repeated the word and to speak it in a kind of expressionless monotone, so that it would become like the tom-tom beat of *The Emperor Jones.* It was pointed out to him that by the third repetition the audience would be tittering, so he abandoned the idea. (Gelbs, p. 453) Again the repetitive word can be meaningless, only an interjection, as with "Ay-eh" in *Desire Under the Elms.* "Ay-eh" is a New Englandism

---

[6] Lawrence Langner, *The Magic Curtain* (New York, 1951), p. 405.

still used; it signifies "Yes" or "Yeah" and is a kind of assentual grunt delivered in a slurred drawl. His typist told him that this seemed to be an odd spelling of "Yeah," but O'Neill assured him that "Ay-eh" was just what he wanted. (Gelbs, p. 558) What he meant to convey by it evidently was not only the historical flavor of New England but also some of the qualities of its life, namely, a kind of inarticulate and unlovely monotony, under which raged the lust and the greed of the individual characters. So too in *Mourning Becomes Electra,* another New England play, he thought he had hit upon the right rhythm of prose—"monotonous, simple words driving insistence—tom-tom from 'Jones' in thought repetition." (Gelbs, p. 725) Again the repetition could be musical, "Shenandoah" in *Mourning Becomes Electra;* or literary, the fragment from Carlyle's *French Revolution* in *The Iceman Cometh* or from Swinburne in *Long Day's Journey;* or a fragment of his own bad "poetry" as in *Lazarus Laughed* or *The Fountain.*

O'Neill's relationship with words is a curious phenomenon. That he had only "a touch of the poet" he was the first to recognize and lament. Indeed he doubted that even the "touch" was there. When James Tyrone tells Edmund (Eugene O'Neill) in *Long Day's Journey* that he has the makings of a poet, Edmund replies:

> The *makings* of a poet. No, I'm afraid I'm like the guy who is always panhandling for a smoke. He hasn't even got the makings. He's got only the habit. I couldn't touch what I tried to tell you now [he has been trying to tell his father, not very convincingly, of the mystic rapture he felt aboard ships]. I just stammered. That's the best I'll ever do. I mean, if I live. Well, it will be faithful realism at least. Stammering is the native eloquence of us fog people. [IV]

Actually, O'Neill was not nearly so bad a writer as his critics tend to think, and he was a good deal better than he would allow himself to think. He did have a real mimetic genius for the patois and slang of American speech of the turn of the century and the Twenties, of which *Hughie* is the finest example. He could do quite believable Negro, Swedish, and Irish dialects. Nevertheless it is true that throughout most of his first career, when he was trying to project deep emotions in conventional, educated, normative English, he very often fell back right into the rhetorical patterns of the Fechter version, which consists of stringing together in a fragmenatry manner a series of fairly neutral and abstract nouns and/or adjectives and indicating their desired intensity by repeated exclamation points. Surely, Fechter's "Saved! The world is mine!" or "Ha! Have at thee!" is the parent of Lazarus' "Laugh! Laugh with me! Death is dead! Fear no more!" And, in his despair of ever escaping this kind of stale rhetoric, O'Neill made a suggestion about a proposed production of *Lazarus Laughed* such as no other serious writer of a serious play probably ever made, to wit, that the speeches of Lazarus himself be translated into Russian and that Chaliapin be engaged to play the title role—this before an English-speaking audience. According to O'Neill, it would all "probably be a lot clearer to them in Russian!" (Gelbs, p. 603) But, it should be added, O'Neill was not always as inarticulate as this in his first career, and he almost completely escaped the rhetoric of nineteenth century melodrama in his second career.

In the use of temporal rhythms O'Neill's inheritance from *The Count of Monte Cristo* was twofold and polar. The first and most obvious rhythm was long term and involved a lengthy passage of time, e.g., that eighteen-year gap between Acts I and II of *Monte Cristo*. The modern stage generally, and because of Ibsen principally, has tended to be Aristotelian and to concentrate the action in a day or a few days, with the past being filled in by exposition. In his last plays, like *Long Day's Journey* and *A Moon for the Misbegotten*, O'Neill too instinctively came to this form because of the explosive emotional power that it alone can give. But in his early and middle career he was Shakespearean rather than Sophoclean, dealing out time gaps with the prodigality of *Monte Cristo* itself. In *Beyond the Horizon* there is a three-year gap between Acts I and II and a five-year one between II and III. In *The Straw* four months elapse between Acts I and II and another four between II and III. *Diff'rent's* two acts take place respectively in 1890 and 1920, and the play was originally entitled "Thirty Years." In *Gold* six months pass between Acts I and II and a year between III and IV. In *The First Man* there is a time lapse from the fall of one year to the spring of another between Acts II and III. *The Fountain* has a twenty years "or so" gap; *All God's Chillun Got Wings* stretches out over a nine-year, then a five-year, and finally a two-year period. *Desire Under the Elms* takes something like a year; *Marco Millions*, twenty-three years; *The Great God Brown*, from the adolescence of the principals to their middle age; *Strange Interlude* is the lengthiest of all—something like twenty-seven or twenty-eight years must pass, roughly from 1917-18 to 1945; *Dynamo* encompasses almost twenty months; and *Mourning Becomes Electra* over a year. At the same time it should be pointed out that interspersed with these alexandrine monsters are plays that are compressed—*The Emperor Jones, Anna Christie, The Hairy Ape*, and, relatively speaking, *Lazarus Laughed*. But even in these plays, *The Emperor Jones* excepted, there is some passage of time, either days or weeks, between acts. Aristotelian unity, precisely and exactly followed, was reserved for the last masterpieces.

The eighteen years pass in *Monte Cristo* for three reasons: so that Dantes can suffer through them and hence earn his revenge; so that Albert, already conceived, can be born and grow up; and so that the rest of the characters can age. Most of the time O'Neill's motivations for time lapses were as simple as this. Time and again it is either gestation (*Desire Under the Elms*) or the growth to maturity of a child (*The Fountain* or *Strange Interlude*) that necessitates the time gap. O'Neill was not above using in *The Fountain*, his most *Monte Cristo*-esque production, the "recognition" scene whereby the protagonist sees in a younger person an image of his own past. This occurs when the aging Ponce de Leon sees the now grown daughter of the woman who had once been his beloved; the scene could well have been written by Fechter and would certainly have been played superbly by James O'Neill:

> *The murmur of the crowd increases.* JUAN *sinks on the bench before the fountain, oblivious to it, lost in gloomy thought.* BEATRIZ DE CORDOVA *appears attended by her duena, and a crowd of richly dressed nobles. She is a beautiful young girl of eighteen or so, the personification of youthful vitality, charm and grace. The nobles point out* JUAN *to her. She dismisses them, motioning for them to be quiet—then comes in approaches* JUAN *keeping the fountain between them. She holds a sealed document in her hand. Finally she calls in a trembling, eager voice.* BEATRIZ. Don Juan! (JUAN *whirls on the bench and stares through the fountain at her. He utters a stunned exclamation as if he saw a ghost. His eyes are fascinated by her beauty. Then suddenly she laughs—a gay, liquid, clear note—and coming quickly around confronts him*) It is I, Don Juan. JUAN. (*stares at her still fascinated—then, reminded, springs to his feet and bows low with his old mocking gallantry*) Pardon! I am bewitched! I thought you were the spirit of the fountain. [3]

Suffering and aging—in O'Neill the two are one—are the other two products of the passage of time in O'Neill's plays. In fact this is what you might say "happens" in all of O'Neill's elongated plays. Occasionally, someone makes a physical and spiritual comeback, as does Darrell in Act VIII of *Strange Interlude*. But this is rare, and by the last scene of the play Darrell is harassed once more.

The other temporal impulse from *The Count of Monte Cristo* is the quite opposite movement—the fast-moving, the sudden, and the dramatic. In Scene 2 of Act II of *Monte Cristo* Dantes' friend and fellow prisoner, Faria, who had been carrying on a fairly vigorous conversation with Dantes, suddenly announces he is dying and then proceeds to do so. In most of O'Neill's early long plays characters change too suddenly—perhaps a fault of most young playwrights. In *The First Man* Mrs. David-

son, a New England *grande dame,* very unconvincing, the representative
of upper-class narrowness and convention, suddenly turns noble at the end
of the play and becomes an authentic *grande dame.* Or people change because O'Neill says they have, but are only shown to have done so because
the dramatist has allowed a certain amount of time to pass, without dem-
onstrating any particular psychological cause-and-effect to explain the
change. Reuben in *Dynamo* is introduced as a confused, hypersensitive,
cowardly young man. He goes away, time passes, and he returns tough,
sure, and hard. A few months pass and he becomes a lean, burning ascetic. All these metamorphoses are supposed to be explained by deep-set
psychological drives, but they are not: they just happen.

It was the ending, however, of *Monte Cristo,* with its fast-paced melodramatic hammer-strokes, that sounded deepest in O'Neill's memory in
his first career, and comes to the surface, appropriately enough, in the
worst plays of that period, *Dynamo* and *Days Without End.* The impact
of the end of the "Fechter version" depends upon two of the most ele-
mentary of dramatic devices: a death and a revelation, happening suddenly and in succession. It is ironic but somehow logical that O'Neill
should have fallen back on these devices when struggling with the conclusion to his two last plays that deal with modernity, a sphere so far
removed from *Monte Cristo. Dynamo* is simultaneously O'Neill's *Pierre*
and his *The Education of Henry Adams.* Like *Pierre* it is almost incon-
ceivably weird and tortured and confused in meaning; and, like *The
Education of Henry Adams,* it has the dynamo as its symbol and emblem
of the modern world. It is powerful, but it is also melodramatic and
finally unconvincing, and Fechter himself could not have improved upon
the ending. In quick succession Reuben shoots Ada and immolates himself on the dynamo; and it is revealed, rather confusedly, that Mrs. Fife,
Ada's mother, is a sort of human equivalent to the dynamo, or conversely,
that the dynamo is some kind of Earth Mother. Thus we have two deaths
and one revelation. *Days Without End* is, if anything, even a worse play
than *Dynamo,* if not so equivocal in meaning. It constitutes the end of
O'Neill's first career. If he had died at this time, he would have finally
been written down as an interesting, inventive, but not first-rank talent.
Days Without End, which is O'Neill's own "answer" to *Dynamo,* is about
a man regaining his faith. Again, and even more unmistakably, the ending is by way of Fechter. John Loving, the protagonist, is in a Catholic
church. His skeptical self, an actual alter ego named "Loving," is trying
to prevent "John" from regaining his lost faith. They stand before a
gigantic cross. Meanwhile, back at Loving's apartment, Elsa, his wife, lies
near death from a self-induced illness incurred upon hearing of John's
infidelity to her. Then come the hammer-strokes: "Loving" falls dead,

killed by "John's" renewed faith. The corpse lies at the foot of the cross, while "John," standing, stretches out his arms to it. It is sunrise and the rays of the sun illuminate the cross. Father Baird, a Catholic priest and "John's" uncle, hurries in; here are the final lines:

Father Baird. *(finally taps him gently on the shoulder)* Jack.
John Loving. *(still in his ecstatic mystic vision—strangely)* I am John Loving.
Father Baird. *(stares at him—gently)* It's all right now, Jack. Elsa will live.
John Loving. *(exaltedly)* I know! Love lives forever! Death is dead! Ssshh! Listen! Do you hear?
Father Baird. Hear what, Jack?
John Loving. Life laughs with God's love again! Life laughs with love!

CURTAIN

Here then we have one death and two revelations. This ending O'Neill later called "phoney" and, as with *Dynamo*, repudiated the play as a whole. But having gotten them both out of his system, he went on to write *A Touch of the Poet, The Iceman Cometh, Long Day's Journey into Night, Hughie,* and *A Moon for the Misbegotten.* The observance of the unities of time, place, and action, the finely developed characters, the plausible dialogue, the unmelodramatic plots (*A Touch of the Poet* perhaps excepted), and the quiet and sad endings of these plays are at the opposite pole, dramatically speaking, from the "Fechter version." They thus constitute a triumph for Eugene O'Neill that was denied to his father: a final escape from the Château d'If.

"Eugene O'Neill"

by Hugo von Hofmannsthal

It was at the Salzburg Festival last summer that I first heard the name of Eugene O'Neill. Max Reinhardt was producing one of my plays there; a sort of mystery, a synthetic or symbolic handling of allegorical material, mounted in a church. There were a few Americans in our audience, who aroused my curiosity by relating merely the plots of *The Emperor Jones* and *The Hairy Ape*.

Some time after, I read both these plays; also *Anna Christie* and *The First Man*. These plays and a few others, I am told, have placed Eugene O'Neill in the position of the foremost living American playwright. Judging from those of his plays with which I am familiar, his work is throughout essentially of the theater. Each play is clear-cut and sharp in outline, solidly constructed from beginning to end; *Anna Christie* and *The First Man* as well as the more original and striking *Emperor Jones* and *The Hairy Ape*. The structural power and pre-eminent simplicity of these works are intensified by the use of certain technical expedients and processes which seem dear to the heart of this dramatist and, I may presume, to the heart of the American theatergoer as well; for instance, the oft-used device of the repetition of a word, a situation, or a motive. In *The Hairy Ape* the motive of repetition progresses uninterruptedly from scene to scene; the effect becomes more and more tense as the action hurries on to the end. Mr. O'Neill appears to have a decided predilection for striking contrasts, like that, for instance, between the life of the sea and the life of the land, in *Anna Christie*, or between the dull narrowness of middle-class existence and unhampered morality, in *The First Man*. The essential dramatic plot—the "fable," that is—is invariably linked to and revealed by that visual element which the theater, and above all, I believe, the modern theater, demands. The dialogue is powerful, often direct, and frequently endowed with a brutal though picturesque lyricism.

"Eugene O'Neill" by Hugo von Hofmannsthal. From *The Freeman* (March 21, 1923). (Translation by Barrett Clark, slightly revised by the editor.)

In an American weekly publication I find the following judgment on Mr. O'Neill, written by an intelligent and very able native critic: "He has a current of thought and feeling that is essentially theatrical. Taken off the stage it might often seem exaggerated, out of taste or monotonous." To this just praise—for it is intended as praise—I can heartily subscribe. But the same writer goes on to say, however, that in this dramatist's best scenes there is a power in the dialogue that is found in only one work among thousands. Granting that this is true, it seems to me that the manner in which Mr. O'Neill handles his dialogue offers an opportunity for some interesting speculations of a general character on the whole question of dramatic dialogue.

In my opinion, granting the primary importance of the dramatic fable, or plot, the creative dramatist is revealed through his handling of dialogue. By this, be it understood, I do not mean the lyrical quality or rhetorical power; these elements are in themselves of little importance in determining the value of dialogue. Let us assume a distinction between literature and drama, and say that the best dialogue is that which, including the purely stylistic or literary qualities, possesses at the same time what is perhaps the most important of all: the quality of movement, of suggestive mimetic action. The best dramatic dialogue reveals not only the motives that determine what a character is to do—as well as what he tries to conceal—but suggests his very appearance, his metaphysical being as well as the grosser material figure. How this is done remains one of the unanswerable riddles of artistic creation. This suggestion of the "metaphysical" enables us to determine in an instant the moment a person enters the room whether he is sympathetic or abhorrent, whether he brings agitation or peace, whether he affects the atmosphere about us, making it solemn or trivial, as the case may be.

The best dialogue is that which charges the atmosphere with this sort of tension; the more powerful it is the less dependent does it become upon the mechanical details of stage-presentation.

We ought not too often to invoke the name of Shakespeare—in whose presence we all become pygmies—but for a moment let us call to mind that Shakespeare has given us practically no stage directions; everything he has to say is said in the dialogue; and yet we receive pure visual impressions of persons and movement; we *know* that King Lear is tall and old, that Falstaff is fat.

Masterly dialogue resembles the movements of a high-spirited horse; there is not a single unnecessary movement, everything tends toward a predetermined goal; but at the same time each movement unconsciously betrays a richness and variety of vital energy that seems directed to no special end; it appears rather like the prodigality of an inexhaustible abundance.

In the best works of Strindberg we find dialogue of this sort, occasionally in Ibsen, and always in Shakespeare; as fecund and strong in the low comedy give-and-take scenes with clowns and fools as in the horror-stricken words of Macbeth.

Measured by this high ideal, the characters in Mr. O'Neill's plays seem to me a little too direct; they utter the precise words demanded of them by the logic of the situation; they seem to stand rooted in the situation where for the time being they happen to be placed; they are not sufficiently drenched in the atmosphere of their own individual past. Paradoxically, Mr. O'Neill's characters are not sufficiently fixed in the past.[1] Much of what they say seems too openly and frankly sincere, and consequently lacking in the element of wonder or surprise: for the ultimate sincerity that comes from the lips of man is always surprising. Their silence, too, does not always convince me; often it falls short of eloquence, and the way in which the characters go from one theme to another and return to the central theme is lacking in that seemingly inevitable abandon that creates vitality. Besides, they are too prodigal with their shouting and cursing, and the result is that they leave me a little cold toward the other things they have to say. The habit of repetition, which is given free rein in the plot itself as well as in the dialogue, becomes so insistent as to overstep the border of the dramatically effective and actually to become a dramatic weakness.

The essence of drama is movement, but that movement must be held in check, firmly controlled.

I shall not venture to decide which is the more important in drama, the driving motive-element of action or the retarding or "static" element; at any rate, it is the combination, the interpenetration of the two that makes great drama. In Shakespeare's plays there is not a line that does not serve the ultimate end, but when one goes through the text to discover this for oneself, one perceives that the relation between means and end is by no means evident: the means seem tortuously indirect, often diametrically opposed to the end. Nineteen lines out of twenty in a comedy or tragedy of Shakespeare are (seemingly) a digression, an interpolative obstruction thrown across the path of the direct rays; retarding motives of every sort impede the onward march of events. But it is precisely these obstacles that reveal the plasticity, the vitality, of the story and character; it is these that cast the necessary atmosphere about the

---

[1] This statement does not conflict with the fact that many O'Neill characters, as well as O'Neill himself, are *fixated* on the past.—EDITOR

central idea of the work. As a matter of fact, the unity of the play lies in these diversified and apparently aimless "digressions."

If one goes through *Anthony and Cleopatra* looking only for the chain of physical events, the hard outlines of the plot, and neglects the indescribable atmosphere of pomp and circumstance, the spectacle of the downfall of pride and the fulfillment of destiny, the contrasting colors of Orient and Occident, all of which is made manifest through the dialogue, what is left? Nothing more than the confusion and incoherence of nine out of every ten motion-picture dramas. Or if one considered the best pieces of Gerhart Hauptmann merely as samples of superficial naturalism, one would find them pedantic and weak in characterization. Or again, take the productions of the doctrinaire naturalist: good examples are the dramatizations of the Goncourt novels. Thirty years ago these played a role of considerable importance, so far as theatrical history is concerned; but there is no life in them, nor was there when they were first produced; they suffer from lack of fresh air. Hauptmann's best plays, on the other hand, are bathed in it; it unifies and breathes vitality into them because it is the breath of life itself, transfused by that secret process which makes all great art, be it drama or canvas, giving it richness, variety and contrast. This is what the painters call "le rapport des valeurs." The plays of Strindberg are unified in this wise, not because of the bare plot on which they are built, but through the medium of an indescribable atmosphere that hovers somewhere between the realm of the actual and the dream-world.

The European drama is an old institution, laden with the experience of years, but as suspicious and watchful as a venerable though not yet impotent human being.

We know that the dynamic element in drama is a vigorous element, eternally striving for ascendancy. But we also know that great drama is and always has been—from the time of Aeschylus down to the present— an amalgamation of the dynamic and (shall we say?) "static" elements, and we are therefore a trifle suspicious of every effort toward the predominance of one element over another. The nineteenth century witnessed many such efforts, and each time great drama disappeared during the process. There is a constant danger that action—whether it masquerade as thesis-play or play of ideas, problem-play or drama of intrigue, or simply as the vehicle of a virtuoso playing with an anecdote—may prevail over the subtle and difficult but indispensable combination of dynamic and "static," the inseparable oneness of plastic form and action.

Sardou, the heir of Scribe, created a type of play the ingredients of which were entirely dynamic; action took the place of all else, and for twenty years Sardou dominated the European theater, while his followers

—the Sudermanns, the Bernsteins, the Pineros—have continued to dominate it to the admiration of the middle classes of all nations and the abomination of the artists! This was the type of play in which the personages were never guilty of any "irrational" exhibition of character: they were the fixed units in a sharply outlined plot, manipulated by the skilled hand of the playwright; and they passed their lives in rooms hermetically sealed against the breath of mortals.

Sardou coined an expression for his style of play: "Life through movement," which was turned against him by his critics, who retorted: "Movement through life." The critics were all true artists: Zola, Villiers de l'Isle-Adam and their followers, among whom was the young Strindberg; but the most influential was Antoine, a man of the theater.

But the pendulum swung back, and for the time being, perhaps, the European drama has gone too far in the opposite direction. It may be that this is the reason why the plays of so powerful a dramatist as Hauptmann are not popular outside Germany; for a large part of the German public is ready and able to listen to plays in which the "static" element is predominant, dramas in which psychological characterization and lyricism are of more importance than plot. Possibly this tendency is even a little overdeveloped.

Judged from this point of view, Hauptmann's plays are the exact antithesis of the plays of Eugene O'Neill. Where Mr. O'Neill reveals the first burst of his emotions in powerful, clean-cut pictures that seem almost like simple ballads in our complex world, Hauptmann applies himself to making his characters plastic; he does this by throwing a half-light over his men and women and allowing the values to appear slowly, to emerge in new and true and wonderful aspects, gradually shown through an accumulation of tiny and seemingly unimportant incidents of everyday life. As a result, Hauptmann's plots do not progress with directness or force; and at first sight his scenes appear to possess neither dynamic nor even truly "static" elements; they seem somewhat confused. But what ultimately strengthens these scenes and gives them the rhythm of life is a steady and unremitting infusion of the essence of life, which is soul. Hauptmann's method is that of Rembrandt the etcher, who works with a fine steel needle. Since Hauptmann continues to work in this fashion, he must necessarily give little thought to his audience; and indeed he is in actual danger of losing sight of them altogether. Meanwhile, he manages to accumulate so much of the spiritual life of his characters that his last acts are filled with an almost explosive force, so that there is no need for the introduction of any mechanical tension. Ibsen has done the same sort of thing in the last act of *The Wild Duck,* and Ibsen is the master from whom Hauptmann has learned most.

In the case of Mr. O'Neill, however, his first acts impress me as being the strongest; while the last, I shall not say go to pieces but, undoubtedly, are very much weaker than the others. The close of *The Hairy Ape*, as well as that of *The Emperor Jones*, seems to me to be too direct, too simple, too expected; it is a little disappointing to a European with his complex background, to see the arrow strike the target toward which he has watched it speeding all the while. The last acts of *Anna Christie* and *The First Man* seem somewhat evasive, undecided. The reason for this general weakness is, I think, that the dramatist, unable to make his dialogue a complete expression of human motives, is forced at the end simply to squeeze it out like a wet sponge.

I have no intention of giving advice to a man of Mr. O'Neill's achievements; what I have said is not said by way of adverse criticism; it is rather the putting together of dramaturgical reflections inspired by a consideration of his plays. His qualities as a dramatist are already very great, and I have no doubt that he will make progress when, in the course of time, which is necessary to each man who creates, he shall have acquired better control over his materials, and above all over his own considerable talents.

Eugene O'Neill:
An Exercise in Unmasking

by Eugene M. Waith

Dramatic inventiveness is O'Neill's surest claim to fame.[1] I include in this term both the feeling for theater which enabled him to hit upon highly effective devices for the staging of his plays, and another kind of imagination which enabled him to find situations corresponding to his various concepts of the human dilemma. The attempt to find answers to all the big questions in life produced some exquisitely painful prose in such plays as *Lazarus Laughed* and *The Fountain,* but it also determined the characteristic form of an O'Neill play. The answers themselves, unsatisfactory as they are, contribute importantly to the success of the best characterizations. I shall have very little to say about either the philosophical or psychological worth of O'Neill's insights. My concern is the way in which these insights are embodied in dramatic form, and here is where his remarkable inventiveness is to be seen. I shall concentrate on an aspect of his technique based on masks.

Masks were used in several O'Neill plays staged in the Twenties: in *The Hairy Ape, The Ancient Mariner, All God's Chillun Got Wings, The Fountain, The Great God Brown, Marco Millions* and *Lazarus Laughed.* In 1932, two years before resuscitating the device in *Days Without End,* O'Neill published his "Memoranda on Masks" in *The American Spectator.* Here he expressed his conviction that masks would be found to be the "freest solution" of the problem of expressing in drama

"Eugene O'Neill: An Exercise in Unmasking" by Eugene M. Waith. From *Educational Theatre Journal,* XIII, No. 3 (October 1961), 182-191. Copyright © 1961 by the American Educational Theatre Association, Inc. Reprinted by permission of the author and the *Educational Theatre Journal.*

[1] This paper was given at the Seminar in Twentieth-Century Drama arranged by the English Graduate Club of Duke University, March 11-12, 1960. I am grateful to Mr. Donald Gallup, Curator of the Yale Collection of American Literature, for making available many items in the O'Neill Collection established by Mrs. Carlotta Monterey O'Neill, and for permission to publish information derived from them.

"those profound hidden conflicts of the mind which the probings of psychology continue to disclose to us." [2] In an oracular style, probably influenced by *Thus Spake Zarathustra,* he gave his "Dogma for the new masked drama.—One's outer life passes in a solitude haunted by the masks of others; one's inner life passes in a solitude hounded by the masks of oneself." But the most significant of the "Memoranda" for the understanding of O'Neill's technique was the question, "For what, at bottom, is the new psychological insight into human cause and effects but a study in masks, an exercise in unmasking?" The mask was a way of getting at the inner reality of character. In fact, it may be said that for O'Neill is was *the* way, for even in the many plays where actual masks are not used, we find the same preoccupation with concealment and discovery. These plays too are studies in masks.

O'Neill was in good company. Some of the liveliest imaginations of an extraordinarily vital period of artistic activity were haunted (to use a wòrd O'Neill liked) by the mask. The director Kenneth Macgowan collaborated with Herman Rosse on a book called *Masks and Demons,* illustrated with reproductions of masks from Greece, Japan, the Congo, and New Mexico. Macgowan suggested a kind of identity between the dramatic process and the uses of the mask in both primitive and civilized societies.[3] In psychology the conception of the mask was prominent. What was the "inferiority complex" but a mask for aggression? Finally, the mask was part of an exciting stylistic revolution in the arts. Macgowan devoted a chapter in *The Theatre of Tomorrow* to expressionism, in which, as he explained, a formal expression of the artist's emotion was subsituted for realistic representation. Gordon Craig, who influenced both Macgowan and Robert Edmond Jones, gave tremendous importance to the mask.

When O'Neill joined in a triumvirate with Macgowan and Jones at the Provincetown Playhouse it was inevitable that he should experiment with masks. In *The Great God Brown,* he used them to bring out, among other things, the divided consciousness of his hero, Dion Anthony, whose name was intended to suggest Dionysus and St. Anthony. Not only does the mask of a mocking Pan conceal and protect the real face of a sensitive and spiritual artist, but the mask itself changes in time from Pan to Mephistopheles. O'Neill attempted to portray by means of the mask the complicated inner tensions of a personality and the development which those tensions produce. Problems of this sort always concerned him. Through his career he dramatized "the divided man," as John Gassner

---

[2] (Nov., 1932), p. 3.
[3] (New York, 1923), pp. xii, 161, 163.

has said,[4] and when he did not use masks he often used analogous devices. The asides in *Strange Interlude* are a clear example. But this rather obvious use of the mask was not the most important one to O'Neill. In a statement given to the New York *Evening Post* he explained that in writing *The Great God Brown* he meant the "background pattern of conflicting tides in the soul of Man" to be "mystically within and behind [the characters], giving them a significance beyond themselves. . . ."[5] Later, in the "Memoranda on Masks" he said he would like to make the masks in this play symbolize more definitely the abstract theme, rather than stress the superficial meaning that people wear masks before other people.[6] In this same article he referred to *Strange Interlude* as an attempt at the "new masked psychological drama . . . without masks," but considered that it was not wholly successful where it tried to probe deeply. Kenneth Macgowan had spoken repeatedly of the mysteriousness of masks.[7] O'Neill said in his statement about *The Great God Brown* that mystery—a meaning felt but not completely understood—was what he wanted to realize in the theater. Here we encounter the extraordinary spiritual zeal which informed some of the theatrical activity of the Twenties. In O'Neill's case the urge to invest the theater with religious significance, though it led to the unmitigated disasters of *Lazarus Laughed* and *Days Without End,* was elsewhere a source of power. He was never content to catch the surface of a character. He must always by some means suggest what lay beneath and beyond in the character's relations to his inmost self, to his family, to society, and finally to the source of all things, whether referred to as God or Life-with-a-capital-L. The title of his first Broadway play was emblematic: *Beyond the Horizon.*

O'Neill arranged Coleridge's *Ancient Mariner* for the Provincetown Players in their 1923-24 season.[8] In the playbill James Light, who made the masks, talked of the spiritual atmosphere in which the mask lives and of their hope that the masks would intensify the theme of the poem. Since the words are entirely Coleridge's, the dramatic version is an excellent example of ways in which the mask could be used as an auxiliary device. We can readily see what elements are intensified by it. Most conspicuous is the supernatural. The Ancient Mariner himself wears no

[4] "Eugene O'Neill: The Course of a Modern Dramatist," *Critique,* I (1958), 10.

[5] Quoted by Barrett Clark, *Eugene O'Neill: The Man and his Plays* (New York, 1933), p. 162.

[6] *American Spectator* (Dec., 1932), p. 2.

[7] *Masks and Demons,* p. 55.

[8] This version was published for the first time by Mr. Donald Gallup in the *Yale Library Gazette,* XXXV (1960), 61-62.

mask, but as he begins his tale his shipmates appear, wearing the masks of drowned men, which are later changed for those of holy spirits and finally angels. Death wears the mask of a black skull, and the Woman's face, though unmasked, is heavily made up to resemble a white skull. A comparable use of the device is found in *The Great God Brown*, where both the mask and the real face of the hero suggest supernatural forces —mocking demon and ascetic saint—at war in the hero's soul. In the case of Cybel, the prostitute, the mask shows her profession, while her own face reveals the spiritual dimension of the Earth Mother—a combination which was bound to appeal strongly in the Twenties, being both shocking and religious. Cybel marked an important advance beyond La Dame aux Camélias, a harlot who was merely good-hearted.

Another element of Coleridge's poem which is intensified by the masks is the contrast between the Mariner and the unthinking mass of mankind. The two wedding guests who go on to the wedding have mask-like faces; the bride and groom, glimpsed for a moment, look like dolls, and the others in the wedding party are seen once as dancing shadows on a windowblind. The third wedding-quest differs from the others in being "naturally alive—a human being," and thus the spell cast over him by the mariner makes clear the connection between genuine vitality and spiritual vision. Not to share in the dream or the intimation of what lies beyond the horizon is to be part of the faceless crowd of "men and bits of paper whirled by the cold wind" in a "twittering world," to borrow Eliot's words. This expressionistic use of masks to suggest the horror of the anonymous crowd is also found in other O'Neill plays. The Sunday morning crowd on Fifth Avenue in *The Hairy Ape* were given masks, and so were the crowds, Jewish, Greek, and Roman, in *Lazarus Laughed*.

Thus, in the plays of the mid-Twenties O'Neill repeatedly used masks not only to present the divided man but to bring out some relationship between the individual and society or between the individual and the realm of the supernatural, and thus to give the characters "a significance beyond themselves." In *Lazarus Laughed* there was a fantastic proliferation of masks, which proved happily to be the flood tide of this phase of O'Neill's experimentation; for as he himself realized later, the device had overwhelmed the drama. The insistence on something beyond the surface was so great that the characters and their actions, instead of gaining an added dimension, lost all reality. One turns with relief back to the first O'Neill play to be produced, the one-act *Bound East for Cardiff*, a mainly realistic play, where the sense of something beyond is given by a simple device. The ship's foghorn, blown at regular intervals, accompanies the action of the play, which is nothing but the death of the injured seaman, Yank, in his bunk below deck. One is never allowed to forget the context in which this action is taking place.

Bound East for Cardiff is a beautiful illustration of another aspect of O'Neill's technique. In speaking of the new psychological insight in the "Memoranda" he used the phrase "an exercise in unmasking." The ship's whistle keeps reminding us of her slow progress through the fog while below deck in the forecastle, Yank is painfully approaching death. Most of the dialogue is his conversation with his mate, Driscoll, to whom, toward the end, he confides his longing to have a farm "way in the middle of the land," far from the sea. It is an unexpected revelation of his character and by its intimacy it brings Driscoll closer to him than ever before. Shortly afterward he dies. As he does so the whistle stops. The fog has lifted. The play is unassuming but powerful, and I believe that the movement of its action is the characteristic movement of an O'Neill play —a movement toward discovery or revelation or both—a kind of unmasking.

Toward the end of an O'Neill play there almost always comes a moment when the principal characters are for the first time fully revealed to the audience, and often it is only then that they fully understand themselves or their relationships to each other and to the world they live in. These recognition scenes are O'Neill's high points and in his best plays they are very moving. However, there are major differences to observe between these recognitions. In some of them there is a final heroic confrontation with the forces of life or destiny; in others, the hero in retreat reaches the final devastating acknowledgement of despair. O'Neill seems to have thought of his characters' coming to terms with life as movement forward or back. In the early versions of *Days Without End* an antithesis is set up between "going back"—refusing in some way to accept the challenge of life—and going "on to Hercules," a curious phrase, intended at one time to be the title of the play, and meaning acceptance of life, even if life itself is meaningless, determination to create goals for oneself, a heroic gesture with overtones of romantic grandeur. Hercules here is the constellation, but suggests also the great hero's final transcendence of a fate which he accepts. In *Days Without End* the choice between two opposite directions is explicit; in other plays it is implied. The backward movement of O'Neill characters is always flight from the problems posed by existence; forward movement is the heroic, sometimes ecstatic, acceptance of them. Both movements may be toward death, but death in significantly different forms.

None of his plays gave O'Neill more trouble than *Days Without End,* which was after all a commercial and artistic failure of the first magnitude. His notes and several early versions, now in the O'Neill Collection at Yale, are most interesting, however. What they reveal has an important bearing on the rest of O'Neill's work. Though in each version there is a choice of a way forward and a way back (which, unlike the way up and the way down, are not at all the same), the specific courses of action to be chosen are altered in a most surprising way. The hero, John Loving, is plagued by his loss of faith (he was born a Catholic), and by the guilt he feels for his unfaithfulness to his wife. Initially O'Neill planned for him to commit suicide at the end in front of a statue of the Virgin—an end which was intended to suggest that mother-worship had turned to death-worship—a return to the protective womb of religion. Next O'Neill decided to make the play "less definitely Catholic," and in the first completed draft the wife dies and the hero curses God. In another version the hero is split in two; the mocking, Mephistophelean part of him finds a death of denial, consistent with his life, while the other part finds faith, even though he also dies. Here the rediscovery of religion has a clearly positive value, even exceeding the value of heroic persistence in the face of meaninglessness—the "On to Hercules" attitude. The symbol of Christ on the cross is substituted for the statue of the Virgin. The religious solution is retained in the final version, though here the hero also achieves reintegration by imposing his will upon his alter ego, and is rewarded by the forgiveness and survival of his wife. The last scene again takes place at the foot of a crucifix, and the acceptance of Christianity is an assertion of life. The point, as this brief consideration of the earlier versions makes clear, is that he was looking for a dramatic solution which would show the *movement* of his hero from the crossroads where we first meet him. Which solution to the philosophical problems O'Neill himself might have chosen at this period of his life I would not presume to guess. He was obviously capable of imagining several.

The characteristic structure of an O'Neill play, then, is determined by a movement toward unmasking, which is often also a movement of the principal characters toward discovery of the stance they must take toward the fundamental problems of existence. In many of the early plays O'Neill chose an episodic form in which he could show the stages by which, in the course of time, the final discovery was reached. Later he reduced the compass of the time to one day, though contriving to retain the same emphasis on the experience of discovery. Even this one day is a journey. Before discussing in more detail *The Great God Brown, The Iceman Cometh,* and *Long Day's Journey into Night,* I shall give some clear-cut examples of the two sorts of character-development of which I have spoken, the movements backwards and forwards.

The Emperor Jones remains one of O'Neill's more impressive plays. When Brutus Jones, the former Pullman porter, who has made himself emperor of an island in the West Indies, is faced with rebellion, he starts immediately on an escape he has planned through the great forest to the coast, where he is to be met by a ship. But what was planned as an escape turns into a retreat from the symbols of civilized success which he has won for himself to fantasies of primitive terror which lie deep within him. The flight through the forest is a fine theatrical symbol for the psychological regression brought about by panic as Jones loses his way in the darkness and hears the drums of the rebelling natives. The use of the tom-tom, beating first at the rate of the normal pulse, and then gradually faster until it stops at the moment of Jones's death, is a theatrical device comparable in effectiveness to the whistle in *Bound East for Cardiff*.

One of the most brilliant revelation scenes in the plays of the early Twenties is the final scene of *All God's Chillun Got Wings,* which has been excellently analyzed by Doris Falk[9] in the light of the psychological problems which are her main concern. Ella, the white girl married to an ambitious Negro, destroys an African mask, which has been established as a symbol of artistic achievement and religious mystery, but which she perversely takes as a symbol of degradation. A quarrel ensues, followed by reconciliation. Ella is a little girl again: "I'll just be your little girl, Jim—and you'll be my little boy—just as we used to be." Jim is seized by a kind of religious ecstasy. On his knees he prays to be made worthy of the child God has given him as a wife, and when she asks him to "come and play," he replies, "Honey, Honey, I'll play right up to the gates of Heaven with you!" What makes the scene particularly effective is his belief, at the very moment when all his hopes have been frustrated, that he has found happiness—that he too has wings. Utter defeat presents itself to him in the guise of victory.

The final moments of these plays reveal the principal characters reverted to savagery or childhood. I shall spend less time in illustrating the contrary movement toward a wider horizon—an acceptance of life which is not resignation. Juan Ponce de Leon, the hero of *The Fountain,* is described as half "ambitious thinker," half "romantic dreamer." The goal he sets himself when he goes on the expedition to find Cathay is glory for Spain and himself, but the self which sets this goal is only half the man, and the less important half. The repressed romantic dreamer is his true self. In an interview at this time O'Neill said that what he tried to put in his plays was an ennoblement of life, an exaltation, an urge to-

[9] *Eugene O'Neill and the Tragic Tension* (New Brunswick, 1958), pp. 87-90.

ward life, which, he made clear, derived in some way from dreaming.[10]
Juan's ambitious self is presented as a "bitter, mocking mask," and only
at the end is the dreamer allowed to emerge. The expedition in search
of Cathay turns into a spiritual quest, and at the moment when Juan's
hopes of glory are defeated he is granted a mystical vision. Though he
finds neither Cathay nor the Fountain of Eternal Youth, he comes at last
to what seems to him the source of life. His voyage of discovery across
unknown seas is the exact opposite of the flight of the Emperor Jones
through the forest.

The relentless forward movement of *Lazarus Laughed* toward more
and more exultant assertion of the value of life is part of what makes it
the tedious play it is. There is no let-up in this yea-saying. Lazarus himself is a cross between Nietzsche's Zarathustra and Molly Bloom: his first
word, like her last, is "Yes!" to be said, according to the stage-direction,
"Suddenly in a deep voice—with a wonderful exultant acceptance in it."
A far more convincing example of acceptance occurs in a far better play,
Desire Under the Elms, in which the two principal characters, Eben and
Abbie, move through a sequence of false attitudes toward each other to
true understanding and love. Like Juan in *The Fountain,* they have
found more than they knew they were looking for.

The Great God Brown enjoyed a run of eight months in 1926 when it
was first produced. When O'Neill was asked to choose a scene from one
of his plays to be included in Whit Burnett's anthology, *This Is My Best,*
published in 1942, he chose one from *The Great God Brown* and said:
"I still consider this play one of the most interesting and moving I have
written. It has its faults of course, but for me, at least, it does succeed in
conveying a sense of the tragic mystery drama of Life revealed through
the *lives* in the play." Though the faults of which O'Neill was aware are
serious ones, it is, as he thought, one of his most interesting plays, and
contains more penetrating analysis of character than many more competent pieces of dramaturgy with which it could be compared.

The central problem of the play is both subtle and complex: it is the
deformation of a creative impulse in a hostile environment. The urge
toward artistic creation is also the urge toward spiritual self-fulfillment,
as in so many O'Neill plays, and therefore the artist (in this case an ar-
chitect) is given the name Dion Anthony, whose religious implications I
have already mentioned. The basic conflict in the play is between his
aspirations, religious and artistic, and the doctrine of success as understood in a materialistic society. Dion's friend, Billy Brown, is the embodiment of worldly success, playing the role of the ant to Dion's grass-

[10] Mary B. Mullet, "The Extraordinary Story of Eugene O'Neill," *American Magazine* (Nov., 1922), p. 118.

hopper. The relationship, as Kenneth Tynan acutely observed in his review of the recent revival, seems to anticipate the mingled love and hate between the two brothers in *Long Day's Journey*. He might have added that in turn it was anticipated to some extent by the relationship between the two brothers in *Beyond the Horizon,* and by the two warring natures within Juan Ponce de Leon or Marco Polo. In none of these other plays, however, did O'Neill attempt to chart so precisely the interaction of the two temperaments.

Yet the two men have a remarkably large area of shared experience. Both love Margaret, Dion's wife; both patronize Cybel; both are architects, and both work in the same office. In fact Dion's designs are apparently passed off as Billy's. In Acts III and IV, after Dion's death, O'Neill uses Dion's mask to show how one character almost fuses with the other; for Billy inherits the mask. This symbolic action has been prepared for at the end of Act II by the revelation that Dion first assumed the mask as a child to protect himself from the cruelty of Billy, who envied his ability to draw and teased him by destroying his pictures. In a sense, Billy and Dion are complementary halves of one personality, for each in some way wishes to be the other. Their conflict is resolved only at the end of the play when Cybel, seeing Billy with Dion's mask, says "You are Dion Brown!" It is Billy, no longer the great god of success, who finally has the mystic illumination which Dion Anthony sought.

In presenting the tortured progress of this divided personality, O'Neill used the mask to show both the reaction of one half to the other, and also the further division within each half. The gradual change of the mask from Pan to Mephistopheles shows the increasing bitterness of Dion's reaction to his alter ego, the complier with the world. Even the spiritual self hidden by the mask follows a parallel course toward the denial of life. Destructive demon is matched with ascetic saint. When Billy inherits the demonical mask, it initiates him into Dion's sufferings, but the final result is not the same. In the last scene, where Billy is stripped bare and without the mask, he seems to have become the Dionysus which Dion potentially was. This dying god is the inner core of the composite character, whose complex reactions to environment have hitherto concealed the truth.

The complications are far too many (I have omitted several) and the dependence on the mask is far too great. Not only is it impossible in the theater to see clearly the changes in the masks which O'Neill prescribes, but the conception is tiresomely schematic. However, the movement of the characters toward their final revelation is handled with greater finesse than in any of the earlier plays.

In two of the later plays, *The Iceman Cometh* and *Long Day's Journey into Night,* an equal complexity of movement is managed without the machinery of masks and without another encumbrance which handicaps many of the plays in the mid-Twenties. In *The Fountain, The Great God Brown, Lazarus Laughed,* and one or two others, O'Neill tries unsuccessfully to elevate certain crucial moments by the use of a rhapsodic, pseudo-poetic prose. He seems to have been aware himself that he never carried it off, for in the "Memoranda on Masks" he has the interesting comment, apropos of a rejected plan to use masks in *Mourning Becomes Electra:* "Masks in that connection demand great language to speak—which let me out of it with a sickening bump!" [11] The connection he had in mind was with Greek tragedy, but more broadly it is true, whether or not he fully realized it, that he was unable to write in the formal style which his experiments in theatrical formalism demanded. In all of these plays an inadequacy of language hampers, to a greater or lesser degree, the success of his dramatic inventiveness. In the two late plays I have just mentioned the realistic style which he could handle well is perfectly suited to his conception and does not prevent him from achieving the effects he strove for in the more obviously contrived plays.

The effectiveness of *The Iceman Cometh* derives from the progressive stripping of the characters, brought about by their interaction. Again O'Neill plays two characters against each other, Parritt and Hickey, but this time, instead of being opposite, they are equivalents whose careers are counterpointed. Hickey suffers from guilt for the murder of his wife, Parritt from guilt for the betrayal of his mother. Between the two, so to speak, is the pivotal character of Larry, a former lover of Parritt's mother. These are the central characters.

The whole movement of the play, which occupies just under two day's time, is like the advance and retreat of a huge wave. The play opens in the torpor of a drunken sleep; as it gathers force the human derelicts in Harry Hope's bar are impelled toward action; at the end most of them are quickly slipping back into drunken stupor; only three of them have been flung free of the wave—Hickey, Parritt, and Larry. When Hickey urges everyone to give up pipe dreams he merely gives added impetus to Parritt's movement toward explanation and ultimately confession. At the same time he urges Larry to give up his pose of noncommitment and pass judgment on Parritt's betrayal. Hickey himself moves toward the shocking discovery that he has always hated his wife. Each of the three pushes the others toward a discarding of illusion which means the admission of failure in life. At the end one has committed suicide, one has given himself up to the police, and the third prays for death.

Long Day's Journey into Night is wave-like in quite a different way.

---

[11] *American Spectator* (Dec., 1932), p. 2.

Each of the principal characters, James and Mary Tyrone and their sons Jamie and Edmund, is borne toward his final destination by a series of impulsions, between which he may even seem to drift in the contrary direction. The rhythm of the play is one of movement regularly interrupted and regularly resumed. It is Mary's backward movement into drug-addiction which dominates the play, and the stages of her regress give the play its structure. The first act ends with Edmund's suspicion that she has begun again; the first scene of the second act with Tyrone's assurance that she has; the second scene with her plan to go to town for more "medicine." In the third act, which is mostly hers, the drug has already made her quite remote. It ends as she goes upstairs for more. At the end of the fourth act she has arrived at her destination—her girlhood in the convent. Her action precipitates a crisis in the family, which is augmented by news from the doctor that Edmund has tuberculosis. Reacting to these emotional stresses, each of the three men comes to a recognition of his aims and motives. For two of them, Tyrone and Jamie, this amounts to a confession of defeat as humiliating as Hickey's or Larry's. For Edmund alone the darkness of the night into which they are all traveling is relieved by sparks of remembered hope.

The fourth act is a series of "epiphanies," managed with superb control of the theatrical medium. It is night, and the fog which Mary loves because "it hides you from the world" has become a dense wall outside the living room where all the action takes place. The act begins with Tyrone and Edmund, the old actor with a miser's love of property and the young poet with tuberculosis. Depressed by the events of the day, and already partly drunk, they drink more and talk until they goad each other to a showdown. They quarrel over Tyrone's stinginess and his possible responsibility for Mary's drug-addiction. Occasionally arresting themselves, but always resuming the quarrel, they finally tell each other the truth. Edmund accuses his father of economizing even on the treatment of his tuberculosis. Tyrone defends himself by self-pitying reminiscences of his youth, and then admits what he has never admitted to anyone before, that he was corrupted by early success and prostituted his talent for financial gain. For the first time in the play his character is fully revealed, and as he voices his regret for the actor he might have been, we realize that his longing for his youth is no less poignant than his wife's.

His admission puts an end to the quarrel, for it elicits sympathy from his son, but it sets in motion another revelation. Moved by his father's memories, Edmund drunkenly describes some extraordinary experiences "all connected with the sea." They are not wrong turnings but moments of illumination when "the veil of things as they seem [is] drawn back by an unseen hand." Earlier in the evening Edmund has told of a walk he has just taken in the fog, trying to lose himself, and feeling like a ghost. As he now speaks of seeing beyond the veil, he also recalls that after the vision the veil always falls "and you are alone, lost in the fog again. . . ." He describes himself romantically as one who will always be a stranger, "a little in love with death." He is somewhat like his father in his self-dramatization and self-pity; somewhat like his mother in his almost voluptuous surrender to the fog; yet, unlike either of them, he is capable of extracting a significance from his experiences which seems to redeem life from utter meaninglessness. Even though he is "a little in love with death," he does not fall back on self-deception, like his father, nor refuse to live in the present, like his mother. There is still the hope of forward movement. His reminiscences not only reveal him but place him in relation to his parents.

When Jamie comes in, an equally remarkable and effective scene ensues, in which the pretenses of Edmund's ne'er-do-well brother are stripped off for the first time. Again we have the halting movement of a quarrel which seems at moments about to end in reconciliation but then resumes. The jerkiness of the movement is accentuated by Jamie's nature, for he is one of O'Neill's divided characters, half mocking cynic, half good fellow. Jamie, like Hickey, conceals hate under the guise of love. He has pretended and partly believed himself that his kid-brother is his best pal, for whom he would do anything, but now with terrifying frankness he proclaims his jealousy and resentment of Edmund, whom he has tried to corrupt in order to keep him from succeeding. "The dead part of me," he says, "hopes you won't get well." Beneath Jamie's rather feckless charm lies a hatred of life so venomous that it would willingly destroy Edmund. This carefully concealed attitude is almost the exact opposite of the one revealed by Edmund to his father in recalling those times when he felt a part of "Life itself." For all his melancholy, Edmund has none of his brother's destructiveness. Rather, he is the creator.

The unmasking of Jamie, one of the most powerful episodes in the play, is almost the end. There remains only the final view of Mary, now thoroughly lost in the dream of her childhood. Her pathetic immaturity is the ultimate truth about her and her oddly remote chatter about the convent marks the end of her journey. In one sense she is a spokesman for the entire family. Each of them, in groping for the truth about himself, has turned back to some part of his past, and since the present which each of them faces is sad, there is special appropriateness in her last lines, which close the play: "Then in the spring something happened to me. Yes, I remember. I fell in love with James Tyrone and was so happy for a time."

This is O'Neill at his best. In these last plays he gave up his reliance on elaborate theatrical contrivance and attempted no forcing of his muse to rhapsodic heights. As a result his genuine gifts are seen to the best advantage. These plays are a kind of unmasking of their author.

Eugene O'Neill

by John Howard Lawson

Eugene O'Neill's career is of special significance, both because of the abundant vigor and poetic richness of his earlier dramas, and because of the confusion which devitalizes his later work. In a sense, O'Neill's case is not typical, because his pre-occupation with the subconscious and with the destiny of the soul seems to be of a special kind and intensity. But this also accounts for the special importance of his work: he reveals the ideas which affect the modern theater in their most intense form.

Shaw's social thought is based primarily on the liberalism of the days prior to 1914. O'Neill's philosophy reflects the period which followed the World War. This has caused him to ignore, to a remarkable extent, the role of conscious will in dramatic conflict. This is of great interest from a technical point of view. O'Neill has made a consistent and impassioned attempt to dramatize subconscious emotions. He frequently uses the terminology of psychoanalysis, and this terminology is often employed in discussions of his work.

But psychoanalysis as a method of psychological investigation has no bearing on O'Neill's plays. His interest in character is metaphysical rather than psychological. He attempts a complete escape from reality; he tries to sever contact with the world by setting up an inner kingdom which is emotionally and spiritually independent.

If we enter O'Neill's inner world and examine it critically, we find ourselves on very familiar ground. O'Neill's philosophy is a repetition of past ideas. In this, he follows the line suggested by Freud, the line of regression, a flight to the past. There is no coordinated system in O'Neill's thought; but it is not difficult to trace the origin of his ideas and to establish their general trend. His plays bear a definite resemblance to the plays of Ibsen's final period. The conception of emotion as an

"Eugene O'Neill." From Chapter V of *Theory and Technique of Playwriting* (New York: G. P. Putnam's Sons, 1936) by John Howard Lawson, pp. 129-141. Copyright 1936 by John Howard Lawson. Reprinted by permission of G. P. Putnam's Sons.

ultimate force is repeatedly stressed. But there is a difference: in the last and most mystical of Ibsen's plays, *When We Dead Awaken,* he shows us man and woman facing the universe with unbroken courage; their will has become impersonal and universal; but the man and woman are still together and still determined to join their will to the universal will; to climb "right up to the summit of the tower that shines in the sunrise."

O'Neill's mysticism goes beyond this. There is no drama of O'Neill's in which an intense love relationship between man and woman is presented as creative or satisfying. The deepest emotional drive in his plays is always based on the father-daughter, mother-son relationship. His use of the Freudian formula serves to negate any conscious struggle on the part of his characters. Their passion is necessarily evil, because it is incestuous; yet it is unavoidable, because it is the condition upon which they are born. His characters are emotional but sterile. In Ibsen's *When We Dead Awaken,* Rubek and Irene face the dual universe with courage and consciousness. O'Neill's later plays contain no character who possesses either of these qualities.

While Ibsen presents emotion as a means of salvation, O'Neill can find no salvation outside of religion. At the close of *Days Without End,* John kills his disbelieving self: "Life laughs with God's love again." In other plays, emotion is shown as destructive (as in *Mourning Becomes Electra*), or as a mad struggle against the power of the machine (as in *Dynamo*). . . .

O'Neill clings to the will to believe; but his system of thought leaves no room for either will or belief. In his plays, the life-force is no part of life; even emotion is negative, working in man's own heart to accomplish his destruction. O'Neill, and many of his contemporaries, conceive of fate in a manner which has no parallel in any previous period of world literature or drama. In all previous epochs, man has been depicted exerting his will against objective forces. The modern fate is both in man and outside him; it paralyzes his mind; his consciousness and his will and his emotions are his worst enemies. It has often been said that "whom the Gods would destroy, they first make mad." This is not a denial of the will, it is an assertion that man's will is his only weapon against the hostility of his environment. The Gods cannot overcome him until he is *made mad;* he is able to fight until some power outside himself destroys his mind and purpose. But the modern fate presupposes madness as man's natural state. It is not a curse which descends upon him and weakens him at a decisive moment of struggle (a sudden breaking down of the will under pressure which is common in human experience); it is a precondition, which makes the struggle useless, because even the *desire* to struggle is aimless.

If O'Neill's plays conformed literally to these ideas, they would not be plays at all. But his work possesses the power and drive of a fine mind and a burning sincerity. The author's creative consciousness and will are in conflict with the sterile thinking which destroys both art and life. This inner struggle is evident in his repeated efforts to dramatize the subconscious. This has led to his interest in the problem of dual personality; he tries to use the physical man as a means of showing us the subconscious man in whom he is chiefly interested. In three plays, he has invented devices for this purpose. In *The Great God Brown* masks are used; in *Strange Interlude* the asides are ostensibly used for the same purpose. In *Days Without End,* the split between the two selves is complete, and two actors play the two parts of the same man.

The most interesting of these, as far as the conscious will is concerned, is *The Great God Brown.* In the other two plays, the asides and the split personality are merely ways of showing what the characters *think* and *want*—which are aspects of the conscious will. In *The Great God Brown,* O'Neill has seriously set himself the task of building a play in which *the conscious will plays no part at all.* The play deserves careful study, because it is the only instance in dramatic history of a sustained attempt along these lines by a competent craftsman. O'Neill's statement of his purpose reminds us of Maeterlinck's desire to present the "intangible and unceasing striving of the soul toward its own beauty and truth." O'Neill says that he wishes to show the "background pattern of conflicting tides in the soul of Man." This pattern is "mystically within and behind" the characters. "It is Mystery—the mystery any one man or woman can feel but not understand as the meaning of any event—or accident—in any life on earth." [1]

Feeling is accepted as the fundamental principle of drama. The "conflicting tides" can have nothing to do with either conscious purpose or logic. Environment is discarded as a factor, because the mystery applies to "any event—or accident—in any life on earth." Evidently the use of masks is intended by the author to show us what is "mystically within and behind" the characters. But this brings us to the first difficulty: the masks do not, and cannot, show us anything of the sort. When a character's mask is off, we see his real self, the conscious desires which he is concealing from other persons—but we cannot see anything else, because neither the character nor the audience can attain consciousness of anything else. O'Neill seems to realize this difficulty, and he is determined to overcome it. He chooses the only means by which it might conceivably be overcome; he goes beyond dual personality and shows us that the "background pattern of conflicting tides" is not individual, but really

---

[1] Prefatory note to Eugene O'Neill's *The Great God Brown* (New York, 1926).

universal. In a word, the soul has only a partial individuality: it follows that the masks, and the personalities behind the masks, are to some extent interchangeable.

Here we face another difficulty: making character interchangeable does not change the character: we are still concerned with conscious motives and aims—to shift them from one person to another may confuse us, but it cannot introduce a new element. In *The Great God Brown*, Dion Anthony represents two personalities. Both of these personalities are abstract: one side is the pagan acceptance of life; the other is the "life-denying spirit of Christianity." Brown also represents two personalities. As the play proceeds all four of these personalities are scrambled. Dion dies in Act III, Brown steals his mask, and decides to appear to Margaret, Dion's wife, as the real Dion: "Gradually Margaret will love what is beneath—me! Little by little I'll teach her to know me, and then I'll finally reveal myself to her, and confess that I stole your place out of love for her." Then he kisses the mask of Dion: "I love you because she loves you! My kisses on your lips are for her!" (It is to be noted that, at this point, a fifth personality, that of Margaret, is scrambled with the other four.) But this is not all. Brown, masquerading as Dion, pretends that he (as Dion) killed Brown (the real Dion). So the police come and kill Brown thinking he is Dion.

The play proves that men without will and environment are not men. As far as the plot has any meaning at all, it is based on relationships which are factual and even obviously melodramatic. It takes no dual, or plural, personality to explain that Brown loves Dion's wife and wants to take his place. There is no mystery in a situation in which a man is killed because he is mistaken for another man. There is no *additional* meaning, no "background pattern" which conforms to the author's intention; the disorganized expressions of purpose, which slip from the characters almost in spite of themselves, are all that distinguish them from lumps of clay. This is evident in the lines quoted: Brown talks about what he, as a person, will *do* in relation to other people.

The Great God Brown has genuine poetic power; it presents O'Neill's confused philosophy with fervor and honesty. The play is undramatic because the philosophy is undramatic. The poetry, as such, has nothing to do with the characters. Like their personalities, the poetry is interchangeable. The play has beauty because, in spite of its confusion, it represents the author's consciousness and will. But it lacks clarity or dramatic truth, because the author's conscious will is concentrated on a refusal of reality.

O'Neill's mode of thought, which is manifested in its most extreme form in *The Great God Brown*, determines the technical arrangement of all his plays. His denial of reality is a denial of logic. This makes unified dramatic development impossible. In the plays following *The Great God Brown*, O'Neill does not persist in his effort to depict only the "conflicting tides in the soul of man"; he tries desperately to find some means by which he can *apply* his philosophy to the living world. *Strange Interlude* is the most important work of O'Neill's later period. Although there are mystic overtones in this play, the plot-structure is rational, and the characters are modern men and women whose problems grow out of definite conflict within a definite environment.

I have already suggested that Nina Leeds is a replica of Hedda Gabler. It may be objected that Nina is more unconventional, less inhibited, more modern, than Ibsen's heroine. To be sure, there is a superficial difference, because the conduct in each case is conditioned by the conventions of the period. But in their attitude toward these conventions, the two women are remarkably similar. Both are free of moral scruples; but both are dominated by fear of conventional opinion, and are never guilty of defying conventions. Hedda sends a man to his death and burns his manuscript without a qualm of conscience; but she is terrified at the idea of a scandal. Nina has no conscience in pursuing her emotional needs; but she never has the courage to speak the truth. Both women have unusually dull husbands; both regard love as a right with which nothing can interfere; both have father complexes; both are driven by a neurotic craving for excitement; both have what O'Neill calls "a ruthless self-confidence"; both have a strong desire for comfort and luxury, which motivates their acceptance of conventionality; at the same time, both are super-idealists, hating everything which is "ludicrous and mean."

Hedda fights to find an outlet for her will. Unable to accomplish this within the restrictions of her environment, she dies rather than submit. Nina never faces her problem in this definite form. Like Shaw's Candida, she is able to achieve a sufficiently satisfactory adjustment within her environment. But Candida expressed her will through a free choice. Nina lives in an emotional trance; she never chooses or refuses; her "ruthless self-confidence" does not involve any choice of conduct; it is her way of justifying her pursuit of emotional excitement, which leads her to accept every sensation which is offered. In Act II, Nina confesses "giving my cool clean body to men with hot hands and greedy eyes which they called love." Throughout the play, her actions involve no independent decisions; she lives for the moment, and follows any suggestion which makes a momentary impression. . . .

This emphasis on pure emotion is a pragmatic application of the mysticism of *The Great God Brown* to the conduct of living people. This accounts for the plot-structure of *Strange Interlude*. The action rests chiefly on a sense of foreboding, the threat of horrors which never materialize. In the first three acts, Nina marries the dull Sam Evans, and intends to have a baby. She learns that there is insanity in her husband's family. We then discover that these three acts have been exposition to prepare for the real event: since the threat of insanity prevents Nina from having a child by her husband, she selects Dr. Darrell as the prospective father. We watch eagerly for the consequences. But one may say, literally, that there are no consequences. In Act V, Nina wants to tell her husband and get a divorce, but Darrell refuses. In Act VI, Darrell threatens to tell Sam, but Nina refuses. In Act VII, the activity centers around the child (who is now eleven); the boy's suspicions threaten to upset the apple cart. But in the next act (ten years later) everybody is on the deck of a yacht in the Hudson river watching Gordon win the big boat race: "He's the greatest oarsman God ever made!"

Now let us consider the asides. It is generally assumed that these serve to expose the inner secrets of character. This is not the case. Nine-tenths of the asides deal with plot and superficial comments. The characters in *Strange Interlude* are very simply drawn; and they are not at all reticent in telling their inmost feelings in direct dialogue. For instance in Act III, Mrs. Evans says: "I used to wish I'd gone out deliberately in our first year, without my husband knowing, and picked a man, a healthy male to breed by, same's we do with stock." Coming from an elderly farm woman, one would reasonably expect this to be an aside, but it is direct dialogue. Mrs. Evans' asides (like those of the other characters) are devoted to such expressions as "He loves her! . . . He's happy! . . . that's all that counts!" and "Now she knows my suffering . . . now I got to help her."

Then are we to conclude that the asides are a whim, a seeking after sensation? Not at all. They serve a very important structural purpose: they are used to build up a sense of foreboding. Again and again there are comments like Darrell's in Act IV: "God, it's too awful! On top of all the rest! How did she ever stand it! She'll lose her mind too!" But the asides have a much deeper use; in every scene, they foretell what is about to happen, and blunt the edge of conflict. What might be a clear-cut scene is diluted by needless explanations and by annotating the emotions.

Thus we discover that both the asides and the length of *Strange Interlude* are dictated by a psychological need—to delay, to avoid coming to grips with reality. The function of the asides is to cushion the action and make it oblique. And this same obliqueness creates the need of spreading the story over nine long acts.

Strange Interlude reaches no climax and no solution. But the final scene contains a fairly thorough summing up of the author's position. It is not enough simply to point out that the play ends on a note of frustration. Frustration is negative, and tends to become merely poetic whimpering. The sense of frustration which we find in O'Neill is based, as we have seen, on a complex system of ideas. The social application of these ideas is of the utmost importance.

The ninth act begins with a scene between the two lovers, Madeleine and Gordon: the essence of this scene is the idea of repetition; the saga of love and passion will be repeated. Marsden enters and offers a rose to Madeleine, saying mockingly: "Hail, love, we who have died, salute you!" One expects the playwright to follow this line of thought, but he turns sharply away from it. The action suddenly concentrates on Gordon's bitterness against his mother, his feeling that she never really loved the man whom he regarded as his father. Nina, tortured for fear Darrell will tell the boy the truth, asks her son a direct question: "Do you think I was ever unfaithful to your father, Gordon?" Gordon is "shocked and horrified . . . he blurts out indignantly: 'Mother, what do you think I am—as rotten-minded as that!' " Here is the ferm of a vital idea—if the conflict between mother and son were developed. But O'Neill cuts it short at this point. Gordon leaves, soliloquizing as he goes: "I've never thought of that! . . . I couldn't! . . . my own mother! I'd kill myself if I ever even caught myself thinking . . . !" Gordon, who represents the new generation, leaves the stage with these negative words. Darrell then asks Nina to marry him and she refuses: "Our ghosts would torture us to death!"

Thus the idea of the repetition of life turns to the negation of life. In all this, O'Neill disregards one simple fact—that Nina has built her life on a lie, and that this accounts for all her troubles. And her son, as he leaves the stage, tells us that he is just as cowardly as his mother: "I've never thought of that! . . . I couldn't!"

Here we see the conception of an absolute fate as it concretely affects a dramatic situation. The fact that both mother and son evade the truth is not regarded as personal cowardice, but as destiny. Gordon does not face his mother and defeat her—as he would be forced to do in life. He coddles his illusion and goes away on his honeymoon. Since feeling transcends fact, it follows that one preserves the quality of one's feeling even when it means denying or avoiding reality.

The last scene of *Strange Interlude* contains a welter of unfinished ideas which indicate the playwright's feverish uncertainty. There are references to religion, science, womanly intuition, "mystic premonitions of life's beauty," the duty "to love, that life may keep on living," etc. The pain of the author's search lends dignity to his confusion. However confused or sublime a playwright's thought may appear, it exhibits his own attitude toward his environment. Nina's aimless and deceitful life is called beautiful because it is lived for emotion. The last act tells us that the eternal aim of life is to repeat the saga of emotion. But Nina's emotions are those of a woman to whom security and leisure are guaranteed. Her emotional life is dependent on the social structure. Everything which she feels or thinks is designed to preserve the permanence of her environment. This accounts for her intense conventionality, and for her conviction that deceit is socially necessary. Again and again, she tells us that all she seeks is happiness; her idea of happiness is erotic. She has no interest in other people, no desire to exert an influence on her environment. She pretends desperately to be a woman without an environment, because this is the only condition under which she can exist at all. If she came into contact with reality, her whole world of leisure and sentiment would fall to pieces. Her insistence on emotion is an insistence on a *fixed social system*.

This meaning is increasingly evident in the trilogy, *Mourning Becomes Electra*, which follows *Strange Interlude*. O'Neill's mysticism leads him back to the world of reality; he is not satisfied with showing the passive drift of emotion, as in *Strange Interlude*. One must go beyond this; one must show activity—this leads to a neurotic vision of reality dominated by blood and force.

In *Mourning Becomes Electra*, O'Neill illustrates the Spenglerian conception of the modern intellect "overpowered by a growing sense of its Satanism." Here violence is not a necessity of the action; it is an end in itself. Charmion Von Wiegand points out that "more normal alternatives of action were open to all the characters than the one they chose of murder and blood or which their author chose for them." [2] It is evident that the characters have no choice whatever; the author's choice of murder and blood springs from the need to justify cruelty and violence as the normal conditions of our existence. The writer's fear of life springs from disturbances and pressures in his environment; since the lack of equilibrium in the environment is due to a process of change, the first step is to invent an eternity ("the electrical display of God the Father") in which change is meaningless; since one cannot invent an eternity out of nothing, the author invents it out of his own experience; his eternity is a crystallization of the environment in what appears to be

[2] Charmion Von Wiegand, "The Quest of Eugene O'Neil," in *New Theatre* (September, 1935).

a permanent form. Ibsen showed us the decay of the middle-class family as part of a system of causes and effects. The causes were increasing tensions in the social structure; the effects were the substitution of lust and greed, hate and egotism, for more normal emotions. This is the environment against which O'Neill rebels and from which he wishes to escape. But he tries to build a world of abstract emotion out of the very emotions from which he is escaping; an eternity of lust and greed, hate and egotism. In *Strange Interlude,* emotion is abstract, a rarefied desire for happiness; therefore Nina's lust and greed, hate and egotism, are sentimentalized and take the form of aspirations. Nevertheless, these are the only emotions of which she is capable. But the playwright cannot stop at this point; he is driven by the need to remedy the maladjustment between himself and his environment; he must go back and try to *explain* the world in terms of lust and greed, hate and egotism. This task was begun in *Desire Under the Elms,* and continued in *Mourning Becomes Electra.*

Mourning Becomes Electra is a much more realistic play than *Strange Interlude.* The action is less diffuse and better integrated. But the movement of events, in spite of its violence, evades progression. The characters have no goal toward which they are moving. Having no attainable social aims, it is impossible for them to have attainable dramatic aims.

The idea of *repetition* as an emotional commentary on the blindness of the life-force occurs throughout O'Neill's work. This idea plays an important part in the concluding scene of *Strange Interlude.* It occurs in its poetic form in Cybel's lines at the end of *The Great God Brown:* "Always spring comes again bearing life! Always again! . . . spring bearing the intolerable chalice of life again."In *Mourning Becomes Electra,* repetition is the basic structural pattern. The length of the triple scheme has no justification dramatically, because it involves no development of the action. The length is dictated by the need to prove that repetition is socially inevitable. In this connection, one may recall the remark of William James that there is nothing the principle of free will could do "except rehearse the phenomena beforehand." The activity of O'Neill's characters is a rehearsal of preconceived patterns; the will plays no part except as a repetition-compulsion, which gives what James called a "character of novelty to fresh activity-situations."

An understanding of the social direction of O'Neill's thought clarifies the connection between *Mourning Becomes Electra* and the two plays which follow—*Ah, Wilderness!* and *Days Without End.* O'Neill, being one of the most sensitive and most genuine artists of our time, is horrified by the picture of reality which he himself has drawn. Unwilling to accept "the intolerable chalice of life" on these terms, he turns in two directions: to the consolations of religion, and to the regularities of small-town life in the pre-war era. These plays do not present a positive denial of force and cruelty as emotional values; such a denial would require the courageous analysis of reality which is the function of the artist. *Ah, Wilderness!* and *Days Without End* are negative and nostalgic; the social thought resolves itself into the wish that religious finality or tender family sentiments might be substituted for the real world. . . .

Eugene O'Neill: The Tragic in Exile

by Richard Hayes

Yes, Ibsen is ugly, common, hard, prosaic, bottomlessly bourgeois—and with his distinction so far *in*, as it were, so behind
doors and beyond vestibules, that one is excusable for not
pushing one's way to it. And yet of his art he's a master—and
I feel in him, to the pitch of almost intolerable boredom, the
presence and the insistence of life. On the other hand, his
mastery, so bare and lean at it is, wouldn't count nearly as
much in any medium in which the genus was otherwise represented. In *our* sandy desert even this translated octopus
(excuse my comparison of habitats! !) sits alone, and isn't
kept in his place by relativity.

The speaker unraveling his pleasure and exasperation with such
mandarin eloquence is Henry James, quite seventy years ago, and standing in point of time and regard to his flinty Northern peer as do we to
the melancholy, ravaged Celt who is the most conspicuous figure in the
landscape of American drama. It is sobering to contemplate Eugene
O'Neill and Ibsen the Norwegian in the clear light of analogy. O'Neill
himself honored Strindberg as his master and source, and indeed sounds
with him at once the note of intolerableness—those disastrous echoes of
private pain and legend out of which each made a kind of tragic music.
Of that pain and legend, in the O'Neill instance, we have known a
surfeit. He stands in hazard of a vulgar canonization: the lineaments of
his life too easily lend themselves to that perverse American relish for
whatever is straining, tumultuous, or incoherent in experience. Pleasur-
ing ourselves, as the late Stark Young wrote of the cabal about O'Neill,
"in his strong moods and his fierce borderings on a rich life," we have
felt "only a small part of his moral and poetic continuity."
Yet the presence persists, the figure: not to be downed. No escape is

possible from it, into style, rhetoric, grace, or even meaning: there is about the man O'Neill something of that rigidity of structure which animates the profound nullity and metaphysical horror of his late plays. He discharges the glamour of obsession: it is his characteristic note, the source at once of his mesmeric command and our secret resentment: his excellence, and its ineradicable defect.

And it is precisely at this impasse that the example of Ibsen is most fruitfully invoked, and read for the chastening lesson it offers in the uses of adversity. More than piety binds the two legendary solitaries. If Ibsen—the platitude has its justice—created the consciousness of modern European drama, then O'Neill is surely to be seen as his loneliest and most intrepid American agent. Both men had their beginnings in commodity theatre (Ibsen in Scribe and Sardou, O'Neill in the gaslit megalomania of his father's *Count of Monte Cristo*), and each enjoyed what no dramatist does today—a theater in which to give visible shape to his first energies. ("He had not only our stage," Edna Kenton wrote in her vivid memoir of O'Neill and the Provincetown, "he had our 'subscription list,' and he used its members, bill after bill, season after season, in ways they could never dream of; played with them, and on them, with never need for a thought of them except as stark laboratory reactions to his own experimentations.")

To O'Neill, the absence of humor, of free imagination, and of style Henry James remarked in Ibsen has often been attributed, and the verbal inadequacy Mary McCarthy sees in the American as "a kind of triumphant catastrophe . . . how is one to judge the great logical symphony of a tone-deaf musician?" had its counterparts in the current objections to Ibsen's spare and strenuous ugliness of surface. O'Neill and Ibsen, finally, and terribly, each spent their last years in zones of inarticulate consciousness, hideously resonant—one cannot but believe—with the revenge nature inflicts on those who too audaciously demand it confront its own unspeakable exactions.

Yet here abruptly analogy ends. For of that consciousness of modern drama he richly created, Ibsen himself is so eminent a force, while one reflects with melancholy how small an impress O'Neill has left—in the shape of a usable past—on the theater which was to succeed his own. It is difficult, at this juncture, to resist the sense that the reputation of O'Neill has been for some time at best a cultural *devoir*, at worst an intellectual embarrassment. Certainly the history of his encounter with the most rigorous critical sensibilities focused on American drama has not been happy. Eric Bentley, "trying to like O'Neill," and conceding him a model of "good sense and honor" in a theater which "chiefly attracts crooks and idiots," sees him still as a classic instance of the betrayal by Big Intentions: "the man who could not be bribed by the Broadway tycoons was seduced by the Broadway intelligentsia." Francis Fergusson has not, to one's knowledge, publicly altered his judgment of the dramatist first proposed three decades ago: "He [O'Neill] has managed to recognize his emotional demands, but he had not reached the further heroism of accepting what becomes of them: of describing them with reference to some independent reality. He has a sense of human needs, but none of human destiny. He offers us the act of seeking, but no disinterested contemplation; himself, therefore, rather than his work."

Nor has the record of production been more inspiriting. Since José Quintero's bold and generous reclamation of O'Neill from genteel obscurity almost a decade ago, he has not at all commanded the kind of retroactive esteem we would flatter ourselves to have accorded him. The unassailable *Long Day's Journey* and Stuart Vaughan's admirable rendering of *The Great God Brown* aside, O'Neill productions in New York have rarely transcended the status of curiosities or occasions of impertinent stellar exhibitionism. Indeed, one is hard put to isolate just what genuine impulse or engagement may have been obscurely dormant among the disfiguring egotisms of the recent revivals of *Strange Interlude* and *Desire Under the Elms*: no more than O'Neill's contemporaries would we seem able to grasp his "moral and poetic continuity," or the singularity of the dramatic mode it imposes.

The O'Neill problem, then, for any theater in which he is to figure as more than a piety or a tedious chauvinism, must be seen as a challenge to dramatic strategies, not to be divorced from that inadequate metaphysics or language on which it is habitual now to rest whatever voids we sense in his work. O'Neill's insensibility to words—to their luster and resistance, their shimmer or weightiness—harassed him all his days. The durable images in his work are visual and aural, or the residue of his capacity for making myths: that effect of a personal pressure passionately exerted. His attempt to realize them in language clots and muddies. At worst—as in *A Moon for the Misbegotten,* or the symbolic insistence of some of the parables of his middle career—insensibility expands into the larger indifference to anything like selection. Ears, mouth, and mind are crammed not with the intense, the difficult, or abstract, but rather with an aimless and liberal redundancy. Even in *Long Day's Journey into Night,* which forges out of domestic speech a kind of tragic poetry of remembrance and loss—even here some excess might be rinsed away, the whole molded to a richer expressiveness and finality. The sense persists that to the later O'Neill the reality of language deteriorated: he saw it only as part of the tedious machinery of making the spirit manifest, and not—as in T. S. Eliot's fine charge to the poetic dramatist—an element in the arrangement of a form to arrest its flow.

Nor does it seem probable that the dramatist's intellectual audacity, never formidable, will much detain the future. Again, it was Stark Young who noted this in the early O'Neill: "the plays," he wrote, "have less of intellect and theory and more of dramatic instinct and personal upheaval . . . the play proceeds, with whatever agreement or tedium it arouses in us as we hear it, but meanwhile, alongside this agreement or boredom, there runs this personal lyricism, the sense of some individual poignancy whose stress and pressure has evolved these scenes." It is here that O'Neill divagates most sharply from the Ibsen pattern. Like the Norwegian, he underwent "phases," but it has not gone unremarked that the O'Neill career is more a sequence of radical starts—fresh departures undertaken with a gathering desperation—than it is an unfolding of energy, the embodiment of a ripening sense of dramatic action.

The early plays of the sea, with their lulling, fogbound lyricism, their realistic annotation of brutality and squalor, gave way to the magnificent linear fables of *The Emperor Jones* and *The Hairy Ape*; these in their time surrendered to the dexterously engineered enterprises in contemporary bourgeois tragedy—the measureless ambitions of *Strange Interlude* and *Mourning Becomes Electra* and the great projected sequence, now lost, on the vanity of the American dream. Indeed, no random, importunate, or fanciful manifestation of the *Zeitgeist* is ever to be found far from some juncture of this pilgrim-playwright's progress. One would like to think it variety, the amplitude of a searching and manifold nature. Yet might it not be confusion? A generation ago, the alert Ludwig Lewisohn remarked how O'Neill returns from each of these excursions "a little disillusioned, a little dissatisfied, a little hopeful that his next experiment will result in something not quite so fragmentary and unfinished from within." And at the end, something like a magnificent exhaustion overtook the dramatist: the last plays stand as a ferocious abolition of action, a mathematic demonstration of the fallacy of the free agent. Not, perhaps, since *Oedipus* has the futility of man's strategies been displayed dramatically with such formal yet unreadable rectitude. Behind those plays lies the memory of Sisyphus and his "unspeakable penalty," as Camus calls it, "in which the whole being is exerted toward accomplishing nothing."

Diminished in mind, then, impoverished in speech, the theater of O'Neill challenges the artist to give body to what is essentially a Manichaean vision—that ancient, somber doctrine which saw matter as irremediably tainted and man as a creature of the prince of darkness. Its romantic agony takes the form of something very like the phenomenon C. S. Lewis has called "the tragic in exile: what happens to certain elements in tragedy when they are rejected by cultured people and abandoned to the masses." The burden of O'Neill's days as an artist was the recognition of that void, and his desperate search to fill it. Hence the rhetorical solipsisms of *Lazarus Laughed* and *Dynamo,* the impetuous, defeating energies of *The Great God Brown* and *Days Without End.* Hence, too, the absence from O'Neill's dramatic texture of anything like a dominant tone, and, for the actor—the despair of realizing that he can make this world "work" only by the marshaling of personal obsession: varieties of realism, however individually effective, will bring him but to chaos. This theatrical mode, so special and unique—not congenial to American sensibility—lies close in pattern to the morality, even to the parable or the allegory. What it invites as style is the investiture of some quality of baroque expression—a considerable degree of artifice, perhaps, of rhetoric and even formal declamation. Only an infusion of a private and chastened lyricism will release from the monochromatic lithography of the O'Neill world—cruelly blocked in its masses of black and white— the tragic hidden unity and design within the whole.

In the end, for O'Neill, nothing worked but memory: not artifice, nor any solacing reason could mediate the authority of his private pain. "He could not believe," Nicola Chiaromonte has noted, "as Rousseau believed, that *it was the fault of others.* In effect, he no longer believes in anything, except in the sequence of cause and effect." Hence the return in age to the crucifying years of "old sorrow," and the "stammering" which would be its "faithful realism"—when time for once had a stop, and the four Tyrones and the bums and whores and derelicts of *The Iceman Cometh* sit in ceremonial postures about the tables of eternity. It was, O'Neill would be first to admit, the best he (and we) can do, and one might imagine him as readily agreeing that art may inhabit more temperate zones than those barren spheres of grief he charted with such remorseless constancy. But then, he was never—like the figure about whom he fashioned *Beyond the Horizon*—"too harmonious a creature of the God of Things as They Are." *Victor Hugo, hélas!* legend records as André Gide's melancholy nomination of the premier poet of France in an age which offered few alternative candidates. It is a sentiment the rue of which would not have eluded the man O'Neill.

Myth as Tragic Structure in
Desire Under the Elms

by Edgar F. Racey, Jr.

It is customary to point to the underlying Oedipal theme of Eugene O'Neill's *Desire Under the Elms* and to link this play with *Mourning Becomes Electra* as evidence of his consuming interest in the Oedipus theme, both as myth and complex. The use of myth, or classical source, in *Electra* is obvious, for O'Neill takes great pains to insure that no one misses the elaborate series of correspondences that his trilogy effects. Less elaborate, but equally effective, is his reliance on the *Hippolytus* of Euripides (and perhaps on Racine's treatment of the theme) in *Desire Under the Elms*.

That the play is a tragedy few will dispute (although early critics tended to see it as a mere shoddy domestic tragedy). It combines a traditional tragic theme (the Oedipus legend) with a dramatic reconciliation in the interests of a higher virtue (Justice). Abbie and Eben, as they are reconciled to their fate (which they *will*), assume a dignity which approaches tragic stature. As they acknowledge their guilt and enter into the process of expiation, their characters tend to become generalized, and O'Neill manages to suggest something approaching the idea of universal justice.

On the bare framework of a New England domestic tragedy, O'Neill has grafted a religious symbology, almost an iconography. The Biblical names, while "locally" motivated (a man like Ephraim Cabot could be expected to name his sons after characters in the Bible), seem to dictate at least some of the actions of the characters, and even take on the beginnings of a dialectic. Thus, Peter ("the rock") is associated throughout the play with rocks and stones:

"Myth as Tragic Structure in *Desire Under the Elms*" by Edgar F. Racey, Jr. From *Modern Drama*, V, No. 1 (May 1962), 42-46. Copyright 1932 by A. C. Edwards. Reprinted by permission of the author and *Modern Drama*.

Here—it's stones atop o' the ground—stones atop o' the stones—makin'
stone walls—year atop o' the year. . . . (I,i)

And it is Peter who first picks up a rock to cast at his father's house.
Simeon, on the other hand, reiterates the idea of an eye for an eye (of
the Indians which they will presumably meet on the way to California,
he retorts that they will repay them "a hair fur a hair") and, in revenge
on his tyrannical father, he threatens to rape his new wife. One recalls
Jacob's "blessing" of his sons:

> Simeon and Levi are brothers; instruments of cruelty are in their habita-
> tions. O my soul, come not thou into their secret; unto their assembly, mine
> honour, be not thou united; for in their anger they slew a man, and in their
> self-will they digged down a wall.
>   Cursed be their anger, for it was fierce; and their wrath, for it was cruel.
> . . . (*Genesis*, XLIX,5)

In *Desire*, it is Simeon who "digs down a wall," tearing the gate off the
hinges, abolishing "shet gates, an' open gates, an' all gates, by thunder!"
   The predominant features of his two eldest sons are combined in
Ephraim: he is hard and stony, and embodies the ancient law of retalia-
tion in kind. He is Ephraim, progenitor of the Tribes of Israel, the
archetypal patriarch (and for O'Neill, the father-figure). His name ("the
fruitful") may be an underlying source of irony by the end of the play,
and it is significant that his "fruitfulness" is the greatest source of his
hubris. He is also identified specifically with God, both in his harshness
and solitude. Like Ezra Mannon, he is the embodiment of that blighting
New England Biblical tradition which represses life.
   Eben (Ebenezer? "store of hope") is a typical O'Neill son. The hope
of the line (Simeon and Peter are patently unfit to carry on the name),
he is condemned to be placed in constant strife with his father, denying
his obvious resemblance to the man he hates. The rivalry is characteristically O'Neill: the father has usurped what the son regards as right-
fully his own (the mother and the land). This pattern of rivalry and
usurpation is repeated in the male Cabot's relationship with Min, the
"scarlet woman"; first Ephraim claimed her, then Simeon, Peter, and
finally Eben, who is enraged on learning that here too, they are "his [the
father's] heirs in everythin'." The pattern will continue with Eben and
Abbie.
   While these quasi-religious elements serve to generate a kind of Biblical atmosphere, and perhaps a kind of primitivism, the play says little
in the way of definite religious conclusions, save O'Neill's reiterated

statement that the restrictive ethic (usually Puritanism) tends to kill off life. Ephraim retires to his stony, solitary existence, submitting once more to the hard God, whom it is his consolation to resemble. The young and life-bearing have been destroyed.

As a classical tragedy, however, *Desire* is both successful and complete. The time is spring, season of awakening and season of ritual. It is the spring which has sent Ephraim out "t' learn God's message t' me in the spring, like the prophets done." It is a spring so compelling in its beauty and life that even Simeon and Peter are moved to utter, from their animal existence, "Purty!" The play will end in late spring a year later.

The situation is the Hippolytus-Phaedra-Theseus plot: the father has returned, bringing with him a young wife, who is immediately attracted to her stepson. The stepson too has responded to the season—his brothers have subjected him to taunts concerning his affair with Min (a possible loose parallel to the gentle banter of Theramenes in Racine's *Phaedra*). Traditionally, Hippolytus was chaste, but the affair with Min affords O'Neill the opportunity to define the usurpation theme.

Like Phaedra, Abbie conceals her growing passion for Eben with the mask of scorn. Like Phaedra, she asks that the son be banished—and for the same reason, plus the fact that Eben is a potential rival for the farm. Like Phaedra, Abbie makes advances, but with more success than her dramatic ancestor. Like Hippolytus, Eben muses constantly on his mother, who was "foreign."

It is in the murder of Ephraim's supposed child that we see O'Neill modifying his prototype to suit his dramatic purposes. The curse on the son, originally uttered by Theseus, is transferred to Eben, who is the rightful father. Ephraim also utters a curse—the curse of God—on his sons, but the crucially dramatic curse is Eben's. Eben's curse is uttered against his son in the throes of error, and rashly; Abbie proves as implacable an instrument of fate as Poseidon. Like Theseus, however, it is Ephraim who is left alone, surveying the wreck of his kingdom.

In the Euripidean version, a sin had been committed against the gods (or rather, Aphrodite imagined herself slighted by Hippolytus' devotion to Artemis). While it is possible to view the "sin" in *Desire* as merely the Freudian sin of repression (leading to symbolic incest), this view, I think, underestimates the design of the play. A sin has been committed, and the sin is Ephraim's. We are reminded of this sin by Eben's continued antagonism, his insistence that the farm is his, and (most strongly) by the "something" which hangs over the play from the opening (and gloriously melodramatic!) stage direction to the final curtain. The "something" is the mother, or rather the wrong done her by Ephraim. Her fiercely maternal presence broods over the play—even the most imperceptive of the brothers feels it. She is sensed most strongly at the moment of Eben's sin, the sin which is the beginning of the retributive process against her oppressor, Ephraim—and she approves of the sin. It is at this moment, of course, that Abbie enacts simultaneously the roles of mother and beloved, and this is the second stage (the first being when he "bought" the farm from his brothers with Ephraim's hoarded gold) of Eben's revenge on his father.

Of frail disposition, gentle, and unused to Ephraim's ways, Eben's mother was forced to work intolerably hard; the work finally killed her. Moreover, there is strong reason to believe that Ephraim has unlawfully taken the farm from the mother, and from the son, on whom it should lawfully devolve. If this is so—that is, if the wrong done the mother hangs over the play like a curse—then Eben and Abbie may be seen as agents of the process of justice, directed against Ephraim. Like Theseus, Ephraim must atone for his rash injustice; it becomes fitting that Ephraim is condemned, ironically, to the land he has stolen.

Without this framework of the curse, the reader is faced with a problem of "dialectical" motivation: Eben and Abbie become simply the victims of their lust, and fail to assume the stature of agents of tragic retribution. They are, of course, "locally" (psychologically, dramatically) motivated: Eben by the Oedipus complex and the desire for revenge, Abbie by her desire to provide Ephraim with an heir, thus assuring her chances of retaining the farm, and both of them by a strong sexual urge. It is precisely in the light of these local motivations that Eben and Abbie are rendered capable of becoming the instruments of a larger process, directed against Ephraim. In this play, the spontaneity with which the characters enter their dialectical roles is ample testimony to O'Neill's dramatic integrity. In some of the plays (particularly *The Great God Brown, All God's Chillun*, and, a times, *Mourning Becomes Electra*), we have the regrettable sense that the characters are being forced more by their dialectical roles than by their psychological drives; in *Desire*, however, this sense is virtually absent.

Tragedy makes its statement in its resolution, and it is here that O'Neill brings together the various threads of the play. Eben and Abbie are reunited in their love, even as they expiate their joint crime of murder. In acknowledging his responsibility in the crime, Eben submits to the ideals of love and justice. In so doing, the two insure Ephraim's complete downfall: his pride in his manhood is destroyed, and he is condemned (after a final effort to escape) to the very thing he has coveted. In the quasi-religious terms of the play, the harsh, puritanical ethic has triumphed—to its own inevitable defeat: Abbie and Eben are destroyed; Ephraim has taken an eye for an eye, but in so doing, he is forced to acknowledge the solitary sterility which has been in fact his lot. Eben is turned from his dream of revenge, for the sake of a higher ideal, but as he turns, he insures the completeness of his mother's revenge. O'Neill's tragic curses do not end with the death of the sinner; they must be expiated in a long and solitary process. Ephraim Cabot, in the rocky solitude of his farm, and Lavinia Mannon, entering for the last time the "whited sepulchre," confront their fates in the only possible way.

Una Ellis-Fermor has pointed out that the symmetry of the tragic form may account for the phenomenon of *catharsis,* that the artistic order of the play may be generalized to a kind of cosmic moral order. With the resolution of this play, justice has been done, even if O'Neill has not achieved the artistic symmetry which apparently he feels is necessary. Eben's and Abbie's last lines (HE: Sun's a-rizin'. Purty, hain't it? SHE: Ay-eh) echo precisely the play's opening lines, and the cycle of retribution, hinted at through use of myth, is artistically completed.

The sheriff, acting as a kind of ironic chorus, underscores the importance of the ownership of the land, which has been the basis of the tragic action. His "wish't I owned it!" is uttered in profound ignorance of the consequences of coveting the farm: desire for the farm prompted Abbie's marriage to Ephraim, and her affair with Eben was initially motivated by her desire to secure her position with Ephraim. Ironically, it is when Eben learns that his father intends to will the farm to his (Eben's) son that he utters the curse. It is when Eben is freed of his desire for the farm, when he returns to Abbie (and the rope), that he assures his salvation. Ephraim, on the other hand, is condemned.

It is perhaps in the tragic aspects of the play that we find sanction for the Old Testament overlay, as hinted in the names of the characters. Throughout the play, it is the Hebraic God who is invoked as a God of wrath and retribution. If O'Neill is attempting to enact a classical tragedy in a modern setting, he needs an ethos which will support a tragic view of life, and the god of inevitable vengeance lends sanction to such an ethos.

In *Desire Under the Elms* and *Mourning Becomes Electra,* perhaps the most extensive explorations of O'Neill's view of the father-son battle/symbolic incest theme, the author has resorted to the use of myth, adopting the structure of classical tragedies. The use of myth, as Eliot has pointed out, affords the artist both the necessary artistic control to explore his subject and the means of generalization. In both plays we see O'Neill creating characters who, by their very natures, are endowed with the necessary motivation to enact the myth; both plays too, though different in many ways, contribute to a unified dramatic vision and testify to the fact that this is the way O'Neill found life.

Anna Christie: Her Fall and Rise

by Travis Bogard

I

In November 1921, "plainly showing all the outward evidence of belonging to the world's oldest profession," Eugene O'Neill's Anna Christie, in the person of Miss Pauline Lord, entered Johnny-the-Priest's saloon and spoke one of the memorable lines of the American drama: "Gimme a whiskey—ginger ale on the side. And don't be stingy, baby." Devotees of the moment have not remembered that Anna Christophersen first took the stage a year earlier in the person of Miss Lynn Fontanne, as a respectable British typist, whose greatest oath was "By Jimminy," and who eagerly refreshed herself from the fatigues of an Atlantic crossing with a cup of her father's scalding tea.

The date was March 8, 1920; the place, Atlantic City; and the play, then titled *Chris Christophersen*,[1] was O'Neill's second long play to receive professional production, *Beyond the Horizon* having opened in New York a month earlier. *Chris* was heralded and reviewed in kindly fashion by the *Atlantic City Press*, but it was evidently in trouble from the first. No doctoring cured it, and the play closed in Philadelphia. Plans to publish it were not carried out, presumably because within the year O'Neill was at work turning Anna from typist to trollop, and, in the process, altering both structure and theme so radically as to make of *Anna Christie* a wholly new play.

Anna Christie exists in two earlier drafts, *Chris Christophersen*, and a later version entitled *The Ole Davil*.[2] The latter, although it was ultimately severely edited and provided with a new ending, is substantially the final version of the play. The significant changes are those O'Neill

"*Anna Christie:* Her Fall and Rise" by Travis Bogard. A paper published here for the first time. Copyright © 1964 by Travis Bogard. Printed by permission of the author.

[1] The short title *Chris* is used in the early reviews and by O'Neill in most of his published references to the play. The spelling of the family name is changed to "Christopherson" in the second version, "*The Ole Davil*."

[2] Eugene G. O'Neill, *Chris Christophersen*, a play in six scenes [1920]; "*The Ole Davil*," a play in four acts [1920]. Both unpublished manuscripts. Library of Congress.

made in remodeling *Chris,* shifting its emphasis, darkening its tone, and deepening its philosophical implications.

Curiously, although *Anna Christie* announced firmly and positively his major theme, O'Neill seems never to have trusted his achievement. At one point in his career he considered excluding it from his published works, and he fought a defense of the play in letters to editors and critics with arguments by which he himself appeared to be only half convinced.[3]

Chris, on the other hand, was a play he liked in spite of its faults. He reluctantly gave up the old man as the central figure, and to the end attempted to force Chris's view of the sea onto the play as a whole. O'Neill understood Chris, sympathized with him, and up to the writing of *Anna Christie* had apparently believed as he did that the sea was a devil, frustrating the hopes of men. Chris was his kind of hero, but Anna was strange, and Mat Burke, when he was finally imagined, was a figure altogether new to O'Neill. Writing as truly as he could, he let Anna and Mat force their way to happiness, yet he mistrusted their future. In defense of the play's ending, he fought his own sense that their marriage was a "Henry Arthur Jones compromise," and he tried to show that what appeared happiness was only another trick of the "ole davil." He even tried to make evidence of tragic fate what is in context an inevitably comic point: the marriage of Catholic Mat to Lutheran Anna. In short, he did all he could to make the play what *Beyond the Horizon* had been, a tragedy of frustrated destinies, when in fact *Anna Christie* from the first made all the essential points of happiness and fulfillment that are to be found in great comedy.

Back of all the protest and pretense lie three matters which perhaps will serve to explain why O'Neill never quite came to terms with his play. First was the memory of a play, Chris's play, which he never managed to write. Second were the defects of *Chris Christophersen.* Third were his own ambitions, his correct but perhaps too self-conscious sense of his importance to the American theater, which led him and his critics to mistrust as facile and unworthy all but the most hope-undermining spectacles.

II

When he came to the writing of *Chris,* O'Neill was a master of the one-act play. In his sea plays, with no obvious emphasis on story, but with a careful evocation of mood, he was able to reveal human beings at a cru-

[3] See O'Neill's account of the circumstances of the production and revision of *Chris* in letters to George Jean Nathan, published in Isaac Goldberg, *The Theatre of George Jean Nathan* (New York, 1926) pp. 146-156.

cial moment when they must yield to the forces of destiny operating upon them. His technique, determinedly untheatrical, enabled him to take from his own experience men he had known, and allow them to sit for their portraits without the distortions of narrative. In detailing the small moment, set, somehow, out of time, he was able to write with a touch of the poet and yet remain true to life as he knew it.

For such a play, old Chris was excellent material. In his days among the down-and-outs, O'Neill had roomed with the original of Chris, and, in an interview, told his story. He was an old sailor whose hatred of the sea was such that he had tried to take the giant step and leave the sea. Yet he knew no other work, and to live was forced to accept a job as a barge captain. His time ashore he spent in Jimmy-the-Priest's saloon, drinking nickel-a-shot whiskey and "razzing" the sea. One Christmas eve, stumbling drunkenly home to his barge, he fell to the ice between the piles and the dock and froze to death.[4]

What O'Neill saw in the man's death is not hard to imagine. In *Bound East for Cardiff*, Yank and Driscoll, their hope of an inland farm cut off by Yank's accident, live through the same cycle of hatred, impotence, and death as did O'Neill's friend. So does Olsen in *The Long Voyage Home*. The sea is the force which, elementally, gives these men their small power; it is their earth, their unacknowledged god. The death of Yank, the frustration of Driscoll and Olsen are the results of the sea's power to reach out and claim those who belong to it. Like the dark gods that bring Brutus Jones to his savage end, the sea has a power beyond consciousness, which binds its citizens to it, often in their own despite. The story of the barge captain, like the others, offered evidence of the sea's way with those who seek to betray it, material ready-made for another one-act play.

In the first scene of *Chris Christophersen*, O'Neill wrote what was substantially that short play. The setting, Johnny-the-Priest's saloon, is filled with longshoremen, sailors, and derelicts. If Chris differs from the others, he does so because of his energy, which appears now as drunken humor, now as obsessive hatred of the "dirty ole davil," the sea. He has sought the land, but finding there no life, has made for himself a crustaceous existence, burying himself between land and water, clinging to his barge as to an intertidal rock.

Neither Anna nor Marthy Owen appear in the first version of this scene. Instead, to Johnny's there come two sailors, Mickey and Devlin, whom Chris had known when he was bosun on the windjammer *Neptune*. They are dismayed to learn that Chris is a barge captain. Had he deserted the sea entirely they would not blame him so much as they do

---

[4] Louis Kalonyme, "O'Neill lifts Curtain on his Earlier Days." *New York Times*, December 21, 1924, IV, p. 7.

when they discover that he, a deep-water sailor, has taken refuge in this contemptible limbo. They bluntly state that he must go with them to find a "tall, smart daisy of a full-rigged ship with skys'ls—a beautiful swift hooker that'll take us flyin' south through the Trades." [5] Chris violently refuses this chance to return, and stumbles home to his barge as the scene ends.

Here in outline is a one-act play about Chris, an adequate companion-piece to the stories of the *Glencairn* crew. Add to what is here the news of Chris's death, and the demonstration of the power of the sea to reclaim its flotsam is complete.

Although it was virtually ready to hand, O'Neill rejected this play. He was ambitious, no doubt, and anxious to master longer forms of drama. In the beginning, this may have been the entire conscious motive for giving Chris a daughter and another destiny. More deeply, however, O'Neill may have felt a need to test Chris's belief that the sea was no better than a malevolent force, waiting to overwhelm those within its reach. That a sailor could not escape its power, he believed. He bluntly equated the sea and fate,[6] but that the fate was inevitably destruction he was perhaps not sure. Robert Mayo in *Beyond the Horizon*, yearning toward the sea, had found in it the source of all his hope. Was this hope merely delusive, a lure toward destruction? His own experience—as that experience can be read in the words of Edmund Tyrone [in *Long Day's Journey into Night*]—had shown him that there were moments when being possessed by the sea seemed the supreme good a man could know. Was the ecstasy of identification between man and the sea only another instance of man's being possessed with a devil who cheated his will by calling to impulses and identities beneath consciousness? In the revisions which followed the failure of *Chris*, centrally the question rises: Is Chris right in thinking the sea implacably malevolent, or can one find happiness by living simply in the sea's drift, empowered by its surge?

III

In *Chris Christophersen* the exploration of this problem confounded itself in ambiguity. Anna comes to her father's barge, cool, poised, ambitious. Night school, shorthand, college courses, a career are what she contemplates. Her father persuades her to take one trip on the barge, and she finds in the quiet, foggy journey a kind of peace, and senses a power which to her is strange but not alien. Nothing disturbs this calm. Even when the barge breaks loose from its tow and drifts into the steamer

---

[5] *Chris Christophersen*, I, i, p. 18.
[6] Cf. O'Neill's letter in defense of *Anna Christie* in the *New York Times*, December 18, 1921, VI, p. 1.

lanes, she cannot think that the sea which has been so unexpectedly peace-giving can lead them to destruction.

Her belief is justified, for, although the barge is rammed and sunk by the freighter *Londonderry*, Anna and Chris are rescued. Almost at once, Anna finds herself attracted by the handsome second mate, Paul Andersen. Chris, in a rage that Anna has fallen in love with a sailor, finally attempts to murder Andersen. He fails, and the play ends with Chris returning to the sea as the bosun on the *Londonderry*, and with Paul, fired by Anna's ambition, determined to become first officer and then captain, so that, exercising a captain's privilege, he may sail the sea with his Viking bride.

Evidently, so much narrative destroyed any hope for a mood-piece about Chris. Indeed, after Anna appears, strong in her direction, moving toward self-fulfillment, Chris can no longer hold stage center. His is a character defined by its lack of will, and, therefore, if truly limned, he can take no action. His antagonism to Anna's bethrothal to a sailor is part of his chronic hatred of the sea, but even in *Chris,* hatred does not lead to action until a gossiping steward maliciously goads him to attempt murder. His acceptance of the marriage comes as he crouches, strangely passive despite the knife in his hand, and is forced to overhear a long love scene. In its structure, the scene is not unlike Act III of *A Moon for the Misbegotten,* but in its effect, because Chris's action is forced on him, it is the merest melodrama, and Chris is reduced to something less than the obsessed, brooding man O'Neill had known, the man who was ripe only for death. To force him, as O'Neill did at first, to violent, self-determining action is to betray the character.

Not only is Chris reduced to something less than tragic, but Anna and Paul are caught up in an insoluble dilemma.

Paul, like Chris, is a refugee from his destiny. Both men have, in the seaman's phrase, "swallowed the anchor." Paul defines the term as meaning "to loose your grip, to whine and blame something outside yourself for your misfortune, to quit and refuse to fight back any more, to be afraid to take any more chances because you're sure you're no longer strong enough to make things come out right, to shrink from any more effort and be content to anchor fast in the thing you are." [7]

Paul's contentment with the second mate's berth is his weakness. This job, like Chris's barge, is an ethical tideflat. It lies between the responsibility of the officers and the physical labors of the crew. It is a peaceful world where a man, freed of ambition, can follow the drift of his life as a "citizen of the sea." Anna's love, however, fires him, as their marriage

[7] *Chris Christophersen,* III, ii, pp. 5-6.

moves Chris, into a less phlegmatic pattern of existence, and the play ends rosily.

Andersen's phrase "citizen of the sea" leads to a second important, but conflicting element of theme. Anna, like her later fallen counterpart, has known nothing of the sea. Yet in the fog, drifting on the barge, she talks as Mickey and Devlin talked in the first scene, urging Chris to return to the sea, his proper world. She, unlike her father, has neither fear nor hatred of the sea. If something happens, she feels it will be God's will. To this, Chris cries out in protest: The sea is not God! But as he speaks, the foghorn of the *Londonderry* is heard for the first time, and shortly thereafter, the barge is sunk and Anna has met Paul Andersen. Clearly, although O'Neill has tied a heavy weight to this orthodox love story, the implications are that the sea *is* God, that its way is not to be resisted, and, considering the ending, that its way is good.

Anna and Paul find that they share this identification with the sea, responding to its power as if that response were an inheritance of their blood. They, like all who are the citizens of the sea, belong to the sea and permit her to transmute her energy into will through them. Such "citizens" are necessarily will-less drifters, but their drift is the sea's drift, and their reward is the special sense of elemental belonging which worship of a nameless god makes possible.

Chris Christophersen is a failure because its two central thematic conceptions refuse to merge. Is Andersen, as a "citizen of the sea," to be condemned because he has "swallowed the anchor?" Is it enough to "belong" in total identification with the god, sharing its will-lessness, or must one take arms against the sea and struggle to shape one's destiny? Andersen's resolution is evidently makeshift. In the perspective of Edmund Tyrone's identification with the sea, and the similar sense of "belonging" to some large elemental force which all of O'Neill's heroes seek, Andersen's "citizenship" is not to be denied its value. Yet O'Neill renounces it, and substitutes instead—the year is 1920—a "go-getter," a sea-going Babbitt, thus dismissing his earlier conviction of the sea's malignancy with the easiest of compromises—the happy ending, based on self-reform to gain the affection of a pretty girl.

IV

The chief cause of this thematic dilemma was evidently the narrative which ran counter to all that O'Neill had thus far achieved as a playwright. In *Beyond the Horizon* and in *Emperor Jones,* which the Provincetown Players had produced in 1920, O'Neill had succeeded in extending to longer forms of drama the qualities of his one-act mood plays.

To let his play evolve from mood rather than from narrative meant first that he had to eliminate the picaresque story elements—the ramming of the barge and all that followed. Then, to strengthen mood, he darkened the play, and, in an effort to let the question of the sea's power dominate, he put the sea into the title role. The play became *The Ole Davil.*

To change Anna's character was a simple matter. In *Beyond the Horizon,* he had studied the effects of the land on a citizen of the sea. The frustration of Robert Mayo, his failure in love and in his work, his death by consumption, roughly parallel the career of the new Anna. The rootless, bitter creature, unable to bespeak her needs, is what the land has produced. Yet her inarticulate longing pulls her toward the sea and redemption. With old Chris, in the first version, O'Neill had discovered that when the derelict was given affections and desires, when he was motivated in a narrative to action, he must move up from the bottom; he could fall no further. So with the second Anna. Conceivably she could have been brought lower. She could have lost Mat, have died of consumption. But such an end would have been moralistic with no true moral point—one more dreary image of the payment of the wages of sin, and little else would have emerged. Since O'Neill did not think of her as a sinner, the image was not worth drawing. The real morality for O'Neill lay in her discovery of the sea, her purgation, her rise to cleanness and to hope. Anna, like Robert Mayo, was the victim of the land, not of the sea. Whatever the sea was to do to her was better than what the land had done, because she belonged to the sea, not the land. Redemptive and gentle, the action of the sea is not that of a devil. So far as Anna alone is concerned, Chris's view of the sea is proved wrong.

But Anna is not alone. The inevitable return to laughter is occasioned in part by the placing of Anna and Chris so low on the scale that they cannot, in action, become significantly less than they are. But additionally, the rise to the happy ending is made inevitable by the presence of Mat Burke, the Irish stoker, devised to replace the Conradian weakling Paul Andersen.

For Mat, as for Chris, there was apparently a living original. O'Neill depicted him as the powerful, inarticulate Driscoll in *Bound East for Cardiff,* and again as Yank in *The Hairy Ape.* "He was a giant of a man," as O'Neill described him. "He thought a whole lot of himself, was a determined individualist. He was very proud of his strength, his capacity for grueling work. It seemed to give him mental poise to be able to dominate the stokehole, do more than any of his mates. . . . He wasn't the type [to] just give up, and he loved life." [8]

Although O'Neill does not make the identification, evidently in this

[8] Kalonyme, *loc. cit.*

man lies the source figure for Mat Burke, more poetically visualized in his powerful love of life in *Anna Christie* than in the *Glencairn* plays or *The Hairy Ape*. Mat is a true "citizen of the sea." In him, the thematic ambiguity which confused the portrait of Andersen is eliminated. Mat is the personification of the sea, and he seems to bring to crucial test Chris's conception that the sea is a devil. It is his voice hailing the barge from the storm-swept open boat that, in the final version, answers Chris's frightened protest, "Dat ole davil, sea, she ain't God!" His strength is comparable to the strength of the waves and tides, and he glories in its power. He is a man incapable of clear thought, of working toward a fixed goal. Nevertheless, his nature is defined, his goal established by his instinctive belief in the vitality and power he shares with the sea. To this force, as to the sea, Anna responds, and he, in turn, comes to her with an instant recognition that she has in her the same cleanness, the same strength.

So long, therefore, as he and Anna maintain the simple directness of this mutual recognition and response, they find happiness. On the land, where alien forces have influence, they lose themselves and one another, until by an act of will, an act of groping but conscious self-renunciation, they assert their love and come again into right relationship with the sea's force. Only by such deliberate acquiescence to fate, O'Neill seems to say, can man at all shape his destiny. By accepting one another, they go with the sea, perhaps to the quick, clean death by drowning Mat speaks of, but surely to happiness.

The ending of *The Ole Davil*, reducing Chris to a subordinate role, makes the point explicitly:

CHRIS (*who has been staring at his beer absentmindedly: moodily with a sort of somber premonition*)
It's funny—you and me shipping on the same boat dat vay. It's queer. It ain't right. Ay don't know—it's dat funny vay ole davil sea do her vorst dirty tricks, yes. It's so.
BURKE (*with a hearty laugh of scorn*)
Yerra! Don't be talking! The sea means good to us only, and let you lave her alone. She'll be welcoming you back like a long-lost child, I'm thinking.
CHRIS (*shaking his head: implacably*)
Dirty ole davil!
BURKE (*shouting to Anna*)
Will you listen to the old bucko, Anna? He's afther putting up his fists to the sea again.
ANNA (. . . *laughing*)
Oh, for gawd's sake! [9]

[9] "*The Ole Davil*," p. 119.

The Ole Davil ends in laughter, and Chris's brooding is seen not as prophecy, but as the merely personal characteristic it essentially is. In this ending, too, the belief is asserted that one should not "put up his fists" against fate but rather trust that the sea means no harm, especially to its lost children, like Anna and Chris. This is the belief that makes happiness possible, and it is the one O'Neill repeatedly sought to deny, both in his final version of the ending, which gave Chris the last brooding word, and also in his subsequent published comment on the play, which maintained that the play is only the gawdy introduction of an unwritten tragedy.[10] Yet neither his comment nor his final effort to give Chris the power of prophecy was sufficient, and the play remains a story of love finding its way over parental and societal opposition, a fact which, in this context, testifies to the benevolence of the sea.

To say why O'Neill so mistrusted what he had done is not entirely possible. In his mind there remained the death of the old Chris, in flight and frustration—the death that came to Brutus Jones and to Robert Mayo in *The Emperor Jones* and *Beyond the Horizon* respectively. Nagging too was the fate of the original of his Mat Burke. This man, so full of the strength of life, had inexplicably killed himself, leaping overboard in mid-ocean. The mystery of his suicide was, by O'Neill's admission, part of the genesis of *The Hairy Ape*. The death of the two men may well have caused him to feel that his story was somehow misshapen: since its achieved theatrical form did not coincide with the facts of his experience, the play's philosophical pattern seemed, somehow, a lie.

Then too, he and his associates, all the critical smart set, looked with mistrust on anything that smacked of the popular theater. Under their tutelage, O'Neill was ambitious for tragedy, impatient with anything less. This, conceivably, led him to distrust his sensibility to such identification of man with natural forces as he was later to describe with entire commitment in the final act of *Long Day's Journey into Night*. In these early years, he had not apparently made Nietzsche's Dionysian immer-

---

[10] Cf. note 6 above. O'Neill's defense of the play states in part: "In the last few minutes of 'Anna Christie,' I tried to show the dramatic gathering of new forces out of the old. I wanted to have the audience leave with a deep feeling of life flowing on, of the past which is never the past—but always the birth of the future—of a problem solved for the moment, but by the very nature of its solution involving a new problem. . . . It would have been so obvious and easy—in the case of this play, conventional even—to have made my last act a tragic one. It could have been done in ten different ways, any one of them superficially right. But looking deep into the hearts of my people, I saw it couldn't be done. It would not have been true. They were not that kind. They would act in just the silly immature, compromising way that I have made them act; and I thought that they would appear to others as they do me, a bit tragically humorous in their vacillating weakness."

sion in life a philosophical basis for his tragic inquiries. As a formulated philosophy, when he came to develop it from Nietzsche, the belonging he sought to describe through Anna and Mat may have seemed more critically impressive, more philosophically trustworthy, than when it was only an ephemeral response to the sea felt by a lost girl on a fogbound barge.

Yet what O'Neill had done was to set forth the positive basis for his later tragedies. His mistrust and his weak defense of the play suggest that he did it without full awareness of his direction. It is on the premise stated for the first time in *Anna Christie*, however, that his later tragedy is established, and the play thus provides an essential bridge from the one-act tragedies of mood to the more mature philosophical narratives. *Anna Christie* says positively what the others state by negative implication: that men are, by a quality in their blood, united with a vital force which is their origin and their end. Taking many forms, called by many names, but related as a god is to man, this force gives men their identity and integrity, and it is the source of their power. To belong completely to the god is to know fully happiness and peace, and, having allowed men ecstatic glimpses of such unity, the god-force becomes the end of man's questing. Yet men, tragically, refuse their destiny and fight against being possessed by the god. They seek identity in nay-saying, integrity in flight from their proper center. In the tragedies written before *Mourning Becomes Electra*, O'Neill's hero is a fugitive who has refused his place, who has, with a heresy that is also self-betrayal, denied his god and dispossessed himself. Robert and Andrew Mayo, Brutus Jones, Jim Harris (*All God's Chillun Got Wings*), Nina Leeds (*Strange Interlude*), and Eben Cabot (*Desire Under the Elms*) all make their fate disaster because they attempt to live against the lines of their destiny as the impulses of their blood mark out that line. In the early plays, only Mat Burke, who is the sea's man, and Ephraim Cabot (*Desire Under the Elms*), whose god is stony earth, trust the divinity to which they belong and willingly live out the full course of their fate.

With Lavinia Mannon, the pattern begins to change: man's will, and therefore man's responsibility, is given more play in the action. The happiness of belonging is not all, nor is it so poetically conceived in terms of Dionysian ecstasy. But for Mat and Anna, trust is enough. To belong to one another is to belong to the sea, and in that, although he fought the conclusion through three versions, O'Neill, in the first phase of his career, could not finally deny that there is happiness.

Amor Fati: O'Neill's Lazarus
as Superman and Savior

by Cyrus Day

"YE HIGHER MEN, LEARN, I PRAY YOU—TO LAUGH!"
—*Thus Spake Zarathustra*

I

O'Neill may be said to have thought emotionally, or—to put it the other way—to have been profoundly moved by ideas. He was an artist and not a philosopher, but he asked himself ultimate questions, brooded over them, sought answers to them in Schopenhauer, Nietzsche, and Lao-tze, and gave them emotional expression in his plays.

Thus Schopenhauer's dictum that tragic heroes, when they are defeated, atone for the crime of existence itself rather than for their own individual sins,[1] is the source of the following remark by the illiterate stoker, Yank Smith:

POLICEMAN. What you been doin'?
YANK. Enuf to gimme life for! I was born, see? Sure, dat's de charge. Write it in de blotter. I was born, get me?

Schopenhauer's pessimism in the idiom of the Brooklyn waterfront is an engaging, even a moving anomaly. The point to be noted here, however, is that a metaphysical abstraction had become so familiar a strand in O'Neill's way of thinking—or better, perhaps, in his way of feeling— that he was able to weave it without self-conscious effort into the emotional fabric of *The Hairy Ape.*

"*Amor Fati:* O'Neill's Lazarus as Superman and Savior" by Cyrus Day. From *Modern Drama,* III, No. 3 (December 1960), 297-305. Copyright © 1960 by A. C. Edwards. Reprinted by permission of the author and *Modern Drama.*
[1] *The World as Will and Idea,* II, 51. Schopenhauer cites Calderon, who expresses a similar thought: "Pues el delito mayor del hombre es haber nacido."

Modern man, we are constantly being reminded, is in desperate need of the spiritual comfort provided by religious certainty, but the acids of modernism have dissolved all but the last vestiges of his faith in transcendence. O'Neill dramatizes this dilemma in *The Great God Brown*. As the curtain rises on the first act, Dion Anthony is sitting at a table, staring into space, his mask hanging on his breast.

Suddenly he picks up a copy of the New Testament, opens it at random, and reads aloud: "Come unto me all ye who are heavy laden and I will give you rest."

His face lights up from within. "I *will* come," he whispers, "but where *are* you, Savior?" A door is heard shutting: someone has entered the house. Dion claps on his mask, ashamed of his credulity, and tosses the Testament aside.

"Blah!" he sneers. "Fixation on old Mama Christianity! You infant blubbering in the dark!" He laughs in bitter self-contempt.

Here, and in *The Great God Brown* as a whole, the metaphysical conflict between Christianity and naturalism is given emotional expression in terms of the psychological conflict that splits the protagonist's ego and eventually destroys him. In other words, *The Great God Brown* is a play about a human being's reaction to a metaphysical dilemma. It is not, strictly speaking, about the dilemma itself, for it is a work of dramatic literature and not a theological tract.

The duality implicit in *The Great God Brown* is resolved in the last act when Brown, Dion's successor, dies with the prayer "Our Father Who Art" on his lips. The omission of the words "in Heaven," and the fact that the prayer is taught him by the Earth Mother, signify that Brown believes in a God, but not in the God of Christianity, and not in the immortality of the individual soul. By way of compensation he finds the justification of life in the biological cycle, eternally repeated, of birth, suffering, and death.

"Who art! Who art!" he cries exultantly.

> BROWN. I know! I have found Him! I hear Him speak! "Blessed are they that weep, for they shall laugh!" Only he that has wept can laugh! The laughter of Heaven sows earth with a rain of tears, and out of Earth's transfigured birth-pain the laughter of Man returns to bless and play again in innumerable dancing gales of flame upon the knees of God! (*He dies.*)
>
> CYBEL. Always spring comes again bearing life! Always again! Always, always forever again!—Spring again!—life again!—summer and fall and death and peace again!—but always, always, love and conception and birth and pain again! bearing the glorious, blazing crown of life again! (*She stands like an idol of Earth, her eyes staring out over the world.*)

This is the tragic culmination of the story: Brown achieves inner peace and dies. But O'Neill's verbal ineptitude comes perilously close to reducing what he intended to be Brown's mystical assertion of his naturalistic faith to a sentimental absurdity. The drama all but evaporates, and only the specious poetry remains.

Just before the final curtain, however—after Margaret has had *her* chance to be poetical—O'Neill reverts to the technique of *The Hairy Ape* and almost salvages the final scene. The police captain, who thinks Anthony has killed Brown (and symbolically he is right), re-enters in order to question Cybel.

> CAPTAIN. Well, what's his name?
> CYBEL. Man!
> CAPTAIN (*taking a grimy notebook and an inch-long pencil from his pocket*). How d'yuh spell it?
>
> (*Curtain*)

Juan in *The Fountain*, an earlier play than *The Great God Brown*, is a divided soul like Dion Anthony and the later Brown, and he too is destroyed by the struggle between his two selves. Before he dies, moreover, he discovers, as Brown does, that God (being) and the phenomenal world (becoming) are one—I do not think I am misrepresenting O'Neill's thesis—and that immortality means the cyclical regeneration of the biological abstraction Man. His conversion to this creed gives him "the calm of deep serenity," and he is reabsorbed by the material universe (*i.e.*, he dies) in a state of ecstatic happiness. The theme of *The Fountain* and the theme of *The Great God Brown*, as expressed in their concluding lines, are thus seen to be identical.

II

Lazarus Laughed reiterates this theme. O'Neill wrote it in 1925 and 1926, immediately after finishing *The Great God Brown* and before beginning *Strange Interlude*. The ideas embodied in it had been germinating in him ever since his New London days, before World War I, when he first read *Zarathustra* and *The Birth of Tragedy*. They are Nietzsche's ideas, for the most part, but O'Neill felt then, and for many years afterward, that they answered various troublesome questions that he and other cosmically alienated moderns were asking themselves in the 1920's.

My object in the present essay is to consider some of the ways in which the influence of Nietzsche's philosophy is revealed in *Lazarus Laughed*. I shall stress, in particular, O'Neill's reinterpretation of Nietzsche's doctrines of the superman,[2] *amor fati,* eternal recurrence, and pity. I shall also (by way of conclusion) touch briefly on O'Neill's failure (I take his failure for granted) to transmute Nietzsche's ideas into effective drama.

O'Neill was under the illusion, when writing *Lazarus Laughed,* that Nietzsche's philosophy of power could fill the vacancy caused by modern man's loss of faith in God and religion. He created Lazarus, therefore, in the image of a Nietzschean superman, assigned him the dual role of savior and tragic hero, and made him the spokesman for the dying Brown's naturalistic creed. This creed, as we shall see, is a variation of Nietzsche's *amor fati,* and O'Neill thought at the time that it could teach modern man how to live joyously and die fearlessly. He did not consider modern Christianity capable of fulfilling either of these primary religious functions.

The will-to-power—the unifying principle of Nietzsche's philosophy— is variously manifested in the attitudes and conduct of all the characters in *Lazarus Laughed.* Lazarus, as superman, spiritualizes and sublimates it. He triumphs over his animal passions through self-discipline and achieves the kind of happiness that accrues to those who are strong enough to perfect and master themselves. He has no desire to master others.

His wife Miriam, a "life-denying" Christian, extirpates the will-to-power. She resigns herself to sorrow and suffering, and she values life on earth only in so far as it is a preparation for life in the world to come. Lazarus affirms life; she negates it and longs for death. Lazarus, symbolically, dresses in white; Miriam dresses in black.

The Romans, Nazarenes, and orthodox Jews represent the generality of men. They do not try either to sublimate or to extirpate their desires; they try instead to overcome and dominate others. When they fail, they are themselves overcome by their own animality. Because they are afraid of death, they kill or threaten to kill their fellow men.

Thus the Nazarenes and orthodox Jews in Act I "raise clenched fists like threatening talons": they mutter and growl, and their "voices sound animal-like in anger." The Romans in Act IV huddle close to the ground like "terrified rats, their voices squeaky with fright," while Caligula, contemptuous alike of them and of himself, addresses them as his faithful scum and his brother swine.

Most men, O'Neill thought, are curs, dogs, roosters, pigs, swine, rats,

---

[2] O'Neill was aware that the authentic superman has nothing in common with the brutal conqueror of Nazi mythology, or the disembodied end-product of Shavian evolution, or the Dionysian pagan who gives free rein to his animal sensuality.

jackals, and hyenas. Only a few have the strength to re-create themselves as supermen. Lazarus is able to do so, and to rise above the animal level, because (having experienced death) he understands two of the cardinal doctrines of Nietzsche's philosophy: *amor fati* and eternal recurrence. *Amor fati*, or love of necessity, may be defined as the superman's attitude toward life and death. On the positive side it implies the joyful acceptance and affirmation of earthly life and of earthly suffering. On the negative side it implies the rejection of the Christian belief in personal immortality. "Remain true to earth," Zarathustra advises, "and believe not those who speak unto you of super-earthly hopes. . . . Ye want to be paid besides, ye virtuous ones? Ye want reward for your virtue?"[3]

"O Curious Greedy Ones," says Lazarus, "is not one world in which you know not how to live enough for you?"

"This life is thy eternal life," says Nietzsche.[4]

"Men must learn to live," says Lazarus.

And believing as he does that earthly life (becoming) is the only reality he can ever know, the superman deliberately immerses himself in it, affirms it, says Yes to it, and not only endures its pains and vicissitudes, but even welcomes them and rejoices in them. "My formula for greatness in man," Nietzsche said, "is *amor fati:* That a man should wish to have nothing altered, either in the future, the past, or for all eternity. Not only must he endure necessity: . . . but he must also love it."[5] *Lazarus Laughed* is the result of O'Neill's intellectual and emotional commitment to this philosophy.

Eternal recurrence, the second of the two doctrines mentioned above, meant one thing for Nietzsche and another for O'Neill. For Nietzsche it meant "the absolute and eternal cyclical repetition of all things":[6] the hypothesis (to express the concept more simply) that all the events of history are destined to be re-enacted, precisely as they first occurred, in the same order and sequence, and not "once only, but again and again, through all eternity."[7] For O'Neill, on the other hand, it meant (in *Lazarus Laughed* as in *The Fountain* and *The Great God Brown*) the cyclical regeneration of the biological abstraction Man. "Men pass! Like rain into the Sea!" Lazarus says. "Man remains! For Man death is not!

[3] *Thus Spake Zarathustra*, Prologue, 3, and II, 27.
[4] *The Twilight of the Idols*, 1927, p. 22.
[5] *Ecce Homo*, II, 10.
[6] *Ibid.*, IV, 3.
[7] *Die Frölichewissenschaft*. Cited by W. A. Kaufmann, *Nietzsche*, 1950, p. 285. Chapter 11, "Superman and Eternal Recurrence," in Professor Kaufmann's study provides an indispensable explanation of the interdependence, in Nietzsche's philosophy, of the doctrine of the superman and the doctrine of eternal recurrence.

Man, Son of God's Laughter, *is!*" Nietzsche deduced the doctrine from the premise that time and space are infinite—O'Neill, from the empirically observed repetition of the phenomena of birth and death. O'Neill's conception of eternal recurrence is more primitive than Nietzsche's. It is analogous in some respects to the myths of cyclical birth and renewal—year-myths, for instance—by means of which archaic man tried to escape from the horrors of becoming and to maintain or establish a meaningful relationship with being. Myths of this kind, variously embedded in Indian and Greek systems of thought, were interpreted by Greek speculation in such a way as to lend the permanence of being to the evanescence of becoming.[8] Nietzsche, according to Professor Kaufmann, thought that his nineteenth century version of the doctrine, based on linear rather than on circular time, achieved the same result:

> [Nietzsche] thought he had succeeded in creating a magnificent synthesis of the philosophies of Heraclitus and Parmenides, of the dynamic and the static world-pictures, of being and becoming: "That *all recurs* is the most extreme *approach of a world of becoming to one of being.*" Nietzsche's doctrine would "*impress*" upon becoming the character of being." In the moment it would find eternity.[9]

Pity, a Christian virtue, has no place in the superman's creed. Nietzsche denounces it on the ground that suffering is a necessary part of the experience of the man who overcomes and perfects himself. Pity condones weakness. It involves a measure of condescension and even of contempt, and is therefore psychologically degrading to those who pity and to those who are pitied. Plato, Spinoza, and Kant are alike, Nietzsche observes, in their deprecation of pity.[10]

Lazarus represses his natural pity when his father and mother and two sisters are slain in a religious riot. Miriam is grief-stricken, but Lazarus cries "Yes! Yes!! Yes!!!" in a triumphant voice and laughs "from the depths of his exalted spirit." When his followers fall on their own swords, Lazarus' laugh is like "a triumphant, blood-stirring call to that ultimate attainment in which all prepossession with self is lost in an ecstatic affirmation of Life."

Miriam, meanwhile, a life-denying Christian who never laughs, is on her knees, a black figure of grief, "her arms raised outward like the arms

---

[8] Mircea Eliade, *Cosmos and History: The Myth of the Eternal Return*, 1959, p. 123. Professor Eliade's book, invaluable to the student of *Lazarus Laughed*, was first published in 1949 as *Le Mythe de l'Éternel Retour*. W. R. Trask's translation first appeared in 1954.

[9] Kaufmann, *Nietzsche*, p. 288.

[10] Kaufmann, *Nietzsche*, p. 319.

of a cross." Caligula, the ape-man, hops up and down, watching for a sign of weakness in Lazarus and, when he thinks he has detected one, taunting him for giving way to pity. But Caligula is mistaken: far from pitying his followers, Lazarus exults in their "victory." They *will* to die, he tells Miriam. They *will* their own annihilation, they *will* to change. Change, he says, has been the rule of life ever since the first squirming specks, our primordial ancestors, crawled out of the sea. Death means change, and in willing to die, Lazarus' followers are synchronizing themselves with the rhythm of the universe. This thought intoxicates them and eliminates any urge they may have to preserve their own inconsequential lives and egos.

The casual reader of *Lazarus Laughed* may wonder why Miriam's longing for death is a denial of life, whereas the suicide of Lazarus' followers is an affirmation of life. The inconsistency, a real one, is the result of the fact that O'Neill uses the word "life" in two different ways. When he says that Christians deny life, he means that they undervalue their earthly, temporal existence. When he says that Lazarus' followers affirm life, he means that they accept the universe. Their laughter is the symbolical expression of their acceptance.

The paradox that suicide can be an affirmation of life is explicable in terms of the philosophy of Schopenhauer. Lazarus laughs when his followers are dying, not because he is a madman or a monster, but because he is a symbol of a concept borrowed by Nietzsche from Schopenhauer and incorporated in *The Birth of Tragedy*. The will-to-live is Schopenhauer's ultimate reality or thing-in-itself. Its manifestations or objectifications are the phenomena (including human beings) of the material universe. As such they are illusions, doomed (because each is competing with the others for existence) to fight with each other and to destroy each other,—in a word, to suffer. When they die, they lose their individual identity and are merged in the eternal, formless reality of the will-to-live from which they sprang. It is in this sense that the self-annihilation of the individual can be called an assertion of life or of the will-to-live, and that the individual can achieve impersonal immortality. And it is in this sense that Lazarus uses the word "life" in his slogan "There is only life." He does not mean either life on earth or eternal life in the Christian sense of the term.

Nietzsche, in *The Birth of Tragedy*, reinterprets Schopenhauer's ideas in terms of the antithesis between man's Apollonian and Dionysian impulses. O'Neill tries to express them in *Lazarus Laughed* by means of the monosyllable "Yes," four or five ambiguous slogans, and Lazarus' mystical (and mystifying) laughter. He never quite succeeds in making his meaning clear.

Schopenhauer's philosophy is dualistic; Nietzsche's, subsequent to *The Birth of Tragedy*, is monistic. There are inconsistencies, therefore, between the parts of *Lazarus Laughed* that stem from *The Birth of Tragedy* and the parts that stem from *Thus Spake Zarathustra* and Nietzsche's later works. One of them is the inconsistency in the use of the word "life."

III

If Jesus had lived longer, Nietzsche maintained, He "would have learned to live, and love the earth—and laughter also! Believe it, my brethren! He died too early; He himself would have disavowed His doctrine had He attained my age." [11] But being immature, He had known only tears when He died, and so taught patience with what is "earthly," and even hatred of it, instead of joyful acceptance.

These remarks explain the significance of what happened when Lazarus first rose from the tomb. An eye-witness, one of the guests in the house of Lazarus' parents, describes the scene as follows:

> Jesus looked into his face for what seemed a long time and suddenly Lazarus said "Yes" as if he were answering a question in Jesus' eyes. . . . Then Jesus smiled sadly but with tenderness, as one who from a distance of years of sorrow remembers happiness. And then Lazarus knelt and kissed Jesus' feet and both of them smiled and Jesus blessed him and called him "My Brother" and went away.

This little tableau is apt to convey the erroneous impression that Lazarus' doctrines are compatible, in O'Neill's opinion, with Christ's. It is clear, however, that it is Jesus who learns from Lazarus, and not Lazarus from Jesus, and that the substance of what he learns is contained in the word "Yes" and in the contrast that is drawn between sorrow and happiness. The implications are that He disavows His gospel of tears and authorizes Lazarus, by giving him His blessing, to preach the Nietzschean gospel of happiness. When He goes away, O'Neill is, in effect, dismissing Him and promoting Lazarus to the position of savior in His place.

O'Neill is much more critical of Jesus' disciples and followers[12] than of Jesus Himself. Mary, for instance—Lazarus' sister—turns Christianity into vindictive intolerance and *ressentiment*. Miriam, his wife, is meek and resigned. As a young woman she symbolizes eternal motherhood, but

---

[11] *Thus Spake Zarathustra*, I, 21.

[12] For an explanation of why Nietzsche calls them Nazarenes, see Kaufmann, *Nietzsche*, pp. 328-331.

because she is a Christian she "denies life," grows rapidly older and older, and dies without having learned to live.

Lazarus grows rapidly younger and younger: he looks like a man of fifty in Act I and like a teen-age boy in Act IV. His naturalistic faith is, symbolically, the fountain of youth that Juan, in *The Fountain,* looks for in a material sense all his life. O'Neill may have been thinking, here, of an ancient version of the myth of eternal return, mentioned by Plato,[13] in which the processes of growth are reversed and the old become young again. Their white hair becomes dark, their bearded cheeks become smooth, and their bodies become soft and small, until they look like newly born infants, and then they disappear altogether. This is what would have happened to Lazarus if he had not been burned at the stake —only, of course, instead of disappearing, he would have returned to some kind of symbolical womb.

A halo surrounds Lazarus' head; a mysterious light emanates from his body; his presence commands attention; he speaks as one having authority; his laughter is enough in itself to convert people to his creed. But after he leaves them, they relapse into their former condition of fear and mutual hatred. His ministry is a failure, for the "greatness of Saviors is that they may not save," and the "greatness of Man is that no god can save him—until he becomes a god." This paradox means that men must "create" themselves by sublimating their will-to-power and overcoming their limitations by their own unaided efforts. "Let it be my pride as Man," Lazarus says, "to re-create the God in me." But the generality of men are "despicable" and cannot transcend their animality. Lazarus himself scores a victory over death—the same sort of victory previously scored by his followers—but his achievement of martyrdom is futile. Caligula—half man and half beast—retains possession of the earth. "Men forget," Caligula observes as the final curtain falls.

Considered as tragic hero rather than as savior, Lazarus suffers from a curious and probably unique handicap: he has already fought the battle with himself that tragic heroes are customarily obliged to fight, and he has already achieved inner peace and died. He is a static character, incapable of learning anything more by suffering than he has already learned. He endures harrowing external calamities, but the tides of inner conflict never sweep through him. The interest of the reader is sustained, therefore—if it is sustained at all—more by curiosity concerning what O'Neill is trying to say than by pity and fear for the self-secure, self-honored Lazarus.

Lazarus is colorless as well as static. He has no personal traits of any

[13] *The Statesman,* 270. See Eliade, *Cosmos and History: The Myth of the Eternal Return,* 1959, pp. 120-121.

distinctive kind; he is not, in fact, a recognizable human being. He is a symbol, an abstraction, a mere mouthpiece—and an inarticulate one at that—for O'Neill's ideas.

IV

And so we are back at the point where we started. *The Great God Brown*, we suggested, is about Dion Anthony's reactions to an idea; it is not, strictly speaking, about the idea itself. The two halves of Dion's personality are pitted against each other in mortal combat, and the idea that divides and conquers him (and his successor Brown) is presented in the form of a dilemma. Dilemmas, having two horns, are the sort of stuff dramatic conflict is made of.

Lazarus Laughed, on the contrary, is a play about an idea rather than about a human being's reactions to an idea. Lazarus is an integrated, undivided character, and the idea he advocates is presented in the form of the undivided truth. Effective drama cannot be erected on such foundations. *Lazarus Laughed* is O'Neill's ugly didactic duckling; it is a tract in the guise of a play. Despite his own emotional involvement, and despite the masks, the crowds, the pageantry, the violence, and—yes—the importance of the subject, O'Neill did not succeed in transmuting his ideas into what the critics of the 1950's have become accustomed to calling viable drama.

Eugene O'Neill's New Play
[*Mourning Becomes Electra*]

by *Stark Young*

Mourning Becomes Electra, a trilogy: *Homecoming, The Hunted, The Haunted,* by Eugene O'Neill. Guild Theatre. October 26, 1931.

To hear the bare story, shortly told, of this new O'Neill play, with all its crimes and murders, may easily bring a flouting smile or recall Mrs. Malaprop's announcement of Sir Lucius' and Bob Acres' duel: "So, so, here's fine work, here's fine suicide, parricide and simulation going on in the fields." [1] The same thing could be said of *Hamlet* or *King Lear* or *Oedipus King,* of course, but this is sure to be the line the jibes will take from such of the play's critics as are unfriendly or impatient or incapable. As to the length of the event, the actual performance at the Guild could be considerably shortened by going faster in many places, though, take it for all in all, the length of the play itself is for the most part organic with both its meaning and its effect. As to its depressing effects, we will come to that later.

The title, as we see, intends to dispose at the start of the relation of *Mourning Becomes Electra* to the Greek drama. The story of the house of Atreus was set down by Homer, Pindar, Aeschylus, Sophocles, Euripides and diverse other Greek writers whose works are not extant. From this house shadowed by an ancient curse, Agamemnon, brother of Menelaus, goes forth to the war at Troy. His wife, Clytemnestra, the sister of Helen, during her husband's absence takes for her paramour Aegisthus and shares the government of Argos with him. In due time Agamemnon, having at the god's behest sacrificed his daughter Iphigenia

[1] A reference to Sheridan's *The Rivals.*

and bringing with him Cassandra, Priam's daughter, returns, and is murdered by Clytemnestra and her lover. Electra, his daughter, is shamed and degraded and prays for the return of her brother Orestes, long ago sent out of the country by his mother and now become a man. Orestes returns, kills Clytemnestra and Aegisthus. He is pursued by the Erinyes, and only after wandering and agony and a vindication of himself before the tribunal of Athena's Areopagus is he cleansed of his sin.

Mourning Becomes Electra begins with the mother and daughter, Christine and Lavinia, waiting there in the house of the Mannons, the return of Ezra Mannon from the war, which with Lee's surrender is about over. A thread of romance is introduced between Lavinia and Peter, and between Lavinia's brother, Orin, and Hazel, Peter's sister. Meanwhile Captain Brant comes to call; he pays a certain court to Lavinia, and she, acting on a cue from the hired man, who has been on the place sixty years, traps him into admitting that he is the son of one of the Mannons who had seduced a Canadian maidservant and been driven from home by his father, Lavinia's grandfather. She has all her data straight now. She has suspected her mother, followed her to New York, where Christine has pretended to go because of her own father's illness, but has in fact been meeting Adam Brant. Lavinia has written her father and her brother, hinting at the town gossip about her mother. We learn that Captain Brant had returned to avenge his mother but instead had fallen passionately in love with Christine, who loves him as passionately as she hates her husband. From this point the play moves on, with the father's hatred of the son, who returns it, the son's adoration of his mother, the daughter's and the mother's antagonism, the daughter's and father's devotion, to Christine's murder of her husband with the poison sent by Brant and substituted for the medicine prescribed against his heart trouble. Part One of the play ends here. Orin returns, after an illness from a wound in the head. Christine tries to protect herself in her son's mind against the plots of Lavinia. Lavinia, in the room where her father's body lies, convinces him with the facts; they trail Christine to Brant's ship, where she has gone to warn him against Orin. Orin shoots Brant. Christine next day kills herself. Brother and sister take a long voyage to China, stop at the southern isles, come home again. Substitutions have taken place, Lavinia has grown like her mother, Orin more like his father. Meanwhile his old affair with Hazel, encouraged at last by Lavinia, who now wants to marry Peter, is canceled; he finds himself making an incestuous proposal to Lavinia and is repulsed by her. He shoots himself. In the end Lavinia, speaking words of love to Peter, finds Adam's name on her lips. She breaks with Peter, orders the blinds of her house nailed shut, and goes into the house, to live there till her death. Justice has been done, the Mannon dead will be there and she will be there.

So bare an account serves the plot a little, but can give scant indication of the direct speeches and actions heavily charged with the burden and meaning of the scenes; nor does it convey the power and direct arrangement of some of them, that, for example, of the brother and sister at Brant's cabin, where the mere visual elements convey as much as the words. The chantey with which this scene opens, the song and the singer's drunkenness, the lonely ship in the dusk, establishing as it does the mood of longing, futility, land chains and the sea's invitation and memory, is a fine idea and greatly enriches the texture of the play.

It will be obvious that the American dramatist, as the Greek did, used a well-known outline which he could fill in to his purpose. Obviously, too, Ezra Mannon is Agamemnon, Captain Brant Aegisthus, Christine Clytemnestra, Lavinia Electra, and Orin Orestes. But to dismiss the matter by saying that Mr. O'Neill has merely repeated the classic story in modern terms is off the track. Let it go at that and you will miss even the really classic elements in the play and get only the Greek side of it that is self-evident and that would be easy for any dramatist to imitate.

The story itself follows the Greeks up to the middle of the third division of the play, and here the incest motive, the death of Orin and the transference of the whole situation and dramatic conclusion from the mother to the sister depart from Aeschylus, Sophocles, and Euripides. Adam Brant's relation to the family adds to the role of the lover the motif of a blood relationship. The old hired man, the confidant, parallels to some extent a Greek device, familiar to us in countless plays. The townspeople and workmen are now and again a kind of chorus. Many of the shadings and themes are from the older plays; for a good example, the servant's line in Aeschylus about the dead killing one who lives, which underlies one of the new play's main themes. The death of the lover, as in Aeschylus and Euripides, not as in Sophocles, comes before that of the mother, which throws the stress where the O'Neill play needs it. The division of the play into three parts is, of course, like the trilogy of the Greek dramatists. On the other hand, the dividing line is much less distinct in *Mourning Becomes Electra*; the final curtain of the first part, for example, falls, it is true, on Mannon's death, as in Aeschylus it does on Agamemnon's, but there is not the same effect of totality because of the stress put on Lavinia; in *Agamemnon* Electra does not even appear.

The magnificent theme that there is something in the dead that we cannot placate falsely is in the Greek plays and in the O'Neill play. The end of the play is by imaginative insight Greek in spirit: Lavinia goes into the house, the blinds are closed forever, the stage is silent, the door shut, the exaltation is there, the completion, the tragic certainty. Finally, the peculiar kind of suspense employed in the play is Greek. The playwright has learned the adult suspense of the classics as compared with the adolescent concept of suspense, hit off happily enough at times, that reigns in the romantic drama of the North. Classic suspense does not depend on a mere crude strain, wondering how things will turn out, however entertaining and often dramatic that effect may be. The classic suspense has even a biological defense: you know that in life you will come to death, but just how the course of all your living will shade and fulfill itself you do not know, and you are borne up by an animal will to survive, a passionate participation, an absorbed contemplation of the course to be run, till the last moment completes itself. In the classic form, where the outcome is already known, lies the highest order of suspense. Knowing how things will end, you are left free to watch what qualities and what light will appear in their progression toward their due and necessary finish. You hang on what development, what procession exactly of logic, ecstasy or fate, will ensue with them, what threads of beautiful or dark will come into their human fabric. Suspense proves thus to be not necessarily a contrivance, effective as that may be; it is an inner quality.

It is interesting in our confused and feministic epoch that this new employment of the theme gives the play to Electra. Nowhere in Greek does this happen. From Sophocles there survives what must be only a section of a trilogy, the *Electra;* and though so much of the torment and waiting has been hers, Electra is at the end let off with a betrothal to Orestes' faithful Horatio, Pylades, and the forebodings and remorse rise in Orestes only, who has struck the death blow on his mother. In Euripides' *Electra* the conclusion is the forebodings of Orestes and the marriage of Electra to Pylades; in his *Orestes* Electra cleaves to her brother, who is in a violent neurotic sickness, quite modernly indicated; they are both in danger from the State for their action, and the whole situation is solved with a trivial and silly denouement, gods from the machine, killings and abductions, wholly undramatic and redeemed, in so far as it is redeemed, only by Euripides' dialectic and poetic glamour. In Aeschylus, Electra appears only in the middle of the trilogy; the central hero is the royal line, represented by Agamemnon and Orestes.

Along with these more accessible and manifest likes and dislikes, there are numerous points about Mr. O'Neill's play that are additions to or changes from the original Greek and that are yet both high creative invention and, in modern terms and material, re-creations in the most profound sense of Greek equivalents. The most brilliant of these is the incest motive, coming toward the last of the play. (We must recall Shelley's remark that of all tragic motives incest is the most powerful, since it brings the passions most violently into play.) For Orestes the gray forms at the back, invisible at first to all but himself, are the Erinyes, the Furies who will avenge the crime he has committed within his own blood. They are the daughters of night, and when they have been appeased, their other selves, the Eumenides, the Gentle Ones, will pass by and leave him peace. For Orin Mannon there comes the sudden form of his desire, incest: the realization and admission of what it has all been about all along, his feelings toward his father, toward his mother, toward Brant, toward Lavinia. This recognition of his obsession is his avenging Erinyes. In this detail alone might rest the argument that Eugene O'Neill, placing a Greek theme in the middle of the last century, has written the most modern of all his plays.

The motives of the resemblance among the three men, Mannon, Orin, and Brant, is a great dramatic image: it provides a parallel to the Greek motive of a cursed house, and at the same time remains modern and fresh. The Greek husband returned from the war with his paramour and after sacrificing his daughter; Mannon's return will bring the son also home again, to a more subtle and complex situation than the other. The Islands of the Blessed, everywhere in Greek dreams, the southern islands that are the symbol of so much modern meaning in *Mourning Becomes Electra,* make a fine motif. The mother in *Mourning Becomes Electra* is not killed by her son but takes her own life; his essential murder, nevertheless, of his mother turns in his mind with a terror more modern but no less destroying; his mind storms with the Furies—"thoughts that accuse each other," as Cicero, writing in the sophistication of four centuries after Sophocles, defined them.

It is not the Guild's fault if there is no overwhelming performance in *Mourning Becomes Electra.* The casting of such a play is very difficult, and doubly so in the absence of any training in our theater that would prepare actors for the requirements of such parts. The best performances came in the scenes between the mother and son, where Mme. Nazimova's sense of theater and her fluid response combined with Mr. Earle Larimore's simple and right attack on his role, were truly convincing, and in the scene between husband and wife, where Mr. Lee Baker gave a wholly right impersonation and the exact dramatic value for the play. Mr. Erskine Sanford turns out admirably in two character parts, the village doctor and the old workman who takes a bet on braving the ghost in the house. Miss Alice Brady had the role of all roles in the play most difficult. Her performance of this modern Electra was sincere, and was sustained at times not only by a sort of *tour-de-force* achievement, but with real physical power, voice and all. In a few scenes she was pathetic as well, clear and moving, and her beauty most impressive. No doubt there was some instruction from the author himself as to keeping the face like a mask, rigid and motionless, as if fate itself were living there in this passionate and resolute being. As for the Greek of that intention, we must recall that in the Attic theater the mask for Electra was very likely one of tortured lines, that the Greek theater changed masks if need be from one scene to another, and that the Greek actor in the part could avail himself of gesture, dance movement, and a thorough training in voice, meter, speech, and singing. Realistically, which is to say, in life, such rigidity never occurs except as a sign of disease. Aesthetically it belongs only in the midst of a general stylistic whole, as in the Greek drama or the Chinese theater that Mei Lan-fang[2] brought to us. Technically it is immensely difficult, and derives not from an actual rigidity at all. Rigidity, masklike to the utmost, if you will, is a form of rhythm, as silence, when perceptible, exists within a rhythm. It is unfair to bring so great an artist as Mei Lan-fang into the argument, but he gave us the whole model for such a problem in acting—the eyes constantly moving, the head imperceptibly in motion, supported by a complete and often almost invisible rhythm of the body, the emotions precise and compelling because of their very abstraction. Miss Brady's performance had several unforgettable moments. On the whole it moved gravely and in a manner remarkably well sustained just below the surface of the motives set for her by the dramatist; but her performance, by failing both the darkness and the exaltation of the part, often made only oppressive and unvaried what should have been burning and unconquerably alive and dominating. When we come right down to it, however, the best acting in the play is Mr. Earle Larimore's. In all his scenes up to the very last part, where he mouths too much and makes faces instead of a more intense concentration on his effects, he is excellent. In the scenes with his mother especially, he contrived by a certain emotional humility before the moment in which he shared to come out securely right.

Out of Mr. Robert Edmond Jone's curtain and four settings, the rooms and the ship seem to me adequate without any haunting of the imagination, the front of the house dramatically right save for the lighting toward the rear, unnecessarily cruel to the actors. Mr. Philip Moeller's directing was admirable all through for its taste and evenness, its clear movement and fine placing of the scene. Its one fault was its tempo. There can be no doubt that Mr. O'Neill's play suffers greatly and will be accused of pretentiousness where it is wholly sincere and

[2] Chinese actor who opened a season of repertory at the Forty-ninth Street Theatre, New York, on February 17, 1930.

direct, because of the slowness with which the speeches are said. Very often the effect is only that of a bourgeois respect for something to be taken as important. If it is the Greek spirit that is sought, the answer is that the Greek reading of lines was certainly formal but not necessarily slow; the chances are, in fact, that in the Greek theater the cues were taken closely in order to keep the music going. And the Greeks had the advantage of music, dancing, and a great declamatory style, the lack of which will have to be balanced by anything rather than this obvious spacing and pausing and frequent monotone that we encounter at the Guild.

In *Mourning Becomes Electra* Mr. O'Neill comes now into the full stretch of clear narrative design. He discovers that in expressive pattern lies the possibility of all that parallels life, a form on which fall infinite shadings and details, as the light with its inexhaustible nuances and elements appears on a wall. He has come to what is so rare in Northern art, an understanding of the depth and subtlety that lie in repetition and variation on the same design.

As to the depressing element of *Mourning Becomes Electra*, I have only to say that it seems to me above anything else exhilarating. There is a line of Leopardi's[3] where he speaks of poetry as "my delight and my Erinyes"; and once, thinking of the eternal silence, he hears the wind among the trees and goes comparing the infinite silence to that voice, and remembers the eternal, and the dead seasons, and the present and living, and the sound of it, *e il suon di lei*. In this immensity his thought drowns, and shipwreck is sweet to him in such a sea. When the play ended, and the last Mannon was gone into the house, the door shut, I felt in a full, lovely sense that the Erinyes were appeased, and that the Eumenides, the Gentle Ones, passed over the stage.

[3] Giacomo Leopardi (1798-1837), Italian poet and scholar.

Trying to Like O'Neill

by Eric Bentley

. . . Last autumn, when I was invited to direct the German language *première* of *The Iceman*, along with Kurt Hirschfeld, I decided I should actually succeed in liking O'Neill. I reminded myself that he had been honored with prefaces by Joseph Wood Krutch and Lionel Trilling, that he had aroused enthusiasm in the two hardest-to-please of the New York critics, Stark Young and George Jean Nathan, and so forth. I even had a personal motive to aid and abet the pressure of pure reason. My own published strictures on O'Neill had always been taken as a display of gratuitous pugnacity, amusing or reprehensible according to my reader's viewpoint. Under a rain of dissent one begins to doubt one's opinions and to long for the joy that is not confined to heaven when a sinner repenteth. Now it is a fallacy that drama critics are strongly attached to their own opinions; actually they would far rather be congratulated on having the flexibility to change their minds. In short, I would have been glad to write something in praise of O'Neill, and I actually did lecture—and speak on the Swiss radio—as an O'Neillite. If this seems disingenuous, I can only plead that I spoke as a director, not as critic, and that it is sometimes a great relief to do so. There is something too godlike about criticism; it is a defiance of the injunction to men: Judge not that ye be not judged; it is a strain. And if it would be subhuman to give up the critical attitude for mere liking and disliking, the directorial, interpretative attitude seems a more mature and challenging alternative.

Both critic and director are aware of faults, but whereas it is the critic's job to point them out, it is the director's job to cover them up, if only by strongly bringing out a play's merits. It is not true that a director accepts a play with its faults on its head, that he must follow the playwright even into what he believes to be error. He cannot be a self-respecting interpreter without following his own taste and judgment. Thus, Hirschfeld and I thought we were doing our best by O'Neill in toning certain things down and playing others full blast. Specifically, there seemed to us to be in *The Iceman Cometh* a genuine and a non-genuine element, the former, which we regarded as the core, being realistic, the latter, which we took as inessential excrescence, being expressionistic. I had seen what came of author-worshipping direction in the Theatre Guild production, where all O'Neill's faults were presented to the public with careful reverence. In order to find the essential—or at least the better—O'Neill we agreed to forego much O'Neillism.

Our designer, Teo Otto, agreed. I told him of Robert Edmond Jone's Rembrandtesque lighting and of the way in which Jones, in his sketches, tried to create the phantasmagoria of a Strindberg dream play, but Otto, though we discussed various sensational ways of setting the play—with slanting floors and Caligari corridors or what not—agreed in the end that we were taking O'Neill's story more seriously if we tried simply to underline the sheer reality, the sheer banality and ugliness, of its locale. Instead of darkness, and dim, soulfully colored lights, we used a harsh white glare, suggesting unshaded electric bulbs in a bare room. And the rooms *were* bare. On the walls Otto suggested the texture of disintegrating plaster: a dripping faucet was their only ornament. A naked girder closed the rooms in from above. And, that this real setting be seen as setting and not as reality itself, the stage was left open above the girder. While Hirschfeld and I were busy avoiding the abstractness of expressionism, Otto made sure that we did not go to the other extreme—a piddling and illusion-mongering naturalism.

To get at the core of reality in *The Iceman*—which is also its artistic, its dramatic core—you have to cut away the rotten fruit of unreality around it. More plainly stated: you have to cut. The play is far too long—not so much in asking that the audience sit there so many hours as on sheer internal grounds. The main story is meant to have suspense but we are suspended so long we forget all about it. One can cut a good many of Larry's speeches since he is forever re-phrasing a pessimism which is by no means hard to understand the first time. One can cut down the speeches of Hugo since they are both too long and too pretentious. It is such a pretentiousness, replete with obvious and unimaginative symbolism, that constitutes the expressionism of the play. Hugo is a literary conception—by Gorky out of Dostoevsky.

We cut about an hour out of the play. It wasn't always easy. Not wishing to cut out whole characters we mutilated some till they had, I'm afraid, no effective existence. But we didn't forget that some of the incidental details of *The Iceman* are among O'Neill's finest achievements. Nothing emerged more triumphantly from our shortened, crisper version than the comic elements. With a dash of good humor O'Neill can do more than with all his grandiloquent lugubriousness. Nothing struck my fancy more, in our production, than the little comedy of the Boer general and the English captain. O'Neill is also very good at a kind of homely genre painting. Harry's birthday party with its cake and candles and the whores singing his late wife's favorite song, "She Is the Sunshine of Paradise Alley," is extremely well done; and no other American playwright could do it without becoming either too sentimental or too sophisticated. We tried to build the scene up into a great theatric image, and were assisted by a magnificent character actor as Harry (Kurt Horwitz). It is no accident that the character of Harry came out so well both in New York and Zurich: the fact is that O'Neill can draw such a man more pointedly than he can his higher flying creations.

I am obviously a biased judge but I think Zurich was offered a more dramatic evening than New York. The abridging of the text did lay bare the main story and release its suspense. We can see the action as presumably we were meant to see it. There is Hickey, and there is Parritt. Both are pouring out their false confessions and professions and holding back their essential secret. Yet, inexorably, though against their conscious will, both are seeking punishment. Their two stories are brought together through Larry Slade whose destiny, in contrast to his intention, is to extract the secret of both protagonists. Hickey's secret explodes, and Larry at last gives Parritt what he wants: a death sentence. The upshot of the whole action is that Larry is brought from a posturing and oratorical pessimism to a real despair. Once the diffuse speeches are trimmed and the minor characters reduced to truly minor proportions, Larry is revealed as the center of the play, and the audience can watch the two stories being played out before him.

A systematic underlining of all that is realistic in the play did, as we hoped it would, bring the locale—Jimmy-the-Priest's—to successful theatrical realization, despite the deletion of much of O'Neill's detail. It gave body and definition to what otherwise would have remained insubstantial and shapeless; the comedy was sharpened, the sentiment purified. I will not say that the production realized the idea of the play which Hirschfeld, Otto, and I entertained. In theater there is always too much haste and bungling for that. One can only say that the actuality did not fall further short of the idea in this instance than in others.

And yet it was not a greater success with the public than the New York production, and whereas the New York critics were restrained by awe before the national playwright, the Swiss critics, when they were bored, said so. My newly won liking for O'Neill would perhaps have been unshaken by the general opinion—except that in the end I couldn't help sharing it.

I enjoyed the rehearsal period—unreservedly. I didn't have to conceal my reservations about O'Neill out of tact. They ceased to exist. They were lost in the routine, the tension, and the delight of theater work. I don't mean to suggest that you could lose yourself thus in any script, however bad; there are scripts that bear down on a director with all the dead weight of their fatuity. But in an O'Neill script there are problems, technical and intellectual, and every one a challenge. I gladly threw myself headlong into that mad joy of the theater in which the world and its atomic bombs recede and one's own first night seems to be the goal toward which creation strives.

The shock of the first night was the greater. It was not one of those catastrophic first nights when on all faces you can see expectancy fading into ennui or lack of expectancy freezing into a smug I Told You So. But, theatrically speaking, mild approval is little better. Theatrical art is a form of aggression. Like the internal combustion engine it proceeds by a series of explosions. Since it is in the strictest sense the most shocking of the arts, it has failed most utterly when no shock has been felt, and it has failed in a large measure when the shock is mild. *The Iceman* aroused mild interest, and I had to agree that *The Iceman* was only mildly interesting. When I read the critics, who said about my O'Neill production precisely what I as critic had said about other O'Neill productions, my period of liking O'Neill was over.

Of course there were shortcomings which could not be blamed on O'Neill. We were presenting him in German, and in addition to the normal translation problems there were two special ones: that of translating contrasting dialects and that of reproducing the tone of American, semi-gangster, hardboiled talk. There was little the translator could do about the dialects. She wisely did not lay under contribution the various regions of Germany or suggest foreign accents, and her idea of using a good deal of Berlin slang had to be modified for our Swiss public. One simply forewent many of O'Neill's effects or tried to get them by non-verbal means—and by that token one realized how much O'Neill does in the original with the various forms of the vernacular spoken in New York. One also realizes how much he uses the peculiarly American institution of Tough Talk, now one of the conventions of the American stage, a lingo which the young playwright learns, just as at one time the young poet learned Milton's poetic diction. In German there seems to be no real equivalent of this lingo because there is no equivalent of the psychology from which it springs and to which it caters. And there is no teaching the actors how to speak their lines in the hardboiled manner. Irony is lost, and the dialogue loses its salt. This loss and that of dialect flavor were undoubtedly great deficiencies. But not the greatest. I saw the production several times and, in addition to the flaws for which we of the Schauspielhaus were responsible, there stood out clearer each time the known, if not notorious, faults of O'Neill. True, he is a man of the theater and, true, he is an eloquent writer composing, as his colleagues on Broadway usually do not, under the hard compulsion of something he has to say. But his gifts are mutually frustrating. His sense of theatrical form is frustrated by an eloquence that decays into mere repetitious garrulousness. His eloquence is frustrated by the extreme rigidity of the theatrical mold into which it is poured—jelly in an iron jar. Iron. Study, for example, the stage directions of *The Iceman,* and you will see how carefully O'Neill has drawn his ground plan. There everyone sits—a row of a dozen and a half men. And as they sit, the plot progresses; as each new stage is reached, the bell rings, and the curtain comes down. Jelly. Within the tyrannically, mechanically rigid scenes, there is an excessive amount of freedom. The order of speeches can be juggled without loss, and almost any speech can be cut in half.

The eloquence might of course be regarded as clothing that is necessary to cover a much too mechanical man. Certainly, though we gained more by abridging the play than we lost, the abridgement did call attention rather cruelly to the excessively schematic character of the play. Everything is contrived, *voulu,* drawn on the blackboard, thought out beforehand, imposed on the material by the dead hand of calculation. We had started out from the realization that the most lifeless schemata in this over-schematic play are the expressionistic ones but we had been too sanguine in hoping to conceal or cancel them. They are foreshadowed already in the table groupings of Act One (as specified in O'Neill's stage directions). They hold the last act in a death grip. Larry and Parritt are on one side shouting their duet. Hickey is in the center singing his solo. And at the right, arranged en bloc, is everyone else, chanting their comments in what O'Neill himself calls a "chorus."

It would perhaps be churlish to press the point, were O'Neill's ambition in this last act not symptomatic both of his whole endeavor as a playwright and of the endeavor of many other serious playwrights in our time. It is the ambition to transcend realism. . . .

It is no use wanting to get away from realism (or anything else) unless you know what you want to get away *to.* Raising a dust of symbols and poeticisms is not to give artistic expression to a sense of mystery. It is merely, in O'Neill's case, to take your eye off the object. (Cf. Ibsen: "To be a poet is chiefly to see.") It seems to me that O'Neill's eye was off the object, and on Dramatic and Poetic Effects, when he composed the Hickey story. Not being clearly seen, the man is unclearly presented to the audience: O'Neill misleads them for several hours, then asks them to reach back into their memory and reinterpret all Hickey's actions and attitudes from the beginning. Is Hickey the character O'Neill needed as the man who tries to deprive the gang of their illusions? He (as it turns out) is a maniac. But if the attempt to disillude the gang is itself mad, it would have more dramatic point made by a sane idealist (as in *The Wild Duck*).

Does O'Neill find the meaning of his story by looking at the people and the events themselves or by imposing it on them? There are ideas in the play, and we have the impression that what should be the real substance of it is mere (not always deft) contrivance to illustrate the ideas. The main ideas are two: first the one we have touched on, that people may as well keep their illusions; second, that one should not hate and punish but love and forgive. The whole structure of the play is so inorganic, it is hardly to be expected that the two ideas would be organically related. The difficulty is in finding what relation they do have. In a way the truth-illusion theme is a red herring, and, as in *Così è (se vi pare)*, the author's real interest is in the love-hate theme. Pirandello, however, presents the red herring *as* a red herring, relates his "false" theme to this real one. O'Neill is unclear because he fails to do so. A high official of the Theatre Guild remarked: "the point is, you aren't *meant* to understand." In Pirandello this is indeed the point of the Ponza/Frola story. Pirandello *makes* the point, and in art a point has to be made before it can be said to exist. For O'Neill it is merely a point he might have made. As things are, it is his play, and not life, that is unintelligible.

The Iceman, of course, has big intentions written all over it. Most of O'Neill's plays have big intentions written all over them. He has written of

> the death of an old God and the failure of science and materialism to give any satisfying new one for the surviving primitive religious instinct to find a meaning for life in, and to comfort its fears of death with. It seems to me [he adds] anyone trying to do big work nowadays must have this subject behind all the little subjects of his plays or novels.

In other words, O'Neill's intentions as a writer are no less vast than Dostoevsky's. *The Iceman* is his version of crime and punishment. What is surprising is not that his achievements fall below Dostoevsky's but that critics—including some recent rehabilitators—have taken the will for the deed and find O'Neill's "nobler conception" of theater enough. "Conception" is patently a euphemism for "intention" and they are applauding O'Neill for strengthening the pavement of hell. In this they are not disingenuous; their own intentions are also good; they are simply a party to a general gullibility. People believe what they are told, and in our time a million units of human energy are spent on the telling to every one that is spent on examining what is told; reason is swamped by propaganda and publicity. Hence it is that an author's professions and intentions, broadcast not only by himself but by an army of interested and even disinterested parties, determine what people think his work is. The realm of false culture thus created is not all on one level; brows here, as elsewhere, may be low or high. No brows are higher indeed than those of the upper stratum of the subintelligentsia. They spend their time seeking sublimities, works which provide the answers to the crying questions of our time, impassioned appeals for justice, daring indictments of tyranny, everything surefire. Seek and you shall find: a writer like O'Neill does not give them the optimism of an "American century" but he provides profundities galore, and technical innovations, and (as he himself says) Mystery. Now there is a large contingent of the subintelligentsia in the theater world. They are seen daily at the Algonquin and nightly at Sardi's. They don't all like O'Neill, yet his "profound" art is inconceivable without them. O'Neill doesn't like *them,* but he needs them, and could never have dedicated himself to "big work" had their voices not been in his ears telling him he was big. The man who could not be bribed by the Broadway tycoons was seduced by the Broadway intelligentsia.

At one time he performed a historic function, that of helping the American theater to grow up. In all of his plays an earnest attempt is made to interpret life; this fact in itself places O'Neill above his predecessors in American drama and beside his colleagues in the novel and poetry. He was a good playwright insofar as he kept within the somewhat narrow range of his own sensibility. When he stays close to a fairly simple reality and when, by way of technique, he uses fairly simple forms of realism or fairly simple patterns of melodrama, he can render the bite and tang of reality or, alternatively, he can startle and stir us with his effects. If he is never quite a poet, he is occasionally able—as we have seen in *The Iceman*—to create the striking theatric image.

But the more he attempts, the less he succeeds. *Lazarus Laughed* and *The Great God Brown* and *Days Without End* are inferior to *The Emperor Jones* and *Anna Christie* and *Ah, Wilderness!.* O'Neill has never learned this lesson. The idea of "big work" lured him out into territory where his sensibility is entirely inoperative. Even his most ardent admirers have little to say in favor of *Dynamo,* the only play where he frontally assails the problem of "the death of an old God and the failure of science." A hundred novelists have dealt more subtly with hidden motives than O'Neill did in his famous essay in psychological subtlety,

Strange Interlude, a play which is equally inferior as a study of upper-class Americans. Then there is his desire to re-create ancient tragedy. Though no one is more conscious than he that America is not an Athens, the "Greek dream"—the desire to be an Aeschylus—has been his nightmare.

The classic and notorious problem about tragedy in modern dress has been that the characters, not being over life-size but rather below it, excite pity without admiration and therefore without terror. Though O'Neill has talked of an "ennobling identification" with protagonists, he has only once tried to do anything about it: only in *Mourning Becomes Electra* are the characters over life-size. Unhappily this is not because of the size of their bones but, as it were, by inflation with gas, cultural and psychological.

The cultural gas is the classic story. The use of classic stories has been customary for so long, and has recently come into such vogue again, that writers have forgotten their obligation to make the stories their own. They figure that the Aeschylean names will themselves establish the dignity and identity of the subject, while they—the modern adaptors—get the credit and draw the royalties. They are not necessarily conscious opportunists. They probably assume, with some psychologists and anthropologists, that archetypal patterns of myth elicit profound responses of themselves, irrespective of presentation; if this were true the poet would be unnecessary; it is a belief not to be discussed by a critic since the very act of criticism presupposes its falsity. If we ask what difference it makes that Orin and Lavinia are versions of Orestes and Electra the answer is that they thereby acquire an artificial prestige. They have become more important without any creative work on the author's part. We now associate them with the time-honored and sublime. They are inflated with cultural gas. It's like finding out that your girl friend is the daughter of a duke. If you are impressionable, you are impressed; she will seem different from now on, clad in all your illusions about nobility.

We are told that myth is useful because the audience knows the plot already and can turn its attention to the how and why. To this I would not protest that all adaptors, including O'Neill, change the mythic plots, though this is true; what I have in mind is, rather, that they do not always change them enough. Events in their works have often no organic place there, they are fossilized vestiges of the older version. We ask: why does this character do that? And the answer is: because his Greek prototype did it. In *Mourning Becomes Electra* the myth makes it hard for O'Neill to let his people have their own identity at all, yet to the extent that they do have one, it is, naturally, a modern and American identity, and this in turn makes their ancient and Greek actions seem wildly improbable. Heaven knows that murders take place today as in ancient times; but the murders in O'Neill are not given today's reality. Instead, the characters are blown up with psychological gas. O'Neill has boasted his ignorance of Freud but such ignorance is not enough. He should be ignorant also of the watered-down Freudianism of Sardi's and the Algonquin, the Freudianism of all those who are ignorant of Freud, the Freudianism of the subintelligentsia. It is through this Freudianism, and through it alone, that O'Neill has made the effort, though a vain one, to assimilate the myth to modern life. Now what is it that your sub-intellectual knows about Freud? That he "put everything down to sex." Precisely; and that is what O'Neill does with the myth. Instead of reverent family feeling to unite an Orestes and an Electra we have incest. *Mourning Becomes Electra* is all sex talk. Sex *talk*—not sex lived and embodied but sex talked of and fingered. The sex talk of the subintelligentsia. It is the only means by which some sort of eloquence and urgency gets into the play, the source of what is meant to be its poetry. The Civil War never gains the importance it might have had in this telling of the story, it is flooded out by sex. "New England," surely a cultural conception with wider reference than this, stands only, in O'Neill, for the puritanic (i.e. sexually repressive) attitude.

O'Neill is an acute case of what Lawrence called "sex in the head." Sex is almost the only idea he has—has insistently—and it is for him *only* an idea. Looking back on what I wrote about him a few years ago, I still maintain that O'Neill is no thinker. He is so little a thinker, it is dangerous for him to think. To prove this you have only to look at the fruits of his thinking; his comparatively thoughtless plays are better. For a non-thinker he thinks too much.

Almost as bad as sex in the head is tragedy in the head, for tragedy too can decline into a doctrine and dwindle into an idea. And when the thing is absent its "idea" is apt to go soft. Tragedy is hard, but the idea of tragedy ("the tragic view of life," "the tragic sense of life" etc.) is seldom evoked without nostalgic longing. And the most decadent longing is the longing for barbarism, *nostalgie de la boue,* such as is voiced by our tragedy-loving poets:

Poetry is not a civilizer, rather the reverse, for great poetry appeals to the most primitive instincts. . . . Tragedy has been regarded, ever since Aristotle, as a moral agent, a purifier of the mind and emotions. But the story of *Medea* is about a criminal adventurer and his gun-moll; it is no more moral than the story of Frankie and Johnny; only more ferocious. And so with the yet higher summits of Greek Tragedy, the Agamemnon series and the *Oedipus Rex;* they all tell primitive horror stories, and the conventional pious sentiments of the chorus are more than balanced by the bad temper and wickedness, or folly, of the principal characters. What makes them noble is the poetry; the poetry and the beautiful shapes of the plays, and the extreme violence born of extreme passion. . . . These are stories of disaster and death, and it is not in order to purge the mind of passions but because death and disaster are exciting. People love disaster, if it does not touch them too nearly—as we run to see a burning house or a motor crash. . . .

Aristotle's view of tragedy is humane, this one—that of Robinson Jeffers—is barbaric without the innocence of barbarism; it is neobarbaric, decadent. O'Neill is too simple and earnest to go all the way with Jeffers. Puritanism and a rough-hewn honesty keep him within the realm of the human. But *Mourning Becomes Electra* does belong, so to speak, to the same world as Jeffers' remarks, a world which titillates itself with tragedy in the head. Your would-be tragedian despises realism, the problem play, liberalism, politics in general, optimism, and what not. Hence *Mourning Becomes Electra* is unrealistic, unsocial, illiberal, unpolitical, and pessimistic. What of the *Oresteia?* It celebrates the victory of law over arbitrary violence, of the community over the individual. It is optimistic, political, social and with permissible license might be called liberal and realistic as well. *O tempora, o mores!* If one does not like O'Neill, it is not really him that one dislikes: it is our age—of which like the rest of us he is more the victim than the master.

Circe's Swine: Plays by Gorky and O'Neill

by Helen Muchnic

When in *The Odyssey* the companions of Odysseus are changed by Circe into swine, they are not deprived of human consciousness; but in Milton's reworking of the episode in *Comus* the men are transformed so thoroughly that they have lost all notion of what has happened to them, and are completely brutish and contented in their pleasures. Milton, that is, in a way consistent with the severity of Puritanism, changed the pathos of a state in which human beings suffer from a sense of their depravity into the greater moral tragedy of a condition so depraved as to make such suffering impossible.[1] Eugene O'Neill's *The Iceman Cometh* and Maxim Gorky's *The Lower Depths* are, it seems to me, a modern instance of much the same contrast. But, although a comparison of these two plays seems clearly indicated, the fullest one that I have seen so far is but a brief discussion in the Russian journal *Zvezda*;[2] there, in the course of a long and generally scornful article on current American literature, Vladimir Rubin concludes that, "If Gorky's play asserts: 'Man—that has a proud sound,' then O'Neill's *The Iceman Cometh* seems to be saying: 'Man—that has a low and infamous sound,' " for "the gloomy moral" of his play "debases man infinitely . . . as a pitiful, will-less toy of fate." It marks, he says, "the final 'spiritual capitulation' of this veteran of American drama." This, of course, is the opinion one would expect from Soviet criticism today; and there is, to be sure, a shade of truth in it. By comparison with Gorky's view of man, O'Neill's is indeed a pessimistic one. But this shadowy truth dismisses with too casual a brutality the realms of concepts here involved. The whole matter is deeper and of a different order than that indicated by Mr. Rubin's remarks.

On the face of it, the plays are very much alike, not only in setting,

"Circe's Swine: Plays by Gorky and O'Neill" by Helen Muchnic. From *Comparative Literature*, III, No. 2 (Spring 1951), 119-128. Reprinted by permission of the author and *Comparative Literature*.

[1] This comparison was made some years ago by Marjorie Nicolson in one of her lectures at Smith College.

[2] Aug. 1948, p. 200.

plot, and structure, but in aesthetic conception; for they seem to be, and yet are not, "slices of life." They are, more accurately, parables of life; and the social outcasts who people Harry Hope's "cheap ginmill of the five-cent whiskey, last-resort variety" and the "cellar, resembling a cave," owned by Kostilev, are not, despite the naturalism of their portraiture, pictures of real men, but symbolic figures in a parable on man's fate. As such they are exceptionally well chosen; the "dregs" of society, as the mark of extreme failure, are distress signals which urge inquiry into the nature of human disaster and the responsibility for it. Both plays are plays of dialogue rather than action, and what is done in them, reversing the usual method of drama, is an illustration of what is said. In each, a group of individuals, loosely bound together by a familiarity which breeds tolerant indifference and boredom and with enough in common to represent mankind by and large, is confronted by a solitary outsider who considers himself, and is considered by the group, to be superior—to this extent, at least, that he is in a position to preach and to exhort them to a new way of life. In both plays this solitary individual is the repository of a "truth" unknown to the others, and in both, after a brief show of impressive authority, he leaves the scene of his activities in the same, or somewhat worse, condition than he had found it. Is the joke, then, on him? Are the tables turned? Is the prophet false, or at any rate, inadequate? And are the benighted souls whom he had tried to save in possession of a reality which his supposedly superior wisdom has not touched? Who, then, is better, and who is right? Who is to be blamed for the melancholy outcome of events, the prophet or those who refuse to become his disciples? The plays strike deep, deeper than their spoken arguments concerning the nature of truth and the value of illusion. Implicit in them are comparisons between theories of life and actual living, between idealism and reality: demands exacted by the mind and those made by the body, hope imposed by the spirit and the limits to hope set by the circumscribed potentialities of man; questions about the nature and the power of the will; and a search for an ethics that might be accepted as both just and possible in a human situation that is seen to be desperate. But here, with the kind of questions posed and the way they are examined, the similarities end. The answers given are amazingly different, and as one studies them one becomes aware that even the questions are not so similar as at first supposed.

Each play is constructed around a central character, and its meaning hinges on the interpretation of this man and of what he preaches, for he comes with a well-defined faith to correct his fellows; it is to him that they are constrained to respond individually and as a group, it is on him that thoughts and emotions converge. He is, in short, a test of moral principles, and the spectator must decide to what degree he should respect and trust him. In their natures, the two characters are entirely different. Gorky's Luke[3] is a wanderer who, not from any newly found faith but from an accumulated store of sanctified dogma, hands out good advice wherever he happens to be to whoever will listen to him. He clucks sympathetically over men's complaints, tells little moral tales by way of illustrating his precepts, and, when the wretches he has been "saving" are drawn into a perilous situation and he himself is in danger of being caught and questioned by the authorities, slips out unperceived; for, with all his show of self-effacing, greathearted sympathy, he is not unmindful of his own safety—and he happens to be traveling without a passport. Hickey, on the other hand, enters with a program of reform, determined to make his friends happy, now that he himself has found happiness; and until the end, when he becomes a self-convicted felon, he has been a respected member of society. Nor is his scheme a ready-made concoction of untested, pious maxims; his recipe is drastic, and he has first tried it on himself. In the case of Hickey, there is no question of hypocrisy, but there is in the case of Luke.

When *The Lower Depths* was first performed in 1902, Luke was presented as a saintly character, and the play was interpreted as a lesson in brotherly love. That had not been Gorky's intention, as he himself explained in interviews at the time and in an article of 1933 in which—having described four types of "consolers," the sincere (an extremely rare variety), the professional, the vain, and finally "the most dangerous, clever, well-informed, and eloquent" of them all, the coldhearted men who cared about nothing so much as their own peace and comfort and consoled only because they could not be bothered with complaints—he declared that Luke belonged in the last division. "In our days," he added, "the consoler can be presented on the stage only as a negative and comic figure."

Gorky had intended Satin to be the real hero, but muffed the effect by leaving him off stage in some of the crucial moments of the play. Satin is in every respect at opposite poles from Luke, whom he appraises with his native acumen and honest incivility. "Pulp for the toothless" he calls him, but admits that in theory, at least, the wanderer has the right idea about man: namely, that man is large and free and must not be hampered. Satin, who sneers when he is sober and is eloquent when drunk, who is not apart from but very much of the group, on the spot when he is needed, sensible, and, above all, realistic in his understanding of what his fellow men can and cannot do, has an undemonstrative, genuine sym-

[3] "Luke" the religious pilgrim is usually called "Luka" in English translations of the play. (EDITOR'S NOTE.)

pathy which is infinitely more valuable than Luke's facile, softhearted, self-protecting kindliness. "You know how to do better than pity," Kleshch says to him, "you know how not to insult." And his rhetorical speech about man, which begins, "What is man? It is not you, not I, not they . . . no! It is you, I, they, the old man, Napoleon, Mahommed . . . all in one! Do you understand? It is—immense . . . ," is the culminating point of the play and the one that states its meaning. From Satin's standpoint Luke's pampering consolations, when they are not positively harmful—as in the case of the Actor, for whose suicide Satin holds the old man responsible—are insulting to man.

In *The Iceman Cometh* Satin's counterpart is Larry, "the only occupant of the room," according to the stage directions, "who is not asleep" when the curtain goes up, and who indeed remains terribly wide awake throughout the play, who speaks "sardonically," with "a comical intensity," considers himself aloof from all human airs, "in the grandstand of philosophical detachment," but cannot help responding to the sufferings of "the breed of swine called men" with a sensitiveness and passion he would gladly suppress. He is discriminating and stern in his judgments and penetrating in his grasp of motives. He is not given to long pronouncements, does not try to influence men, but his influence is felt in what he is and in what he makes people do when they compel him to direct them; and, when he talks, it is with the aptness, wit, and brevity of poetry: "their ships will come in, loaded to the gunwales with cancelled regrets and promises fulfilled and clean slates and new leases"; "when man's soul isn't a sow's ear, it will be time enough to dream of silk purses"; and it is he who finds the right name for the Iceman, when he calls him the Iceman of Death. At the beginning of the play he makes a little speech that could be taken as the theme song of both *The Iceman Cometh* and *The Lower Depths*:

> What's it matter if the truth is that their favoring breeze has the stink of nickel whiskey on its breath, and their sea is a growler of lager and ale, and their ships are long since looted and scuttled and sunk on the bottom? To hell with the truth! As the history of the world proves, the truth has no bearing on anything. It's irrelevant and immaterial, as the lawyers say. The lie of a pipe dream is what gives life to the whole misbegotten mad lot of us, drunk or sober.

The "pipe dream" is the obvious leitmotif of *The Iceman Cometh*, as it is also that of *The Lower Depths*, the real theme of which, according to a splendid analysis by the Soviet Critic Iury Iuzovsky,[4] is the question

---

[4] Iuzovsky, Iury, *Dramaturgia Gor'kovo*, Chast' I (Moscow-Leningrad, 1940), pp. 61-161.

"What is Truth?" The characters of Gorky's play, this writer points out, are divided into well-marked groups with respect to the kind of truth they believe in: those, like the Actor, Pepel, Natasha, and Nastya, for whom illusion is truth; those, on the contrary, who believe only in the "truth of facts," like Bubnov, Kleshch, and the Baron, all of whom delight in pricking, variously, the bubble of man's hope—Bubnov with quiet satisfaction, Kleshch with bitterness, the Baron with a kind of sensual delight, "sneering out of envy," as Luke says of him; and, lastly, Luke and Satin who belong to neither category, and whose position Iuzovsky explains by a reference to Lenin's article, "What Is To Be Done?"—written in the same year as Gorky's drama. "One must daydream," says Lenin in this article, and, quoting the nineteenth century nihilist critic, Pisarev,

> My daydream may be of such a kind as to catch up with the natural course of events, or it may go off completely at a tangent to where the natural course of events can never arrive. In the first instance, the daydream does no harm; it may even support and strengthen the energy of toiling mankind . . . In such day-dreams there is nothing that can prevent or paralyse the strength of workers . . . When there is a point of contact between the day-dream and life, then everything is going well . . .

comments that of the latter kind of daydream there is unfortunately too little in his time. *The Lower Depths,* says Iuzovsky, seems to give symbolic form to this distinction; for, in the difference between Luke's daydream and Satin's, the one of the principle of slavery, the other of freedom, the one leading to a dead end, the other opening a way out, we have the very distinction which Pisarev had noted.

Nevertheless, whether they believe anything or not, the inhabitants of *The Lower Depths* retain, as individuals, a sense of their humanity and they suffer because of it; Circe has not deprived them of consciousness, and, even though they do not do very much, they retain the possibility of action. With the frequenters of Harry Hope's saloon the case is different. They are contented enough in their sodden stupor and are miserable only when, for a brief space, they are jerked into consciousness, for this robs their liquor of its potency to "paralyze." Once they are made to face themselves, the good-natured Americans, thrown into inward conflict by the sudden demonstration that their long-cherished beliefs about themselves are lies, become acrimonious and belligerent; the Russians, even the "romantic" ones, had been too sober and too unhappy from the start for any kind of pretense of mutual regard and general affability. In both plays, it would seem, amicable relations can exist only on the superficial basis of convenient indifference, the "live and let live" philosophy of those who have not chosen, but have been driven, to live together. The Russians have, indeed, much less sense of group solidarity than the Americans; all but wholly unaware of one another and much more callous, they appear to have theories about society but little capacity or desire for social living.

The real difference between the characters in the two plays, however, is not that of social relationships but of the kind of illusion they cherish and the nature of the "truth" they are invited to adopt. If both plays can be said to deal with illusion and reality, these terms have different meanings for their authors. "Truth" or "reality" for Gorky is not a metaphysical but a humanist concept; it involves not so much a recognition of that which is or may be, immutably, as of that which may or may not be done at a given moment. Freedom of will is here based simply on a practical view of possibilities. O'Neill's position is more sophisticated and complex; for him there is no distinction between useful and useless illusions, and no naïve presentation of men as fully expressed by their beliefs. From an objective point of view, the "pipe dreams" here are all useless, but all are tragically inescapable and necessary to those who hold them; they are drawn not from the human consciousness of Circe's victims, nor from their idealistic hopes, but from painful, suppressed memories, the persistent iteration of recurrent images in troubled dreams. Here every man has been involved in something he wants to forget. Circe has helped him to oblivion, and the one real victory of his life is his capacity to forget. These men—all but one—unlike Gorky's, do not complain of the miserable state they are in. Parritt, the notable exception, commits suicide. The men of *The Lower Depths* are vaguely aware of some great solution to existence which they have not yet discovered, and the play exhorts them to seek a way that will lead them to discover it; those of *The Iceman Cometh* have no thought of anything beyond their individual well-being, which by now has been reduced to the form of drunken senselessness, and the play turns out to be a study of the impossibility of getting at the truth, indeed, a warning of the danger of going after it.

It is in keeping with this condition that the "leaders" differ as they do —that the American "prophet" is a salesman, peddling salvation as he peddles wash boilers, required to persuade a sales-resisting audience of the usefulness of his product, while the Russian is a wandering holy man, who preaches and consoles, leading despairing men who are only too ready to believe him along the path of human kindness, soothing them with assurances that their dreams are attainable. Both men are evil, Gorky's shrewdly and irresponsibly, O'Neill's, even in his noxiously commonplace sentimentality, rather pathetically and goodheartedly; for, whereas Luke's words are words only, Hickey is disastrously involved in what he preaches. Comically enough, neither accomplishes what he sets out to do—comically, because our sympathies are not with them. If the tone of the plays is on the whole tragic, the tragedy inheres not in the doom of the central characters but in the pathos of various episodes, and even more in implications, in what is not, rather than in what is, done or said. But if Luke and Hickey fail as prophets, it is not because they have misunderstood the values by which their audiences live—a passion for faith on the one hand, a desire for individualistic self-assertion on the other. Nor is it these premises, but something else, that is proved false in their failure.

What is at issue in Gorky's play is the relative usefulness—and *usefulness* is here the same as ultimate good—of two ideals: one, the Christian ideal of tender, pitying humility and inactive faith, the other, the materialist doctrine of forceful, self-reliant, practical action. In O'Neill's play the issue is the nature rather than the practicability of ideals. Social activity is the sphere of Gorky's thought, self-knowledge of O'Neill's. Though both are concerned with happiness, in *The Lower Depths* happiness is looked on as derivative, dependent on an intellectual grasp of values: let a man become conscious of his dignity and capacity, let him adopt an ideal which is possible for man, and he will realize it as an individual. In *The Iceman Cometh* happiness is seen to be immediate and primary; larger concepts may be valid only as abstract formulations of what men have done: let a man believe only what he has achieved—otherwise he will be ridiculous, self-deceived, and dangerous. The reason Luke fails is that he is neither serious nor honest in his relations with men; but Hickey fails because, in his desire to rouse Circe's victims to their original status as human beings with insight into themselves, he has attempted the impossible, for most of them cannot be roused, and those who can will kill themselves once they have understood what they are. Gorky's "message" is seriously meant as a program of conduct; O'Neill's is a poetic statement of disaster, presented only for the contemplation of those who care to look below the surface of human activity.

Murder is central to both plays; but in *The Lower Depths* it is accidental, based on passion, and is generally conceded to be regrettable, while in *The Iceman Cometh* it is more or less premeditated, rationalized to appear as an act of love, and is not a mere episode but the essence of the play. In fact, *The Iceman Cometh,* the latest of O'Neill's inquiries into the paradoxes of existence, is a prophecy of doom, of the willful and calculated murder by man of what he thinks he loves, a revelation of his unconscious hatreds and desire for death. Always concerned with illusion, O'Neill has presented it in many ways: in pictures of individuals pathet-

ically or tragically frustrated because of some initial mistake they make
about themselves or that others make about them, as in *Bound East for
Cardiff, Before Breakfast, The Rope, Beyond the Horizon, The Straw,*
and *Diff'rent*; in symbols not of individuals but of man overwhelmed by
the force of unconscious primitivism latent in him, as in *The Emperor
Jones* and *The Hairy Ape*; in parables concerning the ethics of Western
civilization, as in *The Fountain, Marco Millions,* and *Lazarus Laughed*;
or in psychological probings of man's soul, as in *Desire Under the Elms,
The Great God Brown, Strange Interlude,* and *Mourning Becomes Electra.*
Despite great variation in focus and interest, certain factors remain constant enough throughout the plays to make O'Neill's work appear as a
continuous philosophic investigation of the riddle of falsehood at the
core of life, in the process of which several partial solutions have been
reached, but no definitive one as yet. His plays are eerie with the ghosts
of terrible dissatisfactions and of desperate guilt; and their darkness is
hardly relieved by a hovering conviction that there is power in love and
that an ultimate beneficent grandeur exists beyond the groping and rag-
ing consciousness of man, for it is in tragedy itself that men are shown
to have attained their desires. Jones, in death, preserves the magnificent
isolation he had wanted; Yank, in the brotherhood of monkeys, "belongs" at last; Ephraim Cabot's desolate farm is still "jim-dandy"; Lavinia Mannon, who has dedicated herself to the punishment of a wrong,
shuts herself away from life as the final phase of her life work—and so
on. In an ironic way, death and suffering are always the price of attainment, while back of this human scene is "an infinite, insane energy which
creates and destroys without other purpose than to pass eternity in avoiding thought," and is sometimes called God. A primitive, necessary, unthinking, intangible essence that insures perpetuity is shown to exist in
opposition to the will of man, who desires extinction. "We're always de-
siring death for ourselves or others," says Nina Leeds. "Our lives are
merely strange dark interludes in the eternal display of God the Father!"

  The Iceman Cometh, perhaps more clearly than any of the other
O'Neill plays, is a morality play, a variation on the ancient motif of the
Dance of Death, with its modern, paradoxical twist of willed chance and
desired catastrope, where each man kills the thing he loves because he
feels guilty of his inability to love enough. Harry Hope's saloon is Everywhere, and the men in it are drowning a secret guilt they cannot understand. Gorky's outcasts, on the other hand, are boldly, openly immoral;
they admit the crimes they have committed and are not ashamed of them,
for their crimes, being offenses not against themselves but against something hateful outside themselves, have, in a way, the aspect of righteous
vengeance. The depths to which they have sunk are only social depths;

what troubles them is a sense not of guilt but of inadequacy, and to find truth is their only salvation. But O'Neill seems to be saying that to live at all man must live on a lie, for the reward of truth is death. Gorky's man can live only by facing himself, O'Neill's cannot live if he faces himself.

The theme of O'Neill's play is not really the difference between illusion and reality, but the difference between two realities: one the reality of belief, the other the reality of the unrecognized and unacknowledgeable forces of existence. Between illusion and reality a man might choose, but O'Neill's two realities are not open to choice; they are related to each other in a fashion so tortuous as to elude consciousness. A man feels and believes the very opposite of what he thinks he feels and believes. And the reason for this is that the ununderstandable necessity to live has imposed on him a habit of unconscious lying; he reiterates a faith in his will to live, in the great capacity and need of love which animates his life, whereas actually his desire is to die and the motivating force of his life is not love but hate. In short, the two realities which inform man's existence are so profoundly contradictory that consciousness must either pass them by, or deal with them in falsehoods, or obliterate itself. Man is, by definition, a deluded being. Thus the poor, harmless souls at Harry Hope's—good-natured, easygoing, and rather appealing with their vague beliefs in love and honor so long as they remain in their drunken stupor—exhibit, as soon as they are forced to consciousness, unsuspected, deep-seated, murderous hatreds. What Hickey's truth brings to light is that everything that seems good covers up basic evil: Hope, whose life of inactivity is postulated on the premise that he is mourning the death of Bessie whom he loved, suddenly finds himself calling her "that nagging bitch"; Jimmy Tomorrow, who thinks he has been drowning his sorrow at Marjorie's defection, admits, to his own surprise, that he never wanted her; Parritt is forced to acknowledge not only that he is guilty of virtual matricide but that this murder was caused by his hatred of his mother; and, as a piece of final irony, Hickey, in the very process of a touching disquisition on his lasting and passionate love of Evelyn, inadvertently blurts out: "You know what you can do with your pipe dream now, you damned bitch!"

In Gorky's view, what men need more than anything is a belief by which to steer their actions, but for O'Neill beliefs are irrelevant to both morality and happiness. Man is born guilty—O'Neill's attempt to rid himself of Puritanism seems to have brought him round to a metaphysical confirmation of its basic tenets—and the more he tries to clear himself of guilt the more entangled he becomes in it. For how shall the kind of truth which consciousness reveals be met except by death? What price life, O'Neill is asking, and is not genial enough to congratulate man on escaping destruction by the skin of his teeth; for, to his severe scrutiny of man, the death wish seems to have moral justification. The last of all illusions is that ideals are something other than Janus-faced inventions, distressing and comforting by turn, without reference to anything beyond themselves other than the reality of man's having to get through his life somehow. In earlier plays there had been a gentler note. "Do not wound me with wisdom," said the wise Kublai of *Marco Millions*, "Speak to my heart!" But now, how shall the heart be spoken to when it has forgotten the only language by which it can be addressed, when all poetic vision has been lost, the great unanalyzable substratum of experience has been given over to dissection, love and hate have become indistinguishable, and the pursuit of happiness has ended not in enjoyment but in oblivion? Gorky's men are more unhappy than O'Neill's, but not so lost.

The essential difference in the two situations is perhaps best embodied in the real heroes of the plays: Satin, ruthless in his appraisal of individual failings but with a native respect for humanity and an ardent faith in its grandeur, and Larry, whose cynical philosophy is coupled with an instinctive sympathy of which he is ashamed, and whose sense of justice is based on a hopeless understanding of human beings. With these characters, it seems to me, their authors are identified: Gorky with the man of action, closely involved in the fate of his fellows, but more clear-eyed, farseeing, and confident than they, and able, therefore, to inspire them by a persuasive vision of their strength; O'Neill with the Grandstand Foolosopher, whose function it is to look unsquintingly on man's depravity and, when called upon, to discharge the unwelcome task not of judging men but of letting them pass judgment on themselves. The high point of Satin's act is a stirring speech on man, of Larry's, his waiting by the window to hear the sound of Parritt throwing himself from the fire escape (for Larry's finest deed is to free a man of guilt by driving him to suicide)—just as the purpose of Gorky's life was to stir men to action, and the function of O'Neill's has been to make them aware of the full meaning of the evil that is in them.

This contrast, to my mind, cannot be fully explained by the fact that O'Neill has long been preoccupied with Roman Catholicism, into which he was born, while Gorky was always an agnostic; for these titles of belief may point to tendencies of thinking and perceiving but can neither describe nor account for an artist's original view of life. Some might say that O'Neill's sophisticated, puritanical condemnation of man has proved to be a wise commentary on Gorky's naïve Homeric pity, history having shown that it is better for men to mope in harmless inactivity than to follow a leader whose promises fail to take account of the nature of human motives, and that Circe's brutes had better be changed back to men before being urged to action. But to say this would be to disregard both the complexity of historical events and the kinds of plays we are here considering: one of them has as its aim to state a temporary ethical problem affecting men in an unsatisfactory society which might be changed; the other, to scrutinize the eternal dilemma of how conscious man is related to unconscious nature—aims so divergent as to make these two samples of Western art in the twentieth century almost as dissimilar as those produced by the cultures of Byzantium and of ancient Greece.

On the Late Plays of Eugene O'Neill

by Tom F. Driver

Death did not lessen Eugene O'Neill's dominance over the serious American theater. He continues to tower over other American dramatists as his characters tower over ordinary mortals. He died in 1953 at the age of 65, having had only one Broadway production of a new play in nineteen years, none thoroughly successful in twenty. Yet anyone who would evaluate the American theater since the Second World War is obliged to reckon with Eugene O'Neill, and that hardly at all because of the 1946 production of *The Iceman Cometh* but rather because of the amazing concentration of his works which began to be produced in 1956. In May of that year, the off-Broadway group at the Circle-in-the-Square gave *The Iceman Cometh* its first successful performance in New York. Once again, as forty years before, O'Neill in an intimate downtown theater set the tone for Broadway to follow. In the fall of 1956, Broadway unveiled *Long Day's Journey into Night*, written in 1940 but published only in 1956. In the spring of 1957, Mr. George Abbott staged a musical version of *Anna Christie*. By May, there was the first New York production of *A Moon for the Misbegotten*. *Ile, Gold,* and *Where the Cross is Made* were done by small groups in the city. *A Touch of the Poet* was published in the summer of 1957. Its American premier was presented in the fall of 1958. No other American dramatist in recent memory has kept so many theaters busy in a two and one-half year period.[1]

The meaning of this revival must be sought partly in the skillful way in which the playwright's widow has managed the "discovery," publicity,

"On the Late Plays of Eugene O'Neill" by Tom F. Driver. From the *Tulane Drama Review*, III, No. 2 (December 1958), 8-20. Copyright © 1958 by the Tulane Drama Review. Reprinted by permission of the author and the Tulane Drama Review.

[1] Since this essay was written (1958), O'Neill has continued to be played in New York, notably in the Actors' Studio Theatre production of *Strange Interlude*, 1962, and the Circle-in-the-Square production of *Desire Under the Elms*, 1963. In 1961, Paul Shyre projected an off-Broadway series of O'Neill productions, of which only one bill was presented: *The Long Voyage Home* and *Diff'rent*. The Lincoln Center Repertory Theatre has produced *Marco Millions* in its first season. Recent O'Neill films include *Desire Under the Elms*, 1958, and *Long Day's Journey into Night*, 1962.

publication, and first performance of those scripts which the public had not formerly known: *Long Day's Journey into Night* and *A Touch of the Poet*. *More Stately Mansions*, performed in Stockholm, as yet to be seen in America. The short play *Hughie* has not been performed in New York. The appetite for O'Neill is being carefully fed. However, it is not possible to exploit interest in an author if no interest is there to begin with, and of present-day interest in O'Neill there cannot be the slightest doubt.

This interest is the more remarkable if we remember how many shots have been taken at the giant and how many have struck their mark. The staunchest supporters, George Jean Nathan and Joseph Wood Krutch, long ago admitted that he lacked facility of language. Neither they nor anyone else claimed for him a great intellect or denied that he often descended to the juvenile and the banal. Few would demur when Harold Clurman writes that "O'Neill could not by any 'universal' standard be called a cultivated man. His view of life is circumscribed, he is often raw, naïve, sentimental and pessimistic in a somewhat adolescent manner." [2]

The success of O'Neill, like that of Tennessee Williams, who in some ways imitated him, comes in spite of serious lapses in taste and theatrical judgment and is therefore due not so much to technical proficiency as to being able to touch upon certain vibrant concerns of the audience. With Williams, the sensitive area reached is the unconscious, especially the unconscious experience of violence. With O'Neill it is preoccupation with death.

It was a mistake of Joseph Wood Krutch to suppose that O'Neill's handling of the death theme resulted in his having written tragedy. George Jean Nathan also concluded that O'Neill was a tragic dramatist. He hailed *The Iceman Cometh* because from it there poured forth "the profound essence of authentic tragedy." [3] John Gassner was on a better track when he compared O'Neill not to Shakespeare but to Webster and Ford, because of O'Neill's "susceptibility to extremes of passion, will, and affliction." [4] Although O'Neill broods over death, it adds nothing but confusion to call him a tragic dramatist.

Mr. Krutch was led astray partly because his own definition of tragedy was inadequate. He wrote, "true tragedy may be defined as a dramatic work in which the outward failure of the principal personage is compensated for by the dignity and greatness of his character." [5] But of course

---

[2] *The Nation*, CLXXXII, 9 (March 3, 1956), p. 182.
[3] *The Theatre Book of the Year*, 1946-1947 (New York: Alfred A. Knopf, 1947), p. 95.
[4] *The Theatre in Our Times* (New York: Crown Publishers, 1954), p. 256.
[5] "Introduction" to *Nine Plays by Eugene O'Neill* (New York: Modern Library, 1941), p. xxi.

"true tragedy" requires a more complex definition than that, one which includes, if Shakespeare and Sophocles are our models, some statement about the ontological basis upon which the affirmative aspects of the tragic action are understood to rest. Lacking such a basis, one is left simply with the fact of man and the fact of death. Mr. Krutch adds "dignity and greatness" of character, but in connection with O'Neill's plays these terms are more obfuscating than enlightening.

O'Neill's question, which in the late plays became sharper and more accurately perceived, was simply how man, bereft of faith in God, might confront the inevitability of death. That was hardly a new question, far too commonplace to please those who put a premium on originality. Moreover, O'Neill's answer to the question was an ancient one, although it has a modern appeal. The mood of the late O'Neill combines Romanticism and Stoicism.

We may trace that mood in the late plays (those written after *Days Without End*) by looking first at the treatment of time in *Long Day's Journey into Night*, then the Freudian echoes in *The Iceman Cometh*, and finally the question of illusion in that play and in *A Touch of the Poet*.

I

It would be interesting to discover whether Eugene O'Neill knew that in his treatment of time he was closer than in any other respect to the Greek drama. He was not successful in finding a modern equivalent for the Greek Fates or for Nemesis. The attempt to make the Oedipus complex perform this service in *Mourning Becomes Electra* succeeded only in reducing the Greek story to the level of rationalistic psychology. Where O'Neill did succeed, however, and for his purposes it was probably the only place necessary for him to succeed, was in his representation of a world in which, as in most Greek tragedy, there is no future.

Long Day's Journey into Night begins in the forenoon. The sun is yet morning-soft when the Tyrone family finishes breakfast. The second act occurs at lunch-time, the third in late afternoon, the fourth at midnight. The visible action thus moves through some fourteen or fifteen hours of the day. At the same time, it moves from uncertainty into certainty, from light into darkness, from possibility into no-possibility. Within this slight movement forward in time, a movement which reveals that time goes forward only to a dead end, there is a greater movement backward into time past. The reaches of past time are virtually limitless. They proceed by memory. As Mary Cavan Tyrone during the day falls deeper and deeper under the spell of narcotics, she reminisces more and more about things that used to be. She returns to the time when her children were young, when her infant boy died, when she married, when she fell in love, when was a girl in school. Since she dominates the play, she carries the others with her, so that they, too, recall the past they have known. In every case, the past had potentiality which the present has lost. James Tyrone had possessed talent as an actor, which has now atrophied. James Tyrone, Jr. had loved his brother; his love is now soured into hatred. Edmund Tyrone had had good health and had been free to sail the sea; today he discovers he must enter a sanatorium for tuberculosis. It falls to Mary Tyrone, the play's chief spokesman, to put the sense of the past into words. "The drug," she explains, "kills the pain. You go back until at last you are beyond its reach. Only the past when you were happy is real.", Later she describes the fateful moments in which she has made those choices or taken those turns from which there is no going back: "Then one day you wake up and discover that you've lost your true self forever." There follows an explicit statement of the play's poignant understanding of time: "The past is the present, isn't it? It's the future, too."

The long day's journey takes us, then, back into the past. Bulky and "real," the past is so overpowering that the future is obliterated. We know, to be sure, that Edmund Tyrone is really Eugene O'Neill and that he will one day get out of the sanatorium and become a great playwright. But this knowledge is not part of the play. It is the basis of an irony the audience supplies, and so it flavors our experience of the play, but it could in no way be said to be more than a faint echo in the play itself.

Formal analysis of Greek drama, for which there is not space in this article, would show that, aside from the tragicomedies of Euripides and the Orestes trilogy of Aeschylus, Greek tragedy tended also to obliterate the future.[6] In Oedipus Rex we see a formal handling of time very similar to *Long Day's Journey into Night*. A few hours' time shown upon the stage are made to enclose many years of past time, the irony being that although we see the past "contained" as it were in the present, actually the present is under the domination of the past, with the result that the present cannot show any action leading to a future. It is the terminal point of action previously taken. Oedipus (leaving aside, as we should, *Oedipus at Colonus*) might also have declared, "The past is the present, isn't it? It's the future, too." And when Mary Tyrone, holding her wedding dress, closes the long day's journey by saying, "We were happy—for

---

[6] This aspect of Greek drama is analyzed in detail in my book, *The Sense of History in Greek and Shakespearean Drama* (New York: Columbia University Press, 1960).

a time," O'Neill might say with Sophocles, "Count no man happy until he is dead."

In *Days Without End,* O'Neill seemed to try the experiment of writing a play in which present action would reverse the past and thus open up the future. The play which shows the moral repentance and personal integration of its protagonist, John Loving, was a failure from every point of view. We must suppose that the notion of an effective action taken in the present was not consistent with the view of the world that O'Neill had adopted, or was coming to adopt. Other efforts in that direction (*Lazarus Laughed, Dynamo*) also fail. The idea of decisive action seems to have been associated in O'Neill's mind with fantasy. In *The Iceman Cometh, A Touch of the Poet,* and *A Moon for the Misbegotten* all thought of taking action to change things is set forth as the product of illusion. The one function of the present is to reveal the past. Only the past is real.

With the Greek Tragedians, the treatment of time, although formally parallel to O'Neill's, was given a different tone by the presence of several factors: (1) the future was closed by Nemesis, a moral agent serving to reinforce an idea of justice; (2) Nemesis did not overtake every man but only the tragic heroes, who therefore became useful exempla for the populace at large; (3) the death of the hero usually brought some benefit to the society of which he was a part, so that the bleakness of his particular fate was transcended by the renewed or restored welfare of the community. These factors were present as long as Greek society possessed sufficient faith in the gods to consider its time-pessimism as a part of the larger picture of justice; but when such faith gave way to skepticism, as it began to do with the Sophists and Euripides, the bleakness of time increased until the appearance of Epicureanism and Stoicism.

Western history since the spread of Christianity has been influenced predominantly by the Judaeo-Christian sense of time, which emphasizes the validity and crucial importance of action taken in the present moment, and which understands the future as open. The secularization of Western culture therefore resulted first in an unbridled optimism, especially in the Enlightenment. This sense of the future open to man if he will but take sufficient measures in the present, may be seen in both tragedy and comedy down through the plays of Bernard Shaw. In Ibsen the beginning of a change to something else is visible. The earlier Ibsen, even in *Ghosts,* which has an *Oedipus*-like structure, is confident of the ability of the present to break with the past. The later Ibsen is much less sure. Strindberg, of course, has no such confidence at all, and Chekhov shows little of it, not because he does not think the future will be different but because he is so conscious of being at the end of an era.

O'Neill, whose affinities with Strindberg are well known, may be said to represent the secularized man of Christendom living at a time when the built-in optimism of Western society is being exhausted. He is unable with the old latent assumptions to cope with the disruptions of an age of violence; and he is even less able to return to religious life, out of which a belief in the future had originally sprung. It was but natural, therefore, to turn to the kind of skeptical reassurance-in-chaos which had sustained the late Classical age, in other words to a new Stoicism. But we will see this more clearly if we look at the resemblance of the late O'Neill to the late Freud.

II

Freudian influence on *Strange Interlude* and *Mourning Becomes Electra* was obvious, notwithstanding the fact that O'Neill is said to have remarked that too much Freudianism was read into the latter play. The Freudian implications of *The Iceman Cometh*, however, do not seem to have been much written about, probably because they have to do not so much with the Freud of the repressed unconscious or the Oedipal complex, with which everyone is familiar, but with the Freud of the death-wish, who is less popular.

What we know of O'Neill's reading makes it appear unlikely that he read much Freud. Even so, a Freudian understanding of man throws light upon the action represented in *The Iceman Cometh*.

Mary McCarthy was right when she called attention to the lack of realism in *The Iceman*. She said that its alcoholics did not seem to get drunk in a normal way and that it displays "none of the terrors of drink." In fact, she declared, "the 'realist' scene . . . is no more than mood or decor." [7] O'Neill was not, in fact, interested in portraying life on the lower West Side but rather in using the materials of life-on-the-skids as a kind of mythical substance, out of which to mould a philosophic view of the world.

The play might be diagrammed with three concentric circles. In orbit on the outer circle are the numerous characters who inhabit Harry Hope's bar, including Harry himself. Each has his own story, but all are similar in that a past which had, or was thought to have had, potentiality has given way to a present in which there is nothing but drink. The alcoholic elixir is made both palatable and potent by illusions or "pipe-dreams." Each character supposes that when he gets ready he can move again into the world of social respectability and accomplishment. Those who inhabit this outer circle are a kind of unenlightened chorus for the

---

[7] *Partisan Review*, XIII, 5 (November-December 1946), pp. 577-579.

play. Their incessant talk, most of it repetitious, is what keeps the play in motion. A successful production of the play, as José Quintero demonstrated at the Circle-in-the-Square, must handle their speeches like themes moving from one instrument to another in an orchestra.

Two of the end-of-the-roaders at Harry Hope's are of particular significance and may therefore be thought of as moving in a circle within the outer one. These are Larry Slade, the detached, cynical, one-time Syndicalist-Anarchist, and Don Parritt, who comes looking for him bringing memories of past agonies. Those on the outer circle return, at the end of the play, to their original condition. Slade and Parritt do not. Parritt leaps from a window and Slade becomes, as he says, converted to death.

The change in Larry, which is connected with the suicide of Parritt, is brought about as the result of the visit of Hickey, whose orbit is at the play's center. Hickey arrives at Harry Hope's for his annual visit, which is usually the occasion of a rousing good party. This time he brings with him not the usual good humor but a newly found gospel of "peace." This peace is to be discovered when one faces the truth about himself, which is what Hickey would enjoin upon all the inhabitants of the bar. He urges them to go out the next day to fulfill the ambitions they all have harbored so long in their "pipe dreams." They follow his advice, only to discover that their ambitions were illusions. The result is indeed peace, but it is the peace of death. They return to the bar in a veritable state of walking death, in which even the booze loses its kick. "What did you do to this booze? . . . There's no life or kick in it now." Only gradually, after Hickey is removed from the scene, do their illusions return and with them the solace of the elixir on which they live.

Hickey's own story, which he narrates in a lengthy speech, is virtually a play within a play, and is the core of the entire business. In it we learn that the peace which has so recently come upon Hickey is strangely the result of his having put his wife to death. It is a tribute to O'Neill's powers of control that the news, when it comes, is not only not shocking but carries with it that quality of the inevitable and the serene which Hickey himself feels it to have. For by this time we have moved far indeed from the natural surroundings of Harry Hope's bar and are deep within the mythical Freudian lands where life is mediated through dreams. If the very setting of the stage is mood and decor, the setting of a myth, Hickey's story reaches the audience as a distant dream which forms the clue to the myth.

We are given the whole history of Hickey's engagement and marriage to Evelyn. She was from the very beginning something far above him in virtue. She was pure, where he was not. She was patient, and understanding, yet she was a rebuke to his venal existence. He would rather have had "some tramp [he] could be [himself] with without being ashamed—someone he could tell a dirty joke to and she'd laugh." At home, Evelyn "kept everything so spotless and clean." In other words, she represented to him both love and judgment, and to this he responded with both love and hate. "You see, Evelyn loved me. And I loved her. That was the trouble. It would have been easy to find a way out if she hadn't loved me so much. Or if I hadn't loved her. But as it was, there was only one possible way."

Hickey and Evelyn are understandable as husband and wife, but they are even more fully understandable if Evelyn, the beautiful, the pure, the loving, who is never seen except through Hickey's eyes, is seen to represent what Freud would have called Hickey's Super-Ego. On this basis all her roles fit together: the ideal morality with which he invests her, the ambivalence which he feels for her, the opposition stressed between her purity and his bodily lusts (the Id), and the direct line from his killing of her to his desire for death himself. Hickey does not give himself up to the police in remorse, repentance, or fear, but in a quiet peace, as if already he were dead.

"It would be counter to the conservative nature of instinct," wrote Freud in *Beyond the Pleasure Principle,* "if the goal of life were a state never hitherto reached. It must rather be an ancient starting point, which the living being left long ago, and to which it harks back again by all the circuitous paths of development. If we may assume as an experience admitting of no exception that everything dies from causes within itself, and returns to the inorganic, we can only say, 'The goal of all life is death,' and casting back, 'The inanimate was there before the animate.' "

In the same book Freud formulated his dualistic view of organic existence in which the life-instincts wage constant battle with the death-instincts. The former he called *Eros.* The latter has come to be known as *Thanatos,* although Freud himself did not use that term. The two instincts were regarded by Freud as having "equal validity and status," although the death-instinct inevitably wins in the end.[8]

The Iceman Cometh is written in a similar Schopenhauerian darkness. As in Freud, the battle between life and death forces moves back and forth from the conscious to the unconscious and among the participants known as Id, Ego, and Super-Ego. Hickey (Ego) desires death unconsciously. His sensual nature (Id) desires unbridled life and convinces Hickey he could live more successfully if his wife Evelyn (Super-

[8] Ernest Jones, *The Life and Work of Sigmund Freud* (New York: Basic Books, 1953-1957), vol. 3, p. 273.

Ego) were removed. Hickey yields, ostensibly to find peace but actually because he knows that this peace will be the prelude to permanent peace (death). The Ego-instincts, said Freud, are death-instincts.

The peace that the salesman Hickey brings with him into Harry Hope's bar is absolute *Thanatos.* If those on the outer circle could be held to the facing of reality long enough, they also would receive the gospel of death, but in them *Eros* is still too strong. It prolongs their life by the expedient means of bringing back their illusions. Larry Slade, on the second circle, is made of sterner stuff. He is the one member of the group who from the beginning had courage to call the shots as he saw them. Therefore since he is able to face reality he becomes Hickey's "one convert to death." Because of it he sends Don Parritt to his destruction as a kind of mercy, watches Hickey go quietly to his end, and will sooner or later go as quietly to his own.

The very baldness and persistence with which O'Neill states the death-life motif in *The Iceman Cometh* has put off many of his critics. The strength in his work, however, comes from just that quality of laying the simplest, most universal, reality bare so that the spectator has no protection from it. The literary canon of decorum is thereby violated, but the bleakness of the vision, which the very notion of decorum would deny, is preserved. With O'Neill, not even art is a protection against the darkness of the night into which we journey. As a matter of fact, art, as he suggested in *A Touch of the Poet,* is but another illusion.

III

The skepticism of O'Neill is nowhere more in evidence than in his handling of the theme of illusion. This is not so much because he sets about to destroy illusion in the name of reality as because the question of illusions is linked to his time-pessimism, with its essentially foreclosed future. Illusion therefore not only includes self-deception or "pipe-dream" but also every kind of hope, excluding only the hope of death. The attitude here is unflinching. We remember Ibsen's greater flexibility, able at one time to oppose illusory "ideals" for the sake of truth itself, but also able, in *The Wild Duck,* to understand the wisdom of the life-illusion when it is a necessary defense against destruction. O'Neill shows no hint of such practical compromise. There is no value according to which illusion (art, self-fulfillment, hope, religious faith—anything future-oriented) might be tolerated. And there is no alternative to illusion but death.

The action of *A Touch of the Poet* is to destroy "Major" Cornelius

Melody's self-delusion. An alcoholic innkeeper near Boston (alcohol is always an escape in O'Neill, never simply a physiological or sociological fact), Cornelius Melody once fought in the Duke of Wellington's army and has never seen fit to give up regarding himself as a distinguished officer, although every shred of distinction has long since left him, if indeed he ever had any. He lives in the past. He rides a thoroughbred mare, which he cannot afford to feed, admires himself vainly in the mirror, recites lines from Byron, and allows his wife and daughter to do all the work. Through the failure of an ill-conceived piece of bravado, his insane attachment to the past is jolted out of him, bringing from his wife the opinion, "All I hope now is that whatever happened wakes him from his lies and mad dreams so he'll have to face the truth of himself in that mirror." He does come home disillusioned. He even shoots his beloved horse, symbol of the romantic days of old. Yet instead of coming to himself he takes on another role, adopting a false brogue and playing the beaten down Irishman with such gusto that his frightened wife and daughter beg him return to his old "self." They regard him as dead.

Although *A Touch of the Poet* is not a well written play, its radical skepticism lends it some strength. What it questions is not simply the romantic psychology of the Boston tavern keeper but also the ability of man to find *any* reality through the way of his imagination. O'Neill seems to insist upon stripping man of every role, every pattern of order, every formation of his mental powers through which he builds those "lies" upon which life and culture depend: that is, those indirections by which we find directions out. All figurative knowledge is here dismissed, so that O'Neill is not only anti-religious, as he has long been known to have been, but also anti-aesthetic.

O'Neill was anti-religious only in so far as the object of the quest is concerned: he was always extremely religious in terms of the quest itself. The letter to George Jean Nathan in which he spoke of finding a substitute for the old, dead God is famous, as is also his remark to Joseph Wood Krutch that he was interested only in the relation of man to God. Henry Hewes is right to speak of the "constant recognition," in *Long Day's Journey into Night,* of "man's quest for religious ecstasy." [9] Where the quest seems ready to discover its object, however, O'Neill was either ill at ease or emphatically negative.

Similarly, O'Neill was dedicated to art in so far as art can be understood as a quest. Writing was his vocation, and few men have labored at it so consistently against such odds. If part of the odds came from ill

[9] *The Saturday Review,* November 24, 1956, pp. 30-31.

health, another part came from the fact that, as Joseph Wood Krutch said, he had no aptitude for writing, no concern with the *mot juste*. I think it safe to say that he had no *confidence* in art as form. His vocation of writing plays was not followed for the purpose of achieving the right forms incarnating the right conceptions but rather to use writing to wrestle with life. This accounts for the strength and weakness of his work. It is weak at almost every point where we care to ask an aesthetic question, and therefore, by implication, where we care to ask the question of what is being affirmed outside of man. It is strong wherever we care to look at man coming to terms with himself in a world of total darkness.

O'Neill thus affords us a clear example of the close, if usually unacknowledged, connection between art and religious or philosophical assertion. To be concerned about the creation of a work of art is to be able to back off far enough from the existential battles to adopt a standing place, on the basis of which the form of the work of art may be established. Those who say, therefore, that O'Neill lacked only the ability to write well miss the point. To be concerned about writing well would have been to deny the very obsession which impelled him to write in the first place. It would have assumed a stasis, a sense of completion or wholeness which his radical pessimism had completely overthrown. In a situation in which the only reality is death and the only question how to meet it, necessarily a tormented question, there are no values, proportions, relationships, traditions, or ultimates according to which the artistic work might be fashioned and judged. The particular existential power of O'Neill's work and its aesthetic ruggedness go hand in hand.

IV

Where it is held that "death is reality" and "reality is also death" three attitudes may be adopted; fear of death, Romantic love of death, and Stoic resignation to death. O'Neill combines the latter two, thereby dispelling fear.

There is that in man, said Freud, which makes him will his own death. The idea is a Romantic one. The quest for death is found alike in Wagner's *Tristan und Isolde,* in Melville's Ahab, and O'Neill's Hickey. The romantic's seach for the absolute leads him beyond all limiting forms to the reality devoid of form, to the ineffable, to the all-transcending sleep. The one moment of peace, also the one moment of lyricism, in *Long Day's Journey into Night* occurs in the speech of young Edmund

Tyrone in which he describes the semi-mystical experience he had while sailing at sea:

> I belonged, without past or future, within peace and unity and a wild joy, within something greater than my own life, or the life of Man, to Life itself! To God, if you want to put it that way . . . It was a great mistake, my being born a man, I would have been much more successful as a sea gull or a fish. As it is, I will always be a stranger who never feels at home, who does not really want and is not really wanted, who can never belong, who must always be a little in love with death!

If this speech is autobiographical it is understated. Eugene O'Neill was more than a little in love with death. When, in the late plays, he did not love death, he faced it with Stoic resignation and courage. In addition to the Thanatos-romanticism of Hickey, *The Iceman Cometh* contains Larry Slade's resignation to death. It would be wrong, of course, to impute to O'Neill the metaphysics and the logical rigor of the Stoics, but he does reflect the Stoic belief that wisdom lies in accepting the inevitable and in ridding oneself of passion and desire. As long as Larry Slade believed that the struggles of life matter, he was filled with disgust for himself and those about him. By converting him to death, Hickey had shown him that none of the struggles of the living have value. He was thereby purged of passion and desire. Perhaps he surpasses Hickey himself, for Larry retains not even the desire to die. Instead, he recognizes that death is the one certainty in an otherwise deluded existence.

In *Long Day's Journey, A Touch of the Poet,* and *A Moon for the Misbegotten,* no character expresses the rejection of life so absolutely as Larry Slade, but each of those plays is written from his perspective. The playwright's rebuke to Cornelius Melody is that he was not strong enough to face truth and die. The sense of pathos in *A Moon for the Misbegotten* arises from the fact that James Tyrone, Jr. did not know that the real substitute for his mother's breast was the tomb of earth. The playwright's courage in *Long Day's Journey* carries him into night.

The shortcoming of Mr. Edwin A. Engel's useful book, *The Haunted Heroes of Eugene O'Neill*,[10] lies in making O'Neill's attitude to death almost entirely a matter of the playwright's individual psychology. "The abiding theme of his plays," Mr. Engel rightly notes, "was the struggle between life and death." [11] But this he describes as "a compulsive preoccupation." [12] The plays are described as "the transmutation of per-

---

[10] Cambridge: Harvard University Press, 1953.
[11] P. 297.
[12] *Loc. cit.*

sonal and private agonies." [13] "Whereas O'Neill thought that he was
digging at the roots of the sickness of today, much of the time he was
really digging at his own roots." [14] The whole thing came about, Mr.
Engel implies, because of illness: "To direct all the tragic incidents, all
human suffering, to a single untragic end, the purgation of the protagonist's (and the author's?) fear of death, would, we surmise, have been
a conception beyond the comprehension of any playwright blessed with
physical and mental health." [15]

Such an *ad hominem* reading of the plays misses the point. There
may indeed be many things in them which are to be explained on the
basis of the playwright's idiosyncrasies, but the struggle between life
and death is not one of them, nor is the purgation of the fear of death.
In these respects, O'Neill is but one of a much larger company today
for whom the ancient life-death battle is the paramount reality. For
these the major problem of man is how he is to find himself in a world
in which the ultimate reality is a return to nothingness. Here the Stoic
virtues of resignation, courage, and purgation of passion become relevant.
The Stoic element in all the nonreligious versions of existentialism is
very strong. Courage and resignation are the only virtues which apply
to Heidegger's situation of being on the edge of the abyss. They are the
first virtues which apply to the world Sartre has described. They are the
starting point for the assertion of manhood proclaimed by Camus. If it
was Kierkegaard who first convinced modern man that his situation is
desperate, O'Neill is but one among many who have answered neo-
Stoically that despair is only to be overcome by having the courage to
acknowledge it as the inescapable fact of our existence.

If Paul Tillich is right that the basic anxiety of our age comes from
the threat of meaninglessness, it is not difficult to see that O'Neill offers
a remedy for that anxiety. His plays declare that the meaning of life is
its inevitable progression toward death. This is not, of course, an assertion which gives meaning to any of the particularities of life. In fact, it
drains them of meaning. But it is a way of redeeming existence from
meaningless anarchy by showing that its pattern is basically simple and
imperturbable. The bleakest philosophy is preferable to chaos.

One of the primary values of the late plays of O'Neill is that they
draw some issues very, very clearly. Their combination of neo-Stoicism
and Thanatos-romanticism forms almost a diametric opposition to religious faith. Their mythical qualities make it clear where the battle
takes place. St. Paul writes, "We wrestle not against flesh and blood but

[13] P. 298.
[14] P. 299.
[15] P. 296.

against principalities and powers. . . ." Almost more than any other modern author, O'Neill makes it clear what these principalities and powers are. They are the forces that play upon his stage, the elemental claims that fall upon his "haunted heroes." When we read the Pauline declaration that "the last enemy that shall be overcome is death," O'Neill enables us to recognize the visage and the strength of the enemy.

I believe O'Neill's stance is wrong. It is responsible for his failure to come to terms with the particularities and contingencies of living which many of us are not ready to declare of no importance. Be that as it may, no other playwright of the American stage has shown us as much of the grandeur of the dramatic imagination. He makes the rest of our theater seem petite, and very timid.

O'Neill's *Long Day's Journey into Night* and New England Irish-Catholicism

by John Henry Raleigh

Eugene O'Neill's *Long Day's Journey into Night* has been rightly praised as his finest play (and tragedy) as well as perhaps the finest play (and tragedy) ever written on this continent. It does not have much competition, to be sure, but whatever competition it may have—*Winterset, Death of a Salesman,* O'Neill's own early tragedies, and the like—is so completely outdistanced that there is no point in making comparisons and contrasts. *Long Day's Journey* stands by itself. All the power in characterization and the compassion for humanity that everyone knew O'Neill always had and which always showed itself, even if fitfully under such lugubrious surfaces as *Lazarus Laughed,* comes out clearly, cleanly, and unambiguously in *Long Day's Journey.* And the considerable talent for humor that manifested itself in *Ah, Wilderness!* is here joined to a somber plot; so that we have the final paradox that this darkest of tragedies is continually breaking out into wild comedy.

O'Neill's severest critics have never denied him, in a word—"Power"; and this is his most "powerful" play. In all his other "powerful" plays, there are always touches or stretches of staginess and awkwardness. But *Long Day's Journey* is clean, almost pure, one might say.

The first question to be asked is where does this clean power come from? It comes, first of all, from the autobiographical sources, as he tells us in the preface, the "old sorrow, written in tears and blood," and the final strength and courage "to face my dead at last and write this play." After Biblical and Greek-Civil War descents into past history (*Lazarus Laughed* and *Mourning Becomes Electra*), after travels in the Orient (*Marco Millions*), after primitivism (*The Emperor Jones* and *The Hairy*

"O'Neill's *Long Day's Journey into Night* and New England Irish-Catholicism" by John Henry Raleigh. From the *Partisan Review,* XXVI, No. 4 (Fall 1959), 573-592. Copyright © 1959 by The Partisan Review. Reprinted by permission of the author and the Partisan Review.

Ape), after racial imbroglios (*All God's Chillun Got Wings*), after nineteenth century New England (*Desire Under the Elms*), after the sea, after Greek masks, after dynamos, after all kinds of themes and devices and bizarre subjects, he finally returned home to New London, Connecticut, to his family, and to himself. As Stephen Dedalus says in *Ulysses*:

> *If Socrates leaves his home today he will find the sage seated on his doorsteps. If Judas goes forth tonight it is to Judas his steps will tend.* Every life is many days, day after day. We walk through ourselves, meeting robbers, ghosts, giants, old men, young men, wives, widows, brothers-in-love. But always meeting ourselves.

For certainly even a most superficial knowledge of the O'Neill family and of the facts of Eugene O'Neill's early life show that the play is very close to being straight autobiography (no matter what discrepancies may ultimately be pointed out). In another sense it does not matter how close to, or how far from, are the facts of O'Neill's life to the facts of the play, for *Long Day's Journey* is more impressive as a cultural document than it is as an autobiographical document. Furthermore, its distinctive qualities are given, not so much by family, as by culture, or by family-culture, since the two cannot be separated. The culture is, of course, New England Irish-Catholicism, and it is this that provides the folkways and mores, the character types, the interrelationships between characters, the whole attitude toward life that informs *Long Day's Journey* and gives it its meaning. As such, *Long Day's Journey* is *the* great cultural expression of American Irish-Catholicism; it puts permanently into the shade all the "stage-Irish-St. Patrick's Day-'Going My Way'-'Mother McCree' " type of sentimentality that has encircled the image of the Irish in America. Just as effectively does it underline the shallowness of the higher level sentimentality of Edwin O'Connor's *The Last Hurrah*, a whimsical account of the farcical and shoddy character and career of Boston's James Michael Curley. The only other American Irish-Catholic document that even approaches O'Neill's in power and truth is the *Studs Lonigan* trilogy of James T. Farrell, but Farrell's novel is tendentious and therefore "dates," and it lacks both the compassion and the humor of O'Neill's picture. Farrell's novel was written in anger—well justified, it should be added—but O'Neill's play was written out of sorrow, forgiveness, and, strangely enough, a kind of joy. Its world therefore exists on a higher level, humanely speaking, than does that of Farrell. In Farrell's novel there are all kinds of things to blame for the vulgarity and pettiness of the characters' lives. In O'Neill there is no pettiness, no real vulgarity, and nothing is to blame except everybody. Social forces, as

such, do not exist and, as in Greek tragedy, we are face to face with
guilty-innocent humanity on the purely personal level. All the terrible
things that members of a family—in this case an Irish family—will do
to one another, often in innocence, and always without reference to
outside people or events, are presented in a relentless and yet com-
passionate honesty. (It should be added, although it will not concern me
here, that the finest primarily comic expression of the same culture is
O'Neill's *Ah, Wilderness!*).

I

When Yeats and Shaw founded the Irish Academy of Letters, they
invited O'Neill to become an associate member, which he did, although
he was an American by birth. For it would be no exaggeration to say
that an American of Irish-Catholic parentage born in New England in
the late nineteenth or early twentieth century was really not American
but Irish.[1] This distinctive, closely knit culture, which is in our day
relaxing, produced a whole gallery of "un-American" types. Here is how
O'Neill describes one of them in *A Moon for the Misbegotten*: he is Mike
Hogan.

> He has a common Irish face, its expression sullen, or slyly cunning, or
> primly self-righteous. He never forgets that he is a good Catholic, faithful
> to all the observances, and so is one of the élite of Almighty God in a world
> of damned sinners composed of Protestants and bad Catholics. In brief,
> MIKE is a New England Irish Catholic Puritan, Grade B, and an extremely
> irritating youth to have around.

But it also produced Eugene O'Neill and the four haunted Tyrones of
Long Day's Journey, end-products, you might say, of the Irish famine of
the late 1840's, which set off the vast migrations to America. James
O'Neill himself was born in County Kilkenny in Ireland, in the year
1849 and came to this country at the age of five, bringing with him the
penuriousness and the land-hunger that obsess James Tyrone, the father
of *Long Day's Journey*. More important, he was a member of a vast
group of immigrants who did not so much leave Ireland as bring Ireland
to America. In New England, in particular, partly because of their
intense clannishness, partly because they were "outsiders," partly because

---

[1] Obviously things have changed, as the smiling face of Senator Kennedy on the cover
of *Life* or *Time* attests. [This was originally written in 1958.]

they found themselves "ruled" by a Protestant Anglophile culture—it was Ireland all over again with the hostile "strangers" in control—the Irish remained "Irish" and did not get assimilated for several generations, sometimes for a half century or more; they were not merged in one or two generations, as were other foreign groups, particularly Northern European ones, in other parts of the country. James Tyrone, of course, was born in Ireland and is a professional patriot who thinks that Shakespeare and the Duke of Wellington were dyed-in-the-wool Irish Catholics. But even his two sons, who are in rebellion and who scorn this patriotic nonsense, are still—hopelessly for them—"Irish," their whole characters being dominated by the passionate tribal and familial customs and resultant character typology in which their souls were forged.

How extraordinarily profound and pervasive were these characteristics can be only fully appreciated when one becomes aware of the fact that historical accounts of the Irish national character, even in medieval and antemedieval times, sound remarkably like a description of the Tyrone family. It would be no exaggeration to say that a straight line can be drawn from the primitive forests of antique Ireland to the haunted New London, Connecticut, residence of the Tyrone family in the twentieth century.

In the first place there were no clans in ancient Ireland, with the family being the basic unit although the family was not a one generation affair. According to Sean O'Faolain in his *The Irish—A Character Study,* the basic family unit was symbolized by the hand: "The limits of the sacred nexus were symbolized by the hand. The palm was the common ancestor; the joints of the finger were his descendents into his grandchildren; the fingernails were his great grand-children." Those families, moreover, were not inclined toward communal enterprises, such as the founding of cities, and it was the Normans, Danes, and Tudors who first constructed every Irish town of any consequence that exists. To these observations by O'Faolain should be added two more by Shane Leslie from his book *The Irish Tangle.* First, there is the immemorial Irish cult of chastity which was, evidently, a pre-Christian phenomenon (although some modern students of Irish culture claim that the ancient "chastity" is really a projection imposed upon the past by modern historians). There was the legend that an Irish girl could travel unmolested throughout the whole of Ireland, carrying a gold ring as a wand; a legendary Irish king was supposed to have drowned nine daughters at Doon in Kerry because one had a lover and he could not determine which one it was. Second, and at the opposite moral pole, there is the constant turbulence and recourse to drink. These national habits are

best underlined by the anecdote concerning the Cromwellian who be-
queathed to an Irish community a supply of dirks and whiskey, hoping
they would all get drunk and kill one another.

Four more observations should be made. First, as Robin Flower points
out in *The Irish Tradition,* medieval Irish love poetry was dominated by
two diametrically opposed impulses: delicate sentiment and beauty, on
the one hand, and the most astringent kind of irony, on the other.
Second—and this scarcely needs documentation—there is the national
concern with betrayal, the "Judas-complex" that dominates Irish life and
literature. For centuries the "informer" was a constant political fact of
the most bitter importance, and in a literary document like *Ulysses* one
can see it as a constant leitmotif of Dublin life; as Mr. Deasy says to
Stephen: "Helen, the runaway wife of Menelaus, ten years the Greeks
màde war on Troy. A faithless wife brought the strangers to our shore
here . . . a woman too brought Parnell low." Joyce himself was deeply
possessed by the national Judas-complex and was always talking of those
who "betrayed" him. (He even used the word "crucified" at times.) Third,
again requiring no documentation, there is the national commitment to
Roman Catholicism, which produced both the most extravagant devotion and the most deeply felt blasphemy, as in *Ulysses,* for example.
Fourth and finally, there is the national preoccupation with rhetoric and
the national eloquence.

Excessively familial; noncommunal; sexually chaste; turbulent;
drunken; alternately and simultaneously sentimental and ironical about
love; pathologically obsessed with betrayal; religious-blasphemous; loqua-
cious: these are some of the historical attributes of the Irish character.
To these nine characteristics should be added a tenth, which was an
emergent, post-famine phenomenon, namely, a tendency toward less and
later marriage on the part of the young men and a tendency, therefore,
for these young men to remain at home with their father and mother.
In short, here is an abstract picture of the Tyrone family, and it is on
these generic lines that the characters, and the interrelationships, in
Long Day's Journey are formed.

There is a further historical complication in the play, which makes the
whole situation much more concrete and which cuts across the generic
abstractions outlined above, in that *Long Day's Journey into Night* also
shows the Irish in the process of assimilation, or, rather—for none of
these characters can properly be called assimilated—in the process of
breaking away from the culture of the "Old Country." There are at
least four levels of this process represented in *Long Day's Journey.* There
is first of all—never seen on the stage but talked about by the Tyrones—
an authentic, unregenerate Irish peasant-farmer—a tenant of the Tyrones

—named Shaughnessy, cunning, crafty, powerful, and possessed of a "terrible tongue." The Tyrones pretend to be shocked but are secretly delighted when they learn that Shaughnessy, just by use of this "terrible tongue," has run a Standard Oil man named Harker off his property although he was quite guilty of what Harker had come to accuse him. This incident, which must have been based on fact, amused O'Neill immensely, and he presented it directly and fully in *A Moon for the Misbegotten,* where he changes "Shaughnessy" to "Hogan" and "Harker" to "Harder." Hogan's verbal assault on Harder is a masterpiece and one of the high points of O'Neill's humor, and Irish mock-eloquence. (What had happened was that Hogan had let his pigs—of course, he keeps pigs —wallow in a pond on Harder's property.) Hogan's peroration is worth quoting; he has accused Harder of giving his pigs pneumonia:

> All prize pigs, too! I was offered two hundred dollars apiece for them. Twenty pigs at two hundred, that's four thousand. And a thousand to cure the sick and cover funeral expenses for the dead. Call it four thousand you owe me. *(Furiously)* And you'll pay for it, or I'll sue you, so help me Christ! I'll drag you in every court in the land! I'll paste your ugly mug on the front page of every newspaper as a pig-murdering tyrant! Before I'm through with you, you'll think you're the King of England at an Irish wake! *(With a quick change of pace to a wheedling confidential tone.)* Tell me now, if it isn't a secret, whatever made you take such a savage grudge against pigs? Sure, it isn't reasonable for a Standard Oil Man to hate hogs.

There is too on stage in *Long Day's Journey* Cathleen the serving girl, ignorant, cheerful, bumptious.

A cut above Shaughnessy-Hogan and Cathleen is James Tyrone himself, who, according to O'Neill, is in fact still a peasant: nerveless, full of vitality, physically powerful, penurious. Still less of the earth is Mary Tyrone, neurotic, idealistic, dope-addicted, religious; further up still are the nihilistic sons, drunken, cynical, libidinous, spouting *fin de siècle* estheticism and pessimism (Swinburne and Nietzsche are the favorites). Nevertheless, the generic outline still stands, despite this historical progression. One is not Irish, it seems, with impunity and even in rebellion, the norms are still there.

II

I shall proceed through my catalogue of attributes, in reverse order, beginning with the tendency for late marriages and subsequent prolonged adolescence.[2] Jamie, thirty-three, and Edmund, twenty-three, are still, from, say, the contemporary American point of view and practice —which seems to be steadily pushing the normal age for marriage back into late childhood—in adolescence, living at home with the father who grudgingly doles out "allowance" money to them. It is true that Jamie is a wastrel and that Edmund is tuberculous; it is true too that both have left home, at one time or another, but like Willie and Biff Loman, they really *cannot* leave home, and they always return. This feeling goes so deep that it is not even explained or discussed by the play; it is a fact, like the weather, the "given" of a situation.

Loquacity, like drink, is one of the national addictions, and this should not be confused with eloquence, which is the property of the French. Irish "eloquence" is highly overrated, as any critical examination of Irish literature will show. Wilde once said to Yeats: "We Irish are too poetical to be poets; we are a nation of brilliant failures, but we are the greatest talkers since the Greeks." Wilde's own "elegance," O'Casey's meanderings, Joyce's purple passages ("his soul swooned slowly"), Synge's "keening," Shaw's attempt to be poetical with Marchbanks, George Moore's sentences ("squeezed" out of a tooth paste tube, as Yeats said), O'Neill's attempts at "poetry": all these—Yeats alone excepted—show a singular poverty of genuine and organic eloquence. The real forte of the Irish is just in talking, and talking in a special way, histrionically: striking a comic pose and exaggerating it into a burlesque. The funniest parts of *Ulysses* —"Cyclops" or "Nausicaa"—consist of just this. And O'Neill is only at ease, rhetorically speaking, in similar situations, as, witness, the Hogan episode quoted above, or the performance of Jamie Tyrone which will be quoted below. Loquacity, besides humorous exaggeration, implies repetition. Critics have complained that *Long Day's Journey* is too long; it all could have been said in shorter compass and could have been, therefore, of greater artistic impact. I don't agree with this criticism from an esthetic point of view, and from the point of view I am adopting— the play as cultural artifact—this criticism is completely off the point. For the motto of the Irish, especially the drinking Irish, is that a thing is not said unless it has been repeated almost *ad infinitum*. This verbal repetitiousness, this insistent urge to exaggerate and repeat, colors Irish

[2] Since writing this, I have read Agnes Boulton's *Part of a Long Story*, and have learned that Edmund (Eugene) had married and divorced before he married her and before the year in which *Long Day's Journey* takes place. As she says: "Who, having seen *Long Day's Journey into Night*, would ever realize that Edmund, the younger son, had been married and divorced and was the father of a child nearly three years old on that August evening in 1912?" (p. 206). But I think my point still stands.

literature as well. O'Casey's autobiographical volumes are filled with it: "But the O'Briens, the Dillons, and the Healys, mudmen, madmen, badmen, bedmen, deadmen, spedmen, spudmen, dudmen, . . ."; or, a description of Hell-Fire ". . . in a sea of fire, surgin', singin', scourgin', scorchin', scarifyin', skimmin', waves o'fire . . ." As O'Casey himself says in *Drums Under the Windows*:

> Keltic blood is usually accompanied by excited brains and a reckless temperament, and is always an excuse for exaggeration. When not whining or wheedling, the Kelt is usually in a state of bluff, or funk, and can always wind up to the kind of rhetoric no housemaid can resist.

In the words of the immortal washerwoman in *Finnegan's Wake*: "Wash quit and don't be dabbling. Tuck up your sleeves and loosen your talktapes." Or in the words of an Irish medieval monk in a verse concerning a cat:

> *Hunting mice is his delight*
> *Hunting words I sit all night*

The dualism of religion-blasphemy likewise runs through the Tyrone family. The father—and this is often true of Irish families—is conventionally pious, without any deep commitment to the Old Faith. He uses his religion in a purely conventional fashion, to blame, for example, the worldly failures of his two sons on the fact that they have both become apostates: "You've both flouted the faith you were born and brought up in—the one true faith of the Catholic Church—and your denial has brought nothing but self-destruction!" The mother, on the other hand, is deeply, neurotically, but still honestly, pious. Like Claudius, she cannot lie to God, He being so real to her. Rather in her case, as might be expected, it is the Virgin Mary who, in effect, usurps the Trinity and becomes "God," for the Virgin is the symbol of female purity and is thus inevitably the patron saint of Irish Roman Catholic convent girls. As such, the Virgin signifies innocence and childhood, the shelter of the convent, the benign smile of the Mother Superior, the loving earthly father at home—in short, the happy times before she married the harddrinking, rather crude, though kindly, James Tyrone, and had encountered the rude male world of tobacco, alcohol, cronies, and sweat, the agonies of childbirth, the failure of children, the black abyss of dope addiction. Yet she cannot pray, although she would like to, for God or the Virgin sees all:

Longingly.
If I could only find the faith I lost, so I could pray again!
She pauses—then begins to recite the Hail Mary in a flat, empty tone.
"Hail, Mary, full of grace! The Lord is with Thee; blessed art Thou among women."
Sneeringly.
You expect the Blessed Virgin to be fooled by a lying dope fiend reciting words! You can't hide from her!

The morphine is a road back to that virginal childhood and her "Long Day's Journey into Night" is a psychological regress to her convent days.

The sons are militantly atheistical. Edmund's favorite author is Nietzsche, whom he quotes: " 'God is dead: of His pity for man hath God died.' " The blasphemous reaction is not emphasized in *Long Day's Journey*, but it is in *Moon for the Misbegotten* where Jamie Tyrone, now in his early forties, plays a leading role. Here he tells of his blasphemous conduct after his mother's death. He had been abstemious for two years, but on the news of his mother's death an intolerable desire for desecration overcame him. He gets drunk, almost breaks out into a diatribe at the wake, and when escorting the coffin, in the baggage car of the train, to the East from Los Angeles, he continues his drinking and has a nightly assignation with a fat, blonde, fifty-dollar whore. In his drunken revels with the blonde he sings the last two lines of a "tear-jerker" song that he knew as a child:

> *And the baby's cries can't waken her*
> *In the baggage car ahead.*

The idea of betrayal, the "turncoat" psychology, permeates all the Tyrones. Everybody has betrayed everybody else. The father betrayed the mother because of his stinginess: when she was in pain once, he hired a cheap doctor, who unscrupulously started her on morphine; and the father will also probably betray Edmund by sending him to a cheap sanatorium. The mother betrayed Edmund just by bearing him, by bringing him into his painful existence. Jamie, in effect, had killed the son Eugene, who died in infancy, after having been visited by the contagious Jamie (who had been told to stay away). Edmund and Jamie fail their parents by their wasted lives, and Jamie betrays Edmund by trying to corrupt him. (They all are always honest enough to admit all these enormities.) The mother betrays them all by beginning to take dope on the day of the "long journey." Culturally, psychologically, they "know" that nobody is to be depended upon, father, mother, sibling. Whatever the weakness is, it will be given in to. The dope addict mother can't be cured—they all know this, and expect it. In fact, they would be disappointed in a deep, obscure sense if she broke off, and they were all to be happy and secure. They don't expect to be happy, for life is not like that. Always there is the fierce, primitive suspicion that no one is to be trusted. The promises to the parents and the relatives, the "pledge" to the priest, the "bargain" with God, about "the drink" (or dope)—all these go out the window, in a moment, when the implacable imagination, the seizure of the nerves, the impossible desire for a nirvana that lies at the bottom of a bottle of whiskey, comes over the Irishman. Then there is the constant chorus: "You drink!" "You failed!" "You'd like to see me dead!" "You take dope!" "Where's the hophead?" says Jamie of his mother.

The combination of sentiment and irony in matters of love is likewise a Tyrone characteristic, and most cogently illustrated by the mother in her relationship to her "loved ones." For she does love them all, deeply, and is quite sentimental about them. In her most sentimental moments she is capable of misty-eyed dreams of the future happiness of the family. Edmund, the gifted son, is an especial love. Yet she is capable of the most searing and corrosive statements to all of them. To Edmund, her beloved, she can say:

> *Turns on Edmund with a hard, accusing antagonism—almost a revengeful enmity.*
>
> I never knew what rheumatism was before you were born! Ask your father!

Throughout the play we find her alternately sentimental and corrosive. As Edmund says of her:

> Deliberately, that's the hell of it! You know something in her does it deliberately—to get beyond our reach, to be rid of us, to forget we're alive! It's as if, in spite of loving us, she hated us.

Love for all of the Tyrones is ambiguous, unresolved tension between tenderness and hate, sentimentality and irony.

It is impossible to estimate accurately the cosmic import of the "bottle" in the lives of the Tyrones (the only reason that the mother does not take to it is because she possesses something stronger). In a way the Irish addiction to drink is a simplifying element in their lives, for this is how all problems are met—to reach for the bottle. When the mother takes to dope on the morning of the "long day," she knows, as a matter of course, that her men will all be drunk by nightfall. "The Bottle" is at the center of the room, and in many ways is the most important object in the room. If not using it, they talk about it. It enters into their very characters; the father's penuriousness is most neatly summed up by the fact that he keeps his liquor under lock and key and has an eagle eye for the exact level of the whiskey in the bottle he has grudgingly set forth. By the same token, the measure of the sons' rebellion is how much liquor they can "sneak." It is doubtful if the phrase and the action of "sneaking a drink" have in any other cultural group the immense significance that they have with the Irish. Allied to this peculiarly Irish custom are the concomitant phrase and action: "watering the whiskey," that is, filling the bottle with water to the level where it was before you "sneaked your drink." (The pathology of this custom is very curious, for obviously you fool nobody since the next person who uses the bottle instantly knows it has been "watered." And it doesn't take much imagination—since you know the habits of your family—to guess who has been doing the "watering." Thus James Tyrone knows that Jamie "waters" his whiskey, and Jamie knows that his father knows. Yet he will continue to do so: a rite that signifies a fictitious secrecy.) In some Irish households whole quarts of whiskey, indeed whole cases of whiskey, would slowly evolve into a watery, brown liquid, without the bottles having ever been set forth socially, so to speak. This act—the lonely, surreptitious, rapid gulp of whisky—is the national rite, and probably deserves a sculptural embodiment, like Rodin's "The Thinker."

The "turbulence" of the Tyrone family hardly needs to be remarked upon. The play is, in part, psychologically speaking, a "free-for-all," with everybody's hand against everybody else. Yet it is not this simple, for their love for one another is equally overpowering. No relationship has any stability and, sometimes, second by second, it alternates between love and hate. Here, for example, is an interchange between James Tyrone and Edmund (they are both drunk, of course); the father speaks first:

> You'll obey me and put out that light or, big as you are, I'll give you a thrashing that'll teach you—!
> *Suddenly he remembers Edmund's illness and instantly becomes guilty and shamefaced.*
> Forgive me, lad. I forgot— You shouldn't goad me into losing my temper.
> EDMUND
> *Ashamed himself now.*
> Forget it, Papa. I apologize, too. I had no right being nasty about nothing. I am a bit soused, I guess. I'll put out the damned light.
> *He starts to get up.*
> TYRONE
> No, stay where you are. Let it burn.

*He stands up abruptly—and a bit drunkenly—and begins turning on
the three bulbs in the chandelier, with a childish, bitterly dramatic self-
pity.*

We'll have them all on! Let them burn! To hell with them! The poorhouse
is the end of the road, and it might as well be sooner as later!

He finishes turning on the lights.

EDMUND

*Has watched this proceeding with an awakened sense of humor—now
he grins, teasing affectionately.*

That's a grand curtain.

He laughs.

You're a wonder, Papa.

TYRONE

Sits down sheepishly—grumbles pathetically.

That's right, laugh at the old fool! The poor old ham! But the final curtain
will be in the poorhouse just the same, and that's not comedy!

Then as Edmund is still grinning, he changes the subject.

For the Irish are just what the popular legend about them says: mer-
curial. As another American Irishman, F. Scott Fitzgerald, once said of
himself: "I was always saving or being saved—in a single morning I
would go through the emotions ascribed to Wellington at Waterloo. I
lived in a world of inscrutable hostiles and inalienable friends and
supporters."

The sexual chastity of the Irish is likewise a motivating force in the
play. In the mother's preoccupation with the Virgin we can see its
feminine manifestation. For while it is never said in so many words, we
can see that one of the mother's basic difficulties lies in that initial rude
shock of the male assault and that the morphine addiction is an effect,
not a cause. For the dope is her way back to her virginal childhood.
Tyrone himself explains that she was not quite the nun-like, little girl
that she now pictures herself. On the contrary, she was attractive, flirta-
tious, almost hoydenish, and she fell immediately and irrevocably in love
with the handsome and charming young actor that was James Tyrone.
Yet the hard facts of the marriage were too much for her, too little prepared for by the sweet, misty existence of the convent. It is after marriage
that she learns that Tyrone had had a mistress, that he drinks, that he
will go out with cronies and get drunk, while she remains alone in a
"cheap" (as she keeps repeating) hotel room. Always in her mind is the
terrible discrepancy between her life as a girl, or her metaphor for it, and
her life as an adult married woman.

The sons, especially Jamie, represent the obverse side of the sexual chastity of the Irish. For while they are anything but chaste, they yet cannot partake of normal sexual relations and connect sex with love. For them it must always be a desecration, consecrated by drink and debauchery. The mother laments the fact that they never have anything to do with "nice" girls. Precisely, because they in their way are devotees of the Virgin too. Yeats said of Dowson: "Sober, he looked on no woman; drunk, he picked the cheapest whore. 'He did not even want them clean,' said a friend. 'I have been faithful to thee, Cynara! in my fashion.'" Jamie Tyrone will have only whores, and only fat ones, and to them he recites, of course, Dowson. As Edmund describes it:

> It's a good likeness of Jamie, don't you think, hunted by himself and whiskey, hiding in a Broadway hotel room with some fat tart—he likes them fat —reciting Dowson's "Cynara" to her.
> *He recites derisively, but with deep feeling.*
> "All night upon mine heart I felt her warm heart beat,
> Night-long within mine arms in love and sleep she lay;
> Surely the kisses of her bought red mouth were sweet;
> But I was desolate and sick of an old passion,
> When I awoke and found the dawn was gray;
> I have been faithful to thee, Cynara! in my fashion."
> *Jeeringly.*
> And the poor fat burlesque queen doesn't get a word of it, but suspects she's being insulted!

Fat, blonde whores: that is the reaction of some Irish males to the sexual prohibitions that his culture imposes on him. This is the Saturday night dream of young Studs Lonigan: going to bed with a buxom blonde. For it is generally buxom women, with marmoreal thighs and full breasts, as if size alone could make up for the imposed frustrations and inhibitions. Abbie in *Desire Under the Elms* is "buxom, full of vitality. Her round face is pretty but marred by its rather gross sensuality." Nina in *Strange Interlude* is "tall with broad square shoulders, slim strong hips and long beautifully developed legs— . . ." But the O'Neill-Irish sexual fantasy receives its proper apotheosis in *Moon for the Misbegotten* in Josie Hogan who is

> five feet eleven in her stockings and weighs around one hundred and eighty. Her sloping shoulders are broad, her chest deep with large, firm breasts, her waist wide but slender by contrast with her hips and thighs. She has long smooth arms, immensely strong, although no muscles show. The same is true of her legs. . . . She is all woman.

Jamie himself says: " 'I like them tall and strong and voluptuous, now, with beautiful big breasts.' " And looking at Josie, this monument of female flesh (which is available to him, if he so desires, but which he has classified as "nice girl"), he murmurs—he is drunk—"You have a beautiful strong body, too, Josie—and beautiful eyes and hair, and a beautiful smile and beautiful warm breasts." It would seem that only a gigantic female breast, cosmic in scope, can make up to the Irish male for his frustrations. And, characteristically, Jamie Tyrone spends the last hours of his fictional existence (the last scene in *A Moon for the Misbegotten*) with his head resting on the bosom of Josie Hogan. Characteristically too, since he has classified her as a "nice girl"—like his mother— a devotee of the Virgin, so to speak, he keeps the relationship scrupulously filial. So too when Joyce came to create his woman of the earth, Molly Bloom, she must be monumental in proportions. The first glimpse that we have of her is through the voyeuristic eyes of Mr. Bloom, at eight o'clock in the morning in the bedroom at 7 Eccles Street (this is the first description in the book of Molly): "He looked calmly down on her bulk and between her large soft bubs, sloping within her nightdress like a she goat's udder."

A secondary creation of the male rebellion against the Puritan aspects of his culture is the "ne'er-do-well." Any large Irish family used to produce at least one of these. (He's usually your "uncle.") He tends to be, of course, unmarried; he is usually good-looking; he has more than his share of the Irish charm; he has a fine sense of humor; and everybody likes him. He is also completely irresponsible, can never hold a job; and devotes himself to liquor and women, although the liquor is usually more important to him. In short, he is Jamie Tyrone. Very often—since he represents in the Irish national drama the Prince of Darkness—he is positively "Mephistophelean," which is the word used to describe Jamie Tyrone. Lest we think this is an artistic stroke of O'Neill's imagination, we may remember that, according to Frank Budgen, Joyce, who was in his own inimitable ways an Irish "ne'er-do-well," was called by the chorus girls in the Stadttheater in Zurich "Herr Satan" and that Budgen's landlady was actually afraid of this satanic gentleman, with his long thin face, thick glasses, high forehead, and jaunty demeanor.

The Tyrones, like their ancient ancestors, are, to a man, noncommunal. Save for the reference to the Standard Oil Company and a trip to the drugstore, modern American society does not exist for them and certainly it plays no role in the play. But it is not only a question of society; other people have no existence for the Tyrones. The father, it is true, has his drunken cronies, but the family has no social life at all, and the two sons and the mother are lone wolves. The mother in particular feels and laments their isolation and loneliness:

> If there was only some place I could go to get away for a day, or even an afternoon, some woman friend I could talk to—not about anything serious, simply laugh and gossip and forget for a while—someone besides the servants—that stupid Cathleen!

Now it is true too that the Irish are indefatigably gregarious—witness the people in *Ulysses*. Yet they are capable, especially in an alien environment, of great isolation and loneliness, as *Long Day's Journey* evidences.

For they are most profoundly and primarily committed—to get to my last point—to the family. Everything pales beside the fact of the *family,* which is the macro-microcosm that blots out the universe and takes the place of Hardy's Cosmic Forces, or Marx's march of history, or Shaw's evolutionary powers, or Sinclair Lewis's middle class, or Arthur Miller's "changing America." They are always swarming all over one another, simultaneously loving and torturing each other. They can't leave one another alone, either in love or hate, yet each assault—"you wish I were dead!" is punctuated by an unabashed sentiment and humorous affection.

It should be said too that the family swarm produced a violently negative reaction as well (not dealt with by O'Neill in *Long Day's Journey*), just as the religious intensity generated the blasphemy. As in the case of the blasphemous reaction, it was the male who rebelled against the dominion of petticoats and the responsibilities of fatherhood that home and offspring imposed. Some of the violence of this reaction can be gauged from a fact of history, rather than poetry, namely, Stanislaus Joyce's account in *My Brother's Keeper* of his own father's successful flight to freedom and ultimate irresponsibility. When Mrs. Joyce lay dying of cancer, John Joyce blurted at her: "I'm finished. I can't do any more. If you can't get well, die. Die and be damned to you!" And within two years after the mother's death, the family was scattered. "I'll get rid of you all," he would say, "and go back to Cork. But I will break your hearts before I go. Oh yes, by God! See if I don't. I'll break your hearts, but I'll break your stomachs first." He succeeded in divesting himself of his "fleas," as he called them in more jocular moments, and had for himself twenty-six or twenty-seven years of freedom before he died and during which time he frequently complained about his being deserted by his unnatural family. For the pressures of the Irish family seem to lead either to total intimacy or to total estrangement.

The peculiarly intimate relationships of the Irish family were given,

I think, by two conditions. First of all, it is a democracy in a wild sort of way. These are not parents and children, each with their appropriate range of personality and behavior. They are all *equal,* and can condemn one another openly, irrespective of age or rank. The children are not children but little adults. The adults are not adults but big children. The second factor is that they have no *prohibitory conventions:* that is, there are no agreed-upon prohibitions, either in the realm of action or the realm of subject matter. There are no certain things that everybody mutually agrees to keep silent about; there is no norm of conduct beyond which one does not venture. Above all, there is no reticence. Everybody says just what he or she thinks; so that one enormity after another is uttered. Yet so deeply are they involved with and committed to one another that these enormities in reality mean nothing. They pass like the air that gave them voice. For while the Irish may know that life is a tragedy—"We begin to live," said Yeats, "when we have conceived life as a tragedy"—they have a deep suspicion that it may well be—for all they know—a farcical comedy. And against Yeats's observation we must place the perhaps better known one of George Bernard Shaw:

> An Irishman's imagination never lets him alone, never convinces him, never satisfies him; but it makes him that he can't face reality nor deal with it nor handle it nor conquer it: he can only sneer at those that do . . . and imagination's such a torture that you can't bear it without whiskey. . . . And all the while there goes on a horrible, senseless, michievous laughter.

These two observations, of Yeats and of Shaw, define precisely the unique quality of the atmosphere in which the Tyrones live, and O'Neill himself puts both observations in the mouths of the two characters in the play, the mother and Edmund, who are the most perceptive and intelligent of the Tyrones. A pessimistic version of Yeats's observation is put, most appropriately, by the mother:

> None of us can help the things life has done to us. They're done before you realize it, and once they're done they make you do other things until at last everything comes between you and what you'd like to be, and you've lost your true self forever.

But Edmund, in the middle of a serious conversation with his father, makes Shaw's point. The father has just turned out a light bulb, and Edmund suddenly realizes the humor of the father's stinginess, which has also caused tragedy:

Edmund suddenly cannot hold back a burst of strained, ironical laughter. Tyrone is hurt.
What the devil are you laughing at?
EDMUND
Not at you, Papa. At life. It's so damned crazy.

And his own bit of philosophy, which verges upon the old-style O'Neill-ian bathos and pseudo-poetry—"I dissolved in the sea, became white sails and flying spray, became beauty and rhythm . . ."—is saved by irony and humor:

> *He grins wryly.*
> It was a great mistake, my being born a man, I would have been much more successful as a sea gull or a fish.

And later on he says of himself: "Stammering is the native eloquence of us fog people."

Constantly—except for the mother—they see the wild humor of the tragic or grotesque things that they do. Thus Jamie on the night of the "long day's journey" behaves characteristically; he gets drunk and goes to Mamie Burns's whorehouse, where he picks "Fat Violet," whom Mamie has threatened to fire because she is bad for business; Jamie takes her upstairs and starts reciting "Cynara."

> She stood it for a while. Then she got good and sore. Got the idea I took her upstairs for a joke. Gave me a grand bawling out. Said she was better than a drunken bum who recited poetry. Then she began to cry. So I had to say I loved her because she was fat, and she wanted to believe that, and I stayed with her to prove it, and that cheered her up, and she kissed me when I left, and said she'd fallen hard for me, and we both cried a little more in the hallway, and everything was fine, except Mamie Burns thought I'd gone bughouse.

Jamie continues:

> This night has opened my eyes to a great career in store for me, my boy! I shall give the art of acting back to the performing seals, which are its most perfect expression. By applying my natural God-given talents in their proper sphere, I shall attain the pinnacle of success! I'll be the lover of the fat woman in Barnum and Bailey's circus!

For they are all animated by a tremendous zest for this life that is so terrible for them, whiskey and all. What they fear is madness and death, and what they fear most of all is suicide (both Edmund and the mother had once made attempts). Drink then is a form of suicide, a day-by-day one, a suicide from which one can awake in the morning. Like gambling, it is suicide without death: and it drowns out that senseless, mischievous laughter always going on high in the background.

III

> The peoples of "the Celtic Fringe," with the Atlantic at their backs and a host of formidable aggressors ever bearing down upon them from the Continent, were naturally inspired to seek imaginative relief from the pressure of an adverse human environment by dreaming of an Elysium hidden in the bosom of the Ocean . . .

Thus Toynbee in *A Study of History* on the Celts: the perpetual imaginative escape from the intolerable situation. And it is obvious that most of the characteristics that I, and others, have ascribed to the Irish are the result of a passionate people being imprisoned by an endless stasis: historical, political, religious, cultural, sexual, and personal, with the resulting ambiguity of a people and a culture that is at one and the same time violently rebellious and anarchic and inhumanly passive and acquiescent, given, culturally, to musing over past glories in a dull and tedious present, as in the "Cyclops" episode of *Ulysses,* or given, personally, to mulling over the personal past, its motivations, its mistakes, its total determinism over the present, as do characters of *Long Day's Journey.* This peculiarly retrospective mood under which the past is both a lost and glorious paradise and an unyielding tyrant who has fixed his inflexible and murderous hold upon the present (the mood of Mary Tyrone, in short) can be described in two ways: either it can be called an absence of the sense of time (time means nothing to the Tyrones), or an overly acute sense of the past, which makes *it* the living and the present. . . . History, collective and individual, is a "nightmare," in Joyce's words, from which nobody can awake.

O'Neill's Search for
a "Language of the Theatre"

by Robert F. Whitman

There were always those who saw Eugene O'Neill's more extreme experiments in dramatic technique as an unfortunate aberration, and viewed with pity the prospect of a man who could write such powerful "theater" as *Anna Christie* or *Desire Under the Elms*, dissipating his energies pursuing some illusory Theater of Tomorrow in *The Fountain* or *Lazarus Laughed*. And when, in the last plays, he apparently returned to the essentially realistic form of his early work, it was looked on by many as a return to sanity. But O'Neill was never one to go backwards; and the fact that many of his experimental plays failed to win the critical acceptance of the earlier, more conventional, works would never in itself have led him to revert to a form he felt he had outgrown. He was always exploring, always hoping to find a medium of communication that would satisfy his needs both as a dramatist and as a man. The search led him into strange ways, and down dead ends; but the diversity and violence of both his techniques and his subject matter tend to hide some of the unifying threads which bind together all his work.

In his letter to George Jean Nathan regarding *Dynamo* he said that he wished to "dig at the roots of the sickness of today as I feel it—the death of the old God and failure of science and materialism to give any satisfactory new one for the surviving primitive religious instinct to find a meaning for life in, and to comfort its fears of death with. It seems to me that anyone trying to do big work nowadays must have this big subject behind all the little subjects of his plays. . . ." [1] O'Neill would settle for nothing less than "big work," and the apparently sensational aspects of

"O'Neill's Search for a 'Language of the Theatre'" by Robert F. Whitman. From the *Quarterly Journal of Speech*, XVI, No. 2 (April 1960), 154-170. Copyright © 1960 by the Speech Association of America. Reprinted by permission of the author and the *Quarterly Journal of Speech*.

[1] *The American Mercury*, XVI (January 1929), 119.

his plays, the crime, moral degeneracy in general, cynicism, all escapes from reality, whether through insanity or drink or drugs, were for him simply the overt symptoms of this "sickness of today." But O'Neill felt that he, as much as anyone, was a victim of this "sickness," and that he knew whereof he spoke. His plays are, in a very real sense, a continuous record of his soul-searching. *Long Day's Journey into Night* is the most frankly autobiographical of them; but to a degree they all are—not in the events, perhaps, but in the conflicts which are presented and in the view of life taken. Nor, in this sense, is there very much development in O'Neill's writing. The problem does not change—"finding a meaning for life and comfort for the fears of death." There *is*, however, a very real development in his awareness of the complexity of the problems he is facing, and of the possible areas where an answer might be found—a development reflected in the changing ways he approaches the basic questions of life. Each play, then, is a new attempt to come to grips with the same old problem.

A "new approach" for O'Neill, however, was not simply a question of new plots or subject matter, but of new techniques. In one of the early playbills of the Provincetown Playhouse he stated that he hoped to create a "new language for the theater." Like most artists' comments on their own work, this is at least half rationalization. He was also trying to create a "new language for O'Neill."

The search led him into many and varied manners of speech: realism, expressionism, naturalism, symbolism, fantasy, poetry, alone and in various combinations, as well as experiments with devices from older dramatic traditions. But behind the apparent diversity was a single impulse: to find an idiom in which to express the human tragedy. And whatever other characteristics O'Neill may have possessed, or lacked, he had a firm grasp of one essential element of tragedy—the eternal conflict between Man's aspirations and some intransigent, ineluctable quality in life which circumscribes and limits him, and frustrates the realization of those dreams which seem to make life worth living.

Almost all of O'Neill's heroes—those that are in the least sensitive—are baffled and hurt by the blank impalpable wall which hems them in, from the Yank of *Bound East for Cardiff*, dying in the fo'castle of a freighter fog-bound in the North Atlantic, or the other Yank, in *The Hairy Ape*, for whom the fog of anonymity is just as real and even more terrifying, to all of the characters who make the Long Day's Journey into Night. There are exceptions, of course: thick-skinned materialists like Marco Polo, who are too obtuse to question that they have found the earthly paradise; stern, monolithic figures, like Ephraim Cabot, who through a hard life and a hard God has become a hard man, almost a part of the rugged stones and soil of his New England farm; or the mystics, like Lazarus, who, with his vision of a supra-mortal unity and sanity, has simply risen above the whole problem. But the vast majority of the characters are painfully aware that reality is never sufficient to their demands upon it, and that the chalice of life is cursed by some inexorable poison which will frustrate our fondest hopes and turn dreams to dust in our grasp.

The sense of having been betrayed by life runs through virtually all the plays and "there ain't much . . . that'd make yuh sorry to lose it." [2] Robert Mayo clings to the hope that "Life owes us some happiness after what we've been through. It must! Otherwise our suffering would be meaningless—and that is unthinkable" (III, 150). Unthinkable, perhaps, but by the end of *Beyond the Horizon* it seems all too possible. For several characters life is only a "rotten dirty joke"; and Mary, in *Days Without End,* cries: "I only know I hate life. It's dirty and insulting—and evil. I want my dream back—or I want to be dead with it!" (III, 550). Christine, in *Mourning Becomes Electra,* says wistfully: "Why can't all of us remain innocent and loving and trusting? But life won't leave us alone. It twists and wrings and tortures our lives with others' lives until —we poison each other to death!" (II, 73). The members of the Tyrone family "poison each other to death," and Edmund has more insight into the truth than he would like. But it is his mother who gives the motif its most explicit and most poignant utterance: "None of us can help the things life has done to us. They're done before you realize it, and once they're done they make you do other things until at last everything comes between you and what you'd like to be, and you've lost your true self forever." [3]

Whether the individual's struggle with life ends in Dion Anthony's self-destruction or Nina Leeds's apathetic surrender or Lavinia Mannon's triumphant acceptance, the inescapable limitations inherent in existence provide the root of his tragedy. In all but the earliest plays, however, O'Neill tends to take this quality of life as "given," to accept the fact that the harm is "done before you realize it," and to turn his attention to the conflicts which this sense of disillusionment and betrayal sets up within the individual. Characteristically, the impulse toward the ideal, frustrated by life, brings cynicism and despair; the impulse toward faith, frustrated by life, leads to skepticism; the impulse to love, frustrated by

---

[2] *Bound East for Cardiff,* in *The Plays of Eugene O'Neill* (3 vols.; New York, 1947), I, 486. References for all the plays up to and including *The Iceman Cometh,* hereafter cited in the text, are to this edition.

[3] *Long Day's Journey into Night* (New Haven, 1956), p. 61. Further page references for the play are to this edition.

life, leads to hate or smothering possessiveness; the impulse to create, frustrated by life, becomes destructive. Both sets of impulses, however, usually exist together, struggling with each other, tearing the possessor to pieces in their mortal opposition. It is this that provides the central tensions of almost all of O'Neill's plays, and the history of his development as an experimenter in dramatic technique is the history of his efforts to objectify this conflict.

Speaking of his early sea plays, O'Neill said that it was "the impelling, inscrutable forces behind life which it is my ambition to at least faintly shadow at their work in my plays." [4] The "force" was essentially external to the individual, and something which he had to fight against—or accept. And both alternatives are represented in the early one-acters. In *Bound East for Cardiff* the "inscrutable forces" are suggested by the fog which surrounds the play, and in which Yank blindly faces death. He is lost, and he knows it, but there is something more than pathos in the way he looks back over an aimless life, trying to find some kind of sense to it. Yank is not exceptionally brave or humble or frightened—he is a little of all three, a "little" man, broken by life and cast aside, without knowing where he is or why. But at the end of the play, when the fog clears, there is also the suggestion that with death came an answer which gave meaning to existence.

A quite different note is caught in the voice of Smitty, in *Moon of the Caribbees*. Baffled though he may have been, Yank did not complain; but throughout the speeches of Smitty there is a whine of self-pity that stands in sharp contrast to the "impelling," eternal forces shadowed forth in the peace of the sea, the moon, and the mournful, primitive chant of the natives. The only actions in which he engages are negative, in rejecting the advances of a native girl, or in drowning his "memories" in alcohol, the most degrading and self-defeating gesture of romantic *weltschmerz*. Smitty is in a fog of his own making. The beauty and sadness and power of life are there, if he could see and respond. But it is too late; in his frustration by life he has been blinded, turned in upon himself, cut off from what is vital and real. Smitty, for all that he is a somewhat shadowy figure, is a type—or represents a phenomenon—in which O'Neill remains interested throughout his work.

Robert Mayo, the hero of O'Neill's first full length play, *Beyond the Horizon,* is like Smitty a bit of a weakling, but he is also capable of something more than self-pity. He is described as having "a touch of the poet" in him, and his aspirations go far beyond Smitty's maudlin pangs of guilt

---

[4] From a letter to Barrett Clark, quoted by Mr. Clark in his *Eugene O'Neill, The Man and His Plays* (New York, 1947), p. 59.

and self-disgust. Early in the play he tells his brother, ("Pointing to the horizon—dreamily"):

> Supposing I was to tell you that it's just Beauty that's calling me, the beauty of the far off and unknown, the mystery and spell of of the East which lures me in the books I've read, the need of the freedom of great wide spaces, the joy of wandering on and on—in quest of the secret which is hidden over there, beyond the horizon? (III, 85.)

O'Neill has little patience with Mayo himself. His longings are "too conscious, intellectually diluted into a vague, intangible wanderlust. His powers of resistance, both moral and physical, would also probably be correspondingly watered. He would throw away his instinctive dream and accept the thralldom of the farm for—why, for almost any nice little poetical craving—the romance of sex, say." [5] But while his aimless yearning to wander may have been romantic self-delusion, the alternative suggested by Mayo's brother, that "you might as well stay here, because we've got all you're looking for right on the farm," O'Neill characterizes as "thralldom." He himself had a profound sympathy with this intense desire for something more, something better, than life can offer, and its inevitable frustration lies at the heart of his vision of man's tragedy.

In these early plays the conflict between human aspirations, whether "immortal longings" or romantic self-delusion, and the forces which prevent their realization is suggested as much by the setting as by the action itself. In *Bound East for Cardiff* it is in the fog which surrounds the dying Yank, in *Moon of the Caribbees* in the distance between Smitty and his surroundings, and in *Beyond the Horizon* it is symbolized by the dark ring of hills which hems in the world of the farm, and the petty demands and frustrations that sap the life of Robert Mayo, and shut out the beauty and wonder of the sunset and the sea and freedom which lie beyond. All of these devices are fairly successful, but insofar as they *are* "things," physical elements in the setting, they seem to suggest that the inhibiting, limiting force lies somehow *outside* of the individual.

It is perfectly possible that this is the way O'Neill saw it at the time. Certainly the barrier between Mayo and the realization of his dreams is part of "life," for he can surmount it only through death. But in death Mayo is freed not only from life, but from himself. It is true that he is beaten down by existence, by the nagging demands of a wife and child, of domineering parents, of economic necessity, and by his own incompatibility with the way of life he has chosen; but the point is that he *did* choose it. Mayo does not fail because he had dreams, or because some

---

[5] Quoted by Clark, p. 66.

power wholly outside himself frustrated them, but because he sold them for something less. As he is dying he makes one last attempt to reach the encircling hills: "I thought I'd try to end as I might have—if I'd had the courage—alone—in a ditch by the open road—watching the sun rise" (III, 167).

The fact that the forces which prevented the realization of Robert Mayo's dreams lie within himself, rather than externally in the "world," or in "fate," does not necessarily make them any less inevitable, for they may well be inherent elements in human nature. But if the essential conflict is, as it would seem, between two antithetical impulses in Mayo's nature, this is not adequately suggested by the controlling symbol, the surrounding hills. In the plays which follow *Beyond the Horizon*, however, we can see O'Neill's efforts to discover a more effective method of indicating the inner nature of this struggle.

The Straw is in the same realistic tradition as *Beyond the Horizon*, but its symbols, if they deserve the name, are much less overt. The sanatorium, in which most of the action takes place, with its suggestions of hopelessness and decay, is analogous to the world enclosed by the hills; but there is an important reversal in the implications of the "inside-outside" relationship. When he leaves the sanatorium, Stephen, the play's hero, is still prisoner to his own egotism, and he wastes his energies in purposeless wandering and self-indulgence. It is only after his return, and after he has found himself by discovering in the dying Eileen something outside his own ego to which he can give himself, that he achieves any kind of self-fulfillment. In other words, he finds the road to "beyond the horizon" not outside his nature, or outside of life, but *within*.

The question of whether man's inability to achieve self-fulfillment springs from some quality in himself or from the nature of the world around him is handled even more explicitly in *Anna Christie*. The sea, with the sinister shroud of fog in which it hides its malignant purposes, suggests all the awful and mysterious forces of nature which thwart man and his hopes. Throughout the play Chris Christopherson, Anna's father, blames the sea for all that has gone wrong in his life, and at the climax of the action, when his failure as a father has become painfully evident, he knows where the fault lies: "It's dat old davil, sea, do this to me! It's her dirty tricks!" (III, 62). The play ends on much the same note, with Chris muttering: "Fog, fog, fog, all bloody time. You can't see vhere you vas going, no. Only dat ole davil, sea—she knows!" (III, 78).

This use of the fog is very much like that in *Bound East for Cardiff*, and from Chris's point of view it still symbolizes a force which baffles his will, and renders his hopes impotent. But it is made perfectly evident in the action of the play that his recriminations against the sea and the fog are simply rationalizations of his own inadequacies, his justification for his fear of life and failure as a man. They become, therefore, without losing any of the mystery or sense of inevitability which we associate with the sea, projections of forces at work within Chris himself. The conflict in Chris which has thus been created is evident in his grudging love for the sea, which slips out in nostalgic reminiscences of his days as bosun on a sailing ship. He has tried to effect a compromise between his instinctive yearning for the freedom of the sea and his fear of its, and life's, dangers by taking a job which lies half way between land and sea, but which is neither fish nor fowl, as captain of a coastal coal barge. But compromise is not resolution, except in the sense that the two antithetical impulses leave him in a state of suspension: a mild, ineffectual little man, beaten by life and whining that it is all the sea's fault. Partly because *Anna Christie* represents a considerable reworking of an earlier play, *Chris Christopherson,* and the dramatic focus has shifted from father to daughter in the process, much of the effectiveness of this split in Chris's character has been lost.

O'Neill solved the problem of emphasis and focus more than adequately in *The Emperor Jones.* It is a one man play, and in Brutus Jones we have a powerful dramatic characterization of an individual destroyed by two conflicting impulses in his nature. There is on the one hand the arrogant, flamboyant, self-confident Emperor, contemptuous of the servility and superstitiousness of his own race, his head filled with the conviction that "for de big stealin' day makes you Emperor and puts you in de Hall o' Fame when you croaks," a lesson learned "in ten years on de Pullman ca's listenin' to de white quality talk" (III, 78); on the other is the bewildered, frightened Negro, victim of his past, both racial and personal.

The Emperor Jones is the first of O'Neill's frankly experimental plays, and while his exploration of expressionistic techniques can probably be attributed to several factors, one of the most important is certainly that it permitted him to explore inner conflicts with greater flexibility and clarity. The essential realism of the early plays allowed for the use of symbolism; but, as we have seen, such "inanimate actors" as the sea and the fog, or visual symbols in the setting, such as the dark ring of hills, too much throw the emphasis on a struggle between the individual and some element in life outside himself. The "visions" in *The Emperor Jones,* which are neither hallucinations nor projections of Jones's "thoughts," reveal the inner springs of his nature as they come in conflict with his assumed, outward character. But the role is not consciously "put on"—Jones thinks of himself as a bold and unscrupulous exploiter, albeit a fraudulent emperor—nor is he at all aware of the impulses which finally destroy him. Since he is dealing with hidden, subconscious elements in man's nature, O'Neill doesn't beat around the bush, trying to slip sly hints into a "realistic" medium, but presents them directly and dramatically.

There are in the play several dramatic devices, almost inanimate actors, which are external to Jones and which do not pertain directly to his nature. But the pulsating rhythm of the native drums, which dominates the action, rapidly becomes a tangible projection of Jones's rising panic—a fact that has led some commentators to see the play simply as a study in the effect of fear on a half-civilized Negro. There is the brooding, mysterious Great Forest in which Jones loses himself—to find himself. It is not just a place *where* something happens to Jones; it is part of *what* happens to him, a primeval, elemental force which literally and figuratively strips him of the superficies of civilization. This is not a play about fear; panic is simply the "acid test" which reduces Jones to his essential nature as Man. Nor is Jones's race important; it is simply that, in the Negro, man's journey from savagery to "civilization" has been tremedously foreshortened. The play is, in essence, the story of "the failure of science and materialism"—the values implicit in "de white quality's" society—"to give any satisfactory new [God] for the surviving primitive religious instinct to find a meaning for life in, and to comfort its fears of death with." (See n. 1.)

It would be foolish to suggest that all, or even the majority, of O'Neill's plays can be fitted into some neat and air-tight formula, or even that they are all "about" the same thing. Nevertheless, many of them possess a basic pattern not unlike that of *The Emperor Jones.* Man, having lost the faith in life and the sense of belonging which were once the concomitants of his primitive oneness with nature, is cast adrift in a storm of conflicting and mutually destructive impulses with no solid faith, no courage of his convictions, no stable set of values to give direction or meaning to them. And, as in that play, the technical devices which O'Neill chooses to employ are his attempt to reveal, as directly as is possible on the stage, both this disassociation or antagonism between man and the world in which he finds himself, and the inner conflicts which this disharmony leaves him prey to.

The most obvious illustration of this is the play which in both subject and technique is what O'Neill himself termed "the direct descendant of *The Emperor Jones*": *The Hairy Ape.* The dramatist described Yank, the hero of the play, as "a symbol of man, who has lost his old harmony with nature, the harmony which he used to have as an animal and has not yet acquired in a spiritual way." [6] The expressionistic techniques are on the whole better integrated than in the earlier play, for the disassociation, the inner conflict, and the futile reversion to a more primitive orientation are all suggested by the action and setting without recourse to interpolated "visions."

When the play opens, Yank, like Brutus Jones, is a creature of twentieth century America. Its values are his values: it lives on steel, he *is* steel, he "belongs." He can be happy as a machine, because the world *is* a machine. The inhuman, mechanistic nature of Yank's universe is powerfully represented by the below-deck setting in which we first see him, which with its harsh metallic clanging, the robot-like movements, and the impersonal "brazen" chanting of commands is reminiscent of the factory scene in *Gas I* of Kaiser's trilogy. But his faith in this world is shattered when a scared, sickly girl, whose only claim to superiority is that her father is a steel magnate, insults him. That she can do this, and get away with it, raises not only doubts as to his importance in the scheme of things, but also the very un-machine-like feelings of hurt pride, revenge, and hate. In the remaining scenes, Yank tries to assert his individuality, his right to "belong," by getting some vague kind of "revenge." But he is faced with a world where "belonging" has lost all vitality and become merely going through the proper motions, where he can have no significance because nothing has. Throughout the play Yank is seen as a vital, almost brutal, figure set against a background of an inhuman, dead, meaningless world: the machine-like stokehole, the gaudy but "relentless" marionettes on Fifth Avenue, the implacable steel bars of his cell, or the cold suspicion and fear in the "Wobbly" headquarters. In the last scene Yank has been driven at last to the ape's cage in the zoo, in the hope that he may find there a creature with whom he is in harmony, that there, at least, he will "belong." But this is not the story of a "natural" man, purposeful even in his animality. If the world is empty, so is Yank; if it has lost its harmony with nature, so has he; and his last vain effort to find something which will give meaning to existence ends in death. And again, as in *The Emperor Jones*, it is primarily through his experimental techniques that O'Neill suggests this sense of man's being cut off from the vital fountainhead of nature and her purposes, and the destructive inner conflicts which that purposelessness creates.

The Fountain is by no means a radically experimental play, but there is an element of fantasy in the visions of the fountain, and that symbol lies at the heart of the play. Ponce de Leon, too, wanders in a futile world where wealth and military reputation and power become tawdry

---

[6] From a statement by O'Neill in the New York *Herald Tribune,* Nov. 16, 1924; see Clark, p. 84.

and empty, but where the absence of other values leaves him cynical and disillusioned. A desperate hope that love will give life meaning sends him off looking for the Fountain of Youth. Lying half-dead at the edge of a small pool in Florida, he "finds" it in a vision, and in the song of the fountain lies the essence of his "discovery":

> Love is a Flower
> Forever blooming
> Life is a fountain
> Forever leaping
> Upward to catch the golden sunlight
> Upward to reach the azure heaven
> Failing, falling,
> Ever returning,
> To kiss the earth that the flower may live.

(I, 439)

In this vision of life and death, growth and decay, aspiration and failure as integral parts of the eternal cycles of nature, where all things must pass away to give place to and nourish the new, Ponce de Leon finds his "belonging." And since the "disassociation" of the other plays has been overcome, and the deep tap-roots with which man is nourished have quickened to life, there is in the latter part of *The Fountain* none of that inner, self-destructive conflict which presented O'Neill with dramatic problems elsewhere.

Much the same point could be made about *Lazarus Laughed,* another play which asserts the ultimate unity of man with nature and the triumph of life over death:

> Believe in the healthy god called Man in you! . . . Believe! What if you are a man and men are despicable? Men are also unimportant! Men pass! Like rain into the sea! The sea remains! Man remains! Man slowly arises from the past of the race of men that was his tomb of death! For Man death is not! Man . . . *is!* (I, 359-360)

Again the conflict is not internal, for Lazarus, thanks to his glimpse beyond the veil, "belongs." But the struggle between this man of vitality and faith in life and the rest of the world, filled with men who through fear and selfishness and conformity have become but dead things, is emphasized by giving the various choruses masks differentiated only as types: the Self-Tortured, the Proud, the Servile, etc. And insofar as the play could be called a tragedy, it is not the tragedy of Lazarus, who triumphs over death in his love of life, but of men who are dead behind their masks from fear of life.

Neither *Lazarus Laughed* nor *The Fountain* is really a tragedy in any sense, however; they both end with an almost mystical affirmation which is too full of joy and acceptance. And if if the joy at times sounds a little forced, that is more a comment on O'Neill than on the nature of the play. *Desire Under the Elms*, written between the other two, also ends on a note of affirmation and acceptance—but it is at the same time a tragedy. And the differences between them are instructive. *Lazarus Laughed* and *The Fountain* can end as they do because Lazarus and Ponce de Leon have both had a revelation of The Secret: that the forces in life which seem to frustrate man's aspirations and creative instincts are only illusions, or rather, that the aspiration and the failure are one in the eternal cycles of nature, and therefore creative in a larger sense.

The affirmation which is implicit in the joy of mutual love at the end of *Desire Under the Elms* is not unlike that of Lazarus or Ponce de Leon. What makes the play tragic is the price at which it has been bought, and the needlessness of paying it. Eben and Abbie—and to a lesser extent Ephraim—are torn by much the same conflicting impulses as most of O'Neill's characters They yearn desperately for beauty and fulfillment and love, but they are confused and afraid, have no faith in these values, and see in the security of possessing the farm itself the only thing that will give life meaning. Their instinctive impulses, turned awry by fear, become suspicion and hate, that is, destructive. Through the first part of the play Eben and Abbie, in spite of their natural mutual attraction, view each other simply as obstacles in the way of possessing the farm; and while their love ultimately asserts itself, the ghost of their earlier distrust, which they have not the faith to exorcise, is not so easily laid. In the end, it is only through an act of violent self-sacrifice that they are freed from their selfishness and disorientation. Their sin, in O'Neill's terms, is not their love but their lack of faith in it, and the murder which that brought about. For this, perhaps, they must suffer, as all who distrust life suffer; but the note on which they leave the stage is not one of resignation to atonement, but of joy in each other, in love, and in the revelation that death, together, has no fears.

Desire Under the Elms is not noteworthy for its technical experiments. We have again an essentially realistic play employing incidental symbols. There are, for instance, the two elms brooding over the house like Nemesis. It seems apparent that these are intended to suggest the spirit of Eben's mother, once filled with a love of life and beauty, but which had been beaten down and destroyed by Ephraim's materialistic possessiveness, and which only finds fulfillment with the consummation of her son's love for Abbie. But the inner conflicts of the characters are not represented by any special technical devices. They are, rather, implicit in the duality of each character's attitudes toward the others. This duality is resolved, at tragic cost, in the case of Eben and Abbie; for Ephraim, it never is.

The masks of *The Great God Brown* represent a much more drastic experimental device for suggesting a similar internal conflict, although in this case it is not a question of one impulse triumphing over others, but of two antithetical impulses distorting and perverting each other, and destroying the individual in the process. O'Neill himself has defined the "hidden theme" of the play, and the forces which constitute its central tension:

> Dion Anthony—Dionysus and St. Anthony—the creative pagan acceptance of life, fighting eternal war with the masochistic, life-denying spirit of Christianity as represented by St. Anthony—the whole struggle resulting in this modern day in mutual exhaustion—creative joy in life for life's sake frustrated, rendered abortive, distorted by morality from Pan into Satan, into a Mephistopheles mocking himself in order to feel alive; Christianity, once heroic in martyrs for its intense faith now pleading weakly for intense belief in anything, even Godhead itself.[7]

This is not, of course, the whole of the play, but it is sufficient to show its continuity with the others. It should be noted, however—and this suggests one of the dangers to which the mask device is open—that the mask-face relationship is not that of appearance-reality. The mask is not simply a superficial facade which the individual "puts on" to hide from the world, but the perversion of a basic side of his personality or nature. Initially—or ideally—the impulses, that of "intense faith" and that of "creative joy in life for life's sake," Christ and Dionysus, Lazarus and Ponce de Leon, are one and the same. But lacking a strong faith, and hurt and disillusioned by the brutality of life and the insensitivity of men, Dion becomes the battleground in which these two forces, no longer unified, each driven by the other to a negative, life-denying extreme, destroy each other in mortal combat. And it is in the gradual changes in the masks that the nature of the impulses and their distortion is revealed dramatically.

The use of masks in *The Great God Brown* was not entirely successful, partly because, as O'Neill complained, the shifts from mask to "face" were not always immediately visible to the audience, and because they suggested a superficiality he did not intend. O'Neill attacked the prob-

7 From a letter to the New York *Evening Post*, Feb. 13, 1926; see Clark, p. 104

lem of how to present the inner conflict dramatically from another direction in *Strange Interlude*. The drama of the Elizabethans, with its
asides and soliloquies, had a tremendous advantage over the modern realistic tradition when it comes to representing the "inner" thoughts and
conflicts of characters. O'Neill, dedicated to exploring any possible "language" which would permit him to speak through the theater, felt he
could adapt these devices to his own uses and the modern idiom. While
Strange Interlude is in other respects a conventional realistic play, the free
use of asides gives the dramatist a flexibility largely lacking in drama tied
to externals. By this device O'Neill can show the "inner" response of a
character to a speech or situation immediately and directly. Nor, as in the
case of the masks, is the difference between the private and the public
speech the distinction between a character's "real" thoughts and some
front he puts up to the world. Sometimes, as was true of the masks, the
distance between the overt speech and the aside suggests the tensions and
conflicts working in the individual. Just as often, perhaps, it is within the
aside itself that the struggle and antithesis are revealed. The aside is not
required to carry the whole burden of defining the nature of the inner
conflict, as to a great extent the masks are in *The Great God Brown*. In
much the same manner as in *Desire Under the Elms,* it is in part the other
characters who identify and characterize the various impulses which haunt
Nina Leeds, driving her on from experience to experience and man to
man in a vain search for something to cling to, something to give life
meaning. On the other hand, it is her asides that give us the necessary
clues to her attitudes toward these characters. For example, in her one
moment of triumphant joy she says to herself:

> My three men!—I feel their desires converge on me!—to form one complete
> beautiful male desire which I absorb—and am whole. . . . Their life is my
> life—I am pregnant with the three!—Husband . . . lover . . . father . . .
> and the fourth, [my son]. . . . That makes it perfect! . . . I should be the
> happiest woman in the world! (I, 135)

As usual, her happiness does not last, because although her love is made
"complete" by including the loves of daughter-lover-wife-mother, the love
is divided among four individuals, which leads to antagonism and conflict. The relationships of each of the four could have been shown by externals, as could the fact that they are separate and hostile, but the fact
that the unity which they potentially represent is what Nina has been
searching for could only be shown by some more intimate exploration of
her mind than conventional "realistic" speech could provide.

In another respect too the use of asides and soliloquies permitted greater flexibility than did the masks of *The Great God Brown*. The latter device does not easily permit shades and gradations between the two extremes. Dion is endowed with two relatively distinct "sets" of impulses or characteristics, mask and non-mask, but it is virtually impossible to show various combinations or modifications of these motives, and rapid vacillation between conflicting impulses becomes mechanically very awkward. The possibilities of this kind of flexibility are demonstrated in *Dynamo*, which employs much of the same kind of "interior monologue" as *Strange Interlude*. The central "inner conflict" of the play is a three-way struggle in Reuben Light among his instinctive yearning for the security of the "old," discarded religion of his parents, his disillusioned rejection of that religion in favor of "facts," a kind of scientific material-ism, and an almost mystical reverence for the "life force" of Electricity. In the end, under the pressure of a desperate need to believe in *something*, the three impulses become fused in an insane worship of the Dynamo itself, in which are combined the protective and creative aspects of the Mother, a vital, elemental force lying at the heart of the natural universe, and a mystical Being which satisfied his "primitive religious instinct." The Dynamo becomes, in other words, at once the grotesque projection and the object of those instinctive, fundamental drives which, when guided by a vision of man's relationship to nature and the cosmos, such as is granted Lazarus and Ponce de Leon, can be creatively and satisfyingly fulfilled, but which can also, when aimless and conflicting, become destructive. At the end of the play Reuben, a bewildered, lost child again, shorn of his cynical self-assurance and torn by opposing impulses, hurls himself onto the electrodes of the dynamo, crying: "I don't want any miracle, Mother! I don't want to know the truth! I only want you to hide me, Mother! Never let me go from you again! Please, Mother!" (III, 488). And she doesn't.

In the physical representation of the dynamo, and in the organization of Act Three, which moves us gradually into the dynamo room, the "inner temple" of Reuben's religion—much in the manner of *The Ghost Sonata*—O'Neill's technique is close to expressionism. But it is still primarily through the asides and soliloquies that the forces which produce Reuben's self-destruction are revealed. Earlier in the play, before these forces have gotten organized, so to speak, and taken a hold on Reuben's mind, the interior monologue is used to make clear the extent to which the foundation for his disorientation was laid by his parents. He is disillusioned in both the life-denying God of his father and the over-possessive love of his mother, and rejects them violently; but at the same time he cannot live without them, and it is the need for security and authority on the one hand and love on the other that sends him whoring after strange gods. Science and materialism have failed to replace the "old God" who is dead, and the blind struggle to find meaning for existence in the vacuum which results—the "sickness of today" O'Neill called it—is just the area which the "interior monologue" was designed to probe.

The idea that spiritual dislocation, disassociation from the vital springs of life, and the repression, fear of life, self-centeredness which are its progeny, are part of modern man's inheritance is developed further in *Mourning Becomes Electra*. It is the curse of the Mannon family: "That's always been the Mannons' way of thinking. They went to the white meetinghouse on Sabbaths and meditated on death. Life was a dying. Being born was starting to die. Death was being born" (II, 54). And this denial of life, and with it love, is handed down from generation to generation: from old Abe Mannon, who had driven out and crushed his younger brother for loving and marrying a servant girl; from Ezra, for whom life was only a kind of death, who felt a numbness in his heart "like a statue of a dead man in a town square" (II, 55), and whose loveless marriage drove his wife to find fulfillment in the arms of his misbegotten cousin; to the family's dead end in Orin and Lavinia. Some of them learn that there is something more to life than guilt and justice and death. Ezra returns from the Civil War, where he has seen too much of death, wanting to think about life, hoping to resurrect love from the ashes of his marriage; and Lavinia finds a moment of freedom on a South Sea Island where they "have never heard that love can be a sin." But in each case it is too late; they have both been the agents, and must become the victims, of the Mannon curse. And the Fate of the play is not some external, impersonal force, in the Olympian sense, but the requital given by life to those who repudiate her, and cut themselves off from her sources. And the curse is not on just a particular family, nor for a patricular sin; it is the sickness of modern man.

The general framework of the *Oresteia,* with its brooding atmosphere of self-destruction, represents the most important experimental device used by O'Neill in *Mourning Becomes Electra*. But while he used none of the more obvious tricks, such as masks or soliloquies, he characterized the play as "unreal realism." This quality is given the play by the fact that, while he does not *use* masks, he suggests them. The Mannon homestead is described as having a "mask-like" quality, and each of the characters that has come under its influence is described in the stage directions as having a "life-*like*" mask. The malevolent spell of the Mannons drives all vitality and "reality" inwards upon itself, leaving only the appearance of life—until the inner demands break through the shell with all the violence of long repression. O'Neill himself explains that "this mask concept is a dramatic arresting visual symbol of the separateness, the fated isolation of this family." [8]—its separateness not simply from other people, but from life.

O'Neill, however, reinforces the effect of the "masks" with other visual impressions, and it is in the description of the women that the conflict between the instinctive love of life, and "oneness" with it, and the Mannon fear of life and suppression of its impulses is most clearly suggested. Christine "has a fine, voluptuous figure and she moves with a flowing animal grace" (II, 9); she has a "sensual" mouth, lively eyes, and rich copper hair, and her mask is less complete than the others'. Her daughter, Lavinia, is physically a complete copy of her mother—but she is herself a Mannon, and "does all in her power to emphasize the dissimilarity rather than the resemblance to her parent. She wears her hair pulled tightly back, as if to conceal its natural curliness" (II, 10), wears plain black instead of her mother's green, and carries herself in the severe, stiff military manner characteristic of the Mannons.

Christine, as we might gather from her description, is less successful than the true Mannons in suppressing her instincts for freedom and love. Lavinia, however, is of the family stock, and like them dedicated to the suppression of any instinctive "love of life" in herself or in her mother. After she has goaded her brother into executing Christine's lover she herself drives her mother to suicide, and as the fatal shot, the ultimate denial of life, echoes from the house, she stands "stiffly erect, her face stern and mask-like," muttering implacably: "It is justice! It is your justice, Father!" (II, 123.)

With all the Mannons except herself and her brother dead, Lavinia feels something in herself freed from a great weight that had held it down. She returns with her brother from a visit to the South Seas completely transformed into the image of her mother, in a green dress, her bronze hair loosened, her eyes and face alive again. But in destroying Christine, and the spontaneous love and vitality and "life" which, however repressed, she represented, Lavinia has proved herself too true a Mannon to escape her heritage. He brother, now the image of their father, fulfills the curse, destroying himself and driving Lavinia, once more stern and stiff and gray, into permanent isolation in the Mannon mansion—the final revenge of life on those who deny it.

The essentially incestuous relationships which control much of the action of the play may send the unwary reader to his Freud, but it will be a fruitless trip. It is true that O'Neill hoped to "get modern psychological approximation of Greek sense of fate" into the play, but he also said that *Mourning Becomes Electra* would have been "almost exactly as it is if I

[8] From O'Neill's "Working Notes and Extracts from a Fragmentary Work Diary," in *European Theories of The Drama*, ed. Barrett Clark (New York, 1947), p. 535.

had never heard of Freud or Jung or the others." [9] It is not a play *about* incest or even neurosis—these are just the symptoms of a much more basic disease. Basic, spontaneous, "natural" drives, thwarted by the Mannon "denial of life," find outlet in tortured, abnormal relationships. And these relationships also serve to illuminate the divisive inner conflicts of the major characters. Christine hates Lavinia for being Ezra's child, and loves Orin because he was born when her husband was away. Lavinia is *like* her mother, but loves her father and his stern morality. Orin looks and acts like his father, but loves his mother, even dreaming of fleeing with her to some "island of freedom and peace." In the third play of the trilogy he loves his sister as both mother and lover, symbols of everything that has been repressed by the Mannon in him, and hates her *because* of the father in him. Lavinia, caught between her maternal and paternal heritage, looks at Orin both as child and as father. Finally, as a single symbol of forces bound together yet in mortal conflict, they are (figuratively) man and wife. Orin says: "Can't you see I'm now in Father's place and you're Mother? That's the evil destiny out of the past I haven't dared predict! I'm the Mannon you're chained to!" (II, 155.) And like their parents before them, they destroy each other.

These obviously neurotic relationships, then, like the "masks" worn by the characters and the house, and the Oresteian parallels—in fact, all the dramatic devices that might loosely be called "unrealistic"—serve primarily to emphasize the self-destructive conflicts which are the consequence of the "denial of life" that is the Mannon curse. Unlike the masks or soliloquies or expressionism of some of the earlier plays, however, these techniques are not obtrusive, do not call attention to themselves *as* techniques. In this respect, *Mourning Becomes Electra* marks a new major stage in O'Neill's search for a "language for the theater" and for himself.

Days Without End, a very different play, and employing other techniques, seems to reflect much the same tendency, although in some respects it appears to be the most extreme experiment of all. The central contrivance of the play is the introduction of the two conflicting impulses of a single individual in the form of two separate characters, the man and a visible "alter-ego"—man's split personality made flesh. John, the hero of the play, is by nature sensitive, loving, artistic, and possesses a faith in life and in God. Disillusioned in both by the death of his mother—as so often in O'Neill, a symbol of "oneness" with life's eternal forces—he gradually builds up a defense against life in the form of an "alter-ego." Ironically named "Loving" (John's last name), this "other self" is callous, cynical, convinced that love is merely lust, that there is "nothing" beyond

---

*From a letter to Barrett Clark; see Clark, p. 136.

life, and that death is the only reasonable escape from it. The relationship between John and Loving, as well as parallels with ideas we have noted in the other plays, are best seen in John's descriptions of an autobiographical character in a novel he is writing: "His experience had left an indelible scar on his spirit. There always remained something in him that felt itself damned by life, damned with distrust, cursed with the inabilty ever to reach a lasting belief in any faith, damned by a fear of the lie hiding behind the mask of truth. . . . Even at the height of his rationalism, he never could explain away a horror of death. . . . And coupled with this was a dread of life, waiting to catch men at its mercy, in their hour of secure happiness—Something that hated life!—Something that laughed with mocking scorn!" (III, 535.) This Something, in the play, is given substance in the figure—whom only he can see—of Loving. He goes on to describe how he found in love a temporary refuge from his fear. But his faith in life—or in love—was not strong enough, and the very intensity of his devotion became the source of new terrors. "He came to be afraid of his happiness. His love made him feel at the mercy of that mocking Something he dreaded. . . . That he had again let love put him at the mercy of life!" Loving tries to convince John that he really hates love, and that the only true "freedom" lies in escaping love, and denying life, in death. In the end, with the help of a priest, John finds a renewed faith in life at the foot of the symbol of a love that transcended death, the cross. Loving "dies," and John Loving becomes a complete personality again, unified in the discovery of His truth: "And thy faith shall make thee whole."

The play is not, as some have taken it, necessarily evidence that O'Neill was toying with a return to Catholicism. In *The Great God Brown* he had treated the saintly—or at least ascetic—element in Christianity as "life-denying." What he seems to be getting at is that some kind of faith *in* life is man's only escape from a destructive disassociation *from* life. The particular form of the faith—in theological terms—is unimportant; all that is really necessary is a kind of mystical recognition, like Ponce de Leon's, of man's essential oneness with the elemental and revivifying processes of Nature, whether symbolized by Christ or by the Fountain.

The device O'Neill uses to reveal both the inner conflict and the ultimate reunification of his hero sounds just as mechanical as the masks or the soliloquies; but once Loving has been accepted as a real and powerful force in John's world, he is really no more obtrusive or artificial than any "type" character. O'Neill has, in *Days Without End,* treated much the same theme as he did in *Mourning Becomes Electra,* although here applied to an individual rather than a family; and he does so in a manner that I think is intended to be more true to the psychological "facts of life" than the somewhat misleading neuroses of the earlier play.

Between the publication of *Days Without End* in 1934 and the appearance of *The Iceman Cometh* in 1946, O'Neill worked on four plays. Their exact dates of composition are not known, but they were all written, or revised from earlier sketches, between 1939 and 1943. They have much in common, and can be treated together as the last stage in O'Neill's development as a dramatist.

In technique this group of plays represents a return to the relatively "pure" realism of his earliest plays. There is much the same kind of organic symbolism as in those, but there are none of the more obvious "tricks" of the later plays, no masks, no asides, no fantasy, no expressionism.[10] But to say they are a "return" to an earlier technique is misleading. In the intervening years O'Neill had developed tremendously, both in his subject matter and in the skill with which he handled his material dramatically. In these last plays he is still concerned with the internal conflicts which earlier had inspired some of his more daring, and obtrusive, experiments; but the tendency, which we noted in *Mourning Becomes Electra* and *Days Without End*, to try and find a more "natural" dramatic medium is realized even more completely in *The Iceman Cometh, Long Day's Journey into Night, A Moon for the Misbegotten,* and *A Touch of the Poet.*

One of the most striking qualities possessed by all of these plays is the really impressive quantity of alcohol consumed in each of them. If it weren't that thin tea looks like Bourbon, not one of the plays could proceed beyond the second act. This phenomenon might be passed off as irrelevant, or at best attributed to some development in O'Neill's personal life, were it not for the fact that it represents the *technique* which was to serve much the same dramatic function as the more mechanical devices of the earlier plays. A man who is drunk is not *expected* to behave naturally or rationally. And liquor breaks down inhibitions, pulls aside the facade which men build up in self-defense and self-delusion and shows us the tormented, divided spirit within. It is only after they have been drinking that we get any real glimpse of what makes the characters in *Long Day's Journey* "tick," that we see the sense of failure beneath James Tyrone's pride, or the love and fear Jamie hides behind a mask of callous cynicism. In *A Moon for the Misbegotten* it is only because Jim is "far gone" that he can open up the festering abscess of guilt and self-hatred

---

[10] It may be objected that *The Iceman Cometh* is hardly "realistic," and approaches fantasy. It is true that the play was conceived as a sort of "modern morality," and that neither the plot nor the somewhat formalized grouping of characters and patterning of speeches represents any "slice of life." However, in language, setting, and structure, it is obviously much closer to *The Long Voyage Home* or *Anna Christie* than to, say, *Dynamo.*

that has in one sense killed him already, and can make the girl who loves him utter the concluding prayer: "May you have your wish and die in your sleep soon, Jim, darling." [11] If it were not for the fact that Con Melody has had more than a touch of the bottle the sudden shifts from his fantastic posing to moments of despair and bitter self-loathing would seem evidence of nothing less than insanity. Liquor, then, serves two functions: it permits the dramatist to show the contrast between a man sober, with his defenses up, and drunk, when his subconscious drives become overt, and allows the rapid juxtaposition of contradictory moods and impulses once a person *is* drunk. It is a device which O'Neill uses for much the same purposes as the more radical innovations, to reveal the conflicts which tear his characters apart and frustrate their potentialities as complete human beings, without appearing arbitrary or mechanical.

But if the use of liquor were *only* a device for subconscious revelation it might be considered just as arbitrary as the masks or the asides. But it is something more. These last four plays are often considered as being among the most pessimistic that O'Neill ever wrote—certainly a reversion from the note of almost lyrical optimism and faith on which *Days Without End* closed. Undoubtedly there are more Lovings than Johns in these plays. In fact, the gloomy tone which is so predominant is due in large part to the fact that all of the major characters are "life-deniers"—the Lovings or Mannons or Caligulas of this world. They are afraid of life, and the death-wish is practically ubiquitous. Loving had had a vision of "the one beautiful, comforting truth of life: that death is final release, the warm, dark peace of annihilation" (III, 534). Larry Slade's quotation from Heine in *The Iceman* would stand as the unspoken creed of many characters:

> Lo, sleep is good; better is death; in sooth,
> The best of all were never to be born.
>
> (III, 591)

Jim Tyrone, in *A Moon for the Misbegotten,* prays that death will come in his sleep to free him from himself and life. His brother, Edmund, in *Long Day's Journey,* is "a little in love with death." "Who," he says, "wants to see life as it is, if they can help it? . . . You see [it] and you die—that is, inside you—and have to go on living as a ghost," as Jim does in the other play. Larry Slade is even more explicit:

> All I know is I'm sick of life! . . . I'm drowned and contented on the bottom of a bottle. Honor or dishonor, faith or treachery are nothing to me

---

[11] *A Moon for the Misbegotten* (New York, 1952), p. 177.

but the opposites of the same stupidity which is ruler and king of life, and in the end they rot into dust in the same grave. All things are the same meaningless joke to me, for they grin at me from the one skull of death. (III, 649)

The speech also suggests the relationship between this fear of existence and alcohol. Afraid of life, and hating it, but equally afraid of death, men try to find at least temporary escape or forgetfulness by hiding at "the bottom of a bottle." But as alcohol only dulls the pain, and doesn't really free them from themselves, they escape even further into a past that never was or a future that never will be. This is conspicuously true of the inhabitants of Harry Hope's saloon, but it is also true in differing degrees of the others. Mary's dreams of becoming a nun, or a great pianist, her husband's pretensions to being the great Shakespearian actor he *might* have been, Con Melody's fatuous role as the proud and noble hero of Talavera, Jim Tyrone's pose as a hard and cynical playboy, are all refuges from life, and the cheapest ticket is a glass of whiskey—or a shot of morphine.

At one point in *Long Day's Journey* Mary Tyrone says:

None of us can help the things life has done to us. They're done before you realize it, and once they're done they make you do other things until at last everything comes between you and what you'd like to be, and you've lost your true self forever. (P. 61)

In case this should be taken as *O'Neill's* justification for Mary, it should be remembered that she is already well on her way into that pipe dream world which is each character's form of self-justification. It is not a question so much of what life has done to them, but of what they have done to life. Each of them has been disillusioned by something, the death of someone loved, or the frustration of some dream of wealth or fame. And with no faith equal to the disappointment, afraid that love or "involvement" of any kind would "again . . . put him at the mercy of life," they have turned on her bitterly, betrayed her, and then built up a pipe dream to excuse their failure as humans, to others and to themselves. And often, when they think they are being most honest about "facing life" they are in fact the most deluded. Larry Slade believes himself to be a detached and cynical observer on the "grandstand of life"; Hickey knows better, but what he doesn't recognize is that his own altruistic murder of his wife, and his equally generous efforts to bring his alcoholic friends back to "reality," spring from his own hatred and fear; Tyrone explains his stinginess, his failure as an actor and as a husband, as things "life" has done to him; Jim debauches himself, turns beauty into sordidness and love into lust, simply to prove to himself that beauty and love have no existence in a meaningless world; and Major Cornelius Melody attributes all his failures to the pride which is the necessary concomitant of being an officer and a gentleman. Edmund describes his mother's retreat into her drug-fantasy as "like a bank of fog in which she hides and loses herself. Deliberately, that's the hell of it! . . . to get beyond our reach, to be rid of us, to forget we're alive! It's as if, in spite of loving us, she hated us!" (p. 139.) Fearing the commitment and responsibility which facing life and love would demand, they are driven to find what Edmund himself sought in the fog: a world where "life can hide from itself" (p. 131).

The real tragedy of these characters is that they have lived so long with their pipe dreams that they have *become* those dreams; the roles are, in a sense, reality, and when the illusion is pricked—often by some drunken insight or confession—nothing remains for them to cling to, unless it is another dream. Larry Slade is dragged from his perch above life, and is forced to admit: "Life is too much for me. . . . I'm the only real convert to death Hickey made" (III, 727). Hickey himself, who has been described as bringing with him "the breath of death," escapes from his self-exposure into insanity. Jim Tyrone has so poisoned himself and his capacity for love that even Josie cannot save him, and although he finds one night of drunken bliss in her arms, she describes him as "already dead." Cornelius Melody kills the "Major" when he realizes that "it was the Major played a game all his life, the crazy auld loon, and cheated only himself." [12] The Major is replaced by plain Con Melody, the Irish peasant and inn-keeper; but even this is in danger of becoming just another pose, although closer to the truth. When his daughter challenges his new role, Melody is described as "visibly crumbling as he listens until he appears to have no character left in which to hide and defend himself. He cries wildly and despairingly, as if he saw his last hope of escape suddenly cut off" (p. 178). But his wife's love, which is part of the "life" he would hide from, appears in the end to be even stronger than his fear. *Long Day's Journey into Night* ends with nothing basically changed—although there has been some self-awareness on the part of the characters. Jamie "gives Edmund a strange look of mingled pity and jealous gloating," and Tyrone, "trying to shake off his hopeless stupor," says of Mary: "Oh, we're fools to pay any attention. It's the damned poison. But I've never known her to drown herself in it as deep as this. Pass me the bottle, Jamie." The play ends with Mary's long monologue from deep inside her "night," the dope-dream of the past. And perhaps she is the luckiest of them all, she and the inhabitants of Harry Hope's "End of the Line Café," who cling grate-

---

[12] *A Touch of the Poet* (New Haven, 1957), p. 170.

fully to Hickey's plea of insanity and drift happily back into their alcoholic never-never land, where all struggle is over.

None of these last four plays ends on the note of mystical affirmation
of *The Fountain* or *Lazarus* or *Days Without End.* If there is any affirmation at all, it is more like that of *Desire Under the Elms* or *The Great
God Brown,* tempered by the tragic fact that the "sickness of today" is so
pervasive and so inbred that its cure, if it comes at all, comes too late. The
problems dealt with in the last plays are much the same as earlier: the
"disassociation" from life, the price which life exacts for her betrayal,
and the inner conflicts which the "failure of science and materialism" to
provide any solid faith in life has produced. It is primarily O'Neill's
methods that are new; for he found in the "escapism" and symptoms of
compulsive drinking and drug addiction both an adequate symbol for the
"sickness of today" and a realistic device for revealing the destructive
clashes of antithetical impulses which are its consequence.

Throughout his life O'Neill sought a dramatic medium with which to
explore the human soul. He tried many methods, some of them as radical
as anything attempted in the American theater. He found, however, that
these had their limitations, were too mechanical, called attention to themselves rather than to what they were intended to reveal, suggested de-
marcations that were too black and white, or forces too much outside his
characters. But he did not return to the realism which was, after all, his
"natural language" until he had found that with it, and the help of
alcohol, he could say the same thing better.

The Nature of O'Neill's Achievement:
A Summary and Appraisal

by John Gassner

Eugene O'Neill died at the age of sixty-five in Boston on November 27, 1953, but he was perhaps the most alive playwright of the Fifties. His work reveals, more than that of any playwright of this decade except O'Casey, those comprehensive interests and intensive explorations of human experience that distinguish a major dramatist. He was indeed one of the very few playwrights of the twentieth century stage who could arouse, with some labor, the same comprehensive interest in life that a dozen or more writers did with more ease in modern fiction. He was certainly the only American to achieve first rank among the century's dramatists. It is remarkable, moreover, that O'Neill should have won his reputation *twice* (once in the Twenties and once in the Fifties, after his death), without coming up to the literary standards of the day or winning the approbation of literary critics.

The return of O'Neill to the American stage in the Fifties and renewed European interest in his work provided a proper occasion for re-examining his reputation. It had been examined about ten years before, when investigation was apparently aimed at demolishing O'Neill's fame. A new generation seemed determined to denigrate O'Neill on every count, even if it had no new culture-hero to substitute. In the face of the onslaught, his friends and admirers could only reflect that these young critics had had few opportunities to see O'Neill's plays in adequate stage productions and that nothing charged against his work was really new.

With the off-Broadway revival of *The Iceman Cometh* at the Circle-in-the-Square in 1956 and the impressive Broadway success of the long-

"The Nature of O'Neill's Achievement: A Summary and Appraisal" by John Gassner. Revised and abbreviated version of the essay "Eugene O'Neill: The Course of a Major Dramatist" in the author's *Theatre at the Crossroads* (New York: Holt, Rinehart & Winston, 1960), pp. 65-76. Copyright © 1960 by Mollie Gassner. Reprinted by permission of Mollie Gassner.

deferred *Long Day's Journey into Night* the same year,[1] O'Neill's return to favor and the discovery of his power by new audiences became apparent. In the season of 1956-57 he was represented on the New York stage alone by no fewer than four productions. Before 1960, two other O'Neill plays were on view in the New York theater as well as abroad: *A Moon for the Misbegotten,* staged in the spring of 1957, and *A Touch of the Poet,* given a star-studded Broadway production in the 1958-59 season.

There can be no doubt that O'Neill represented almost everything that is fundamentally modern about the American theater. He reflected also all that until recently was modern about the European theater in his restless experimentation, his avid cultivation of new ideas, his assertive individualism, and his intense unease. His success is that of a restless spirit honest enough to refuse to feel by rote, and his work is often as provocative as a leading question and as exciting (if also as precarious) as a plunge down a waterfall. His major defect is that he nearly always strains for metaphysical *Angst,* negativeness, and a sense of desolation not always well founded and more conducive to darkness than to light, liberation, and final purgation.

O'Neill dignified the craft of playwriting in America. He made it a calling rather than a trade, and he gave playwrights, hitherto mostly hacks or routine entertainers, a position of some importance in American cultural life. Winner of the Nobel Prize and author of plays staged in nearly all the capitals of Europe, he became America's first dramatist of international standing. Though his power often exceeded his skill, still his craftsmanship was sufficient to carry him through some of the most ambitious projects attempted in the Western theater since Aeschylus wrote trilogies twenty-four hundred years ago. O'Neill represented the avant-garde in this country, if not in Europe, after the First World War. A leader of the experimental Little Theater movement, led by his own play-producing organization, the Provincetown Players, and after 1920 the leading playwright also of the progressive wing of Broadway professionalism, O'Neill sparked a revolt of great moment against middle-class complacency and commonplace realism on the American stage.

Combined with a deeply felt (if also fashionably Bohemian) rejection of Victorian gentility, puritanical prissiness, dollar-idolatry, and the entire cult of go-getting opportunism, O'Neill's lofty individualism placed him in the forefront of those who began to modernize the content of American drama no less than its form. His response to the vogue of depth psychology led him to modernize further both dramatic form and content by attempting to manifest subconscious tensions. The means he

[1] This autobiographical play was written in 1940, but withheld from the public until Mrs. O'Neill allowed the Yale University Press to publish it in 1956.

adopted for this purpose carried him into areas of experimentation which only venturesome playwrights dared enter and where only exceptionally adept ones could survive.

More than any other writer in the American theater he endeavored to give range and significance to the drama. This endeavor alone would justify our sense of indebtedness to him and our readiness to place him in the company of the European theatrical pioneers. But there is another, less easily definable, quality that distinguishes O'Neill. Almost alone among our professional playwrights, he possessed a boundless sense of integrity and self-immolating artistry that he never betrayed.

In an interview with the press on the eve of the premiere of *The Iceman Cometh* in 1946, he reaffirmed his intractable position by calling the United States the "greatest failure" in the world. The reason was "the everlasting game of trying to possess your own soul by possessing something outside of it, too," and America with its immense resources had been especially tempted to play that game. "This was really said in the Bible much better," he added. "We are the greatest example of 'For what shall it profit a man if he shall gain the whole world and lose his own soul?' We had so much and could have gone either way. . . ." O'Neill proceeded, characteristically, to enlarge his indictment to include the whole human race, concluding that, "if humanity failed to appreciate the secret of happiness contained in that simple sentence," it was time to "dump" the human race "down the nearest drain and let the ants have a chance."

O'Neill produced an impression of greatness by virtue of the absolute demands he made upon life and art. He labored his points. He was a Faustian aspirant to greatness whether in entertaining vast expectations for the theater or slim hopes for mankind. The state of damnation was both a psychological and metaphysical reality for him. He certainly had no knack for moderation or finesse. But it is futile to wish that he had composed his plays with less repetition and emphasis; their emotional power and their authenticity are bound up with their insistence and massiveness. O'Neill made the theater rise to both his reasonable and his unreasonable requirements. Intent upon having his grim say despite the effect on dramatic form or length, O'Neill became one of those rare playwrights with whom the practical theater has been compelled to come to terms.

It is apparent, too, that in O'Neill's search for spiritual "values," a term that would be ostentatious if applied to most of his fellow playwrights, he had in view the magnitude of theme and treatment present in the great ages of the theater. And he sought that magnitude not as an imitator but as a strenuously creative dramatist working in the American idiom. The Oresteian trilogy furnishes the basis of *Mourning Becomes Electra,* and it is possible to detect the Hippolytus theme in *Desire Under the Elms.* But classic elevation is barely visible in O'Neill's plays; psychological pressures take the place of Fate, and the dialogue of his plagued characters is generally direct and unadorned. Still it cannot be said that modernity of any kind was in his case a cause for complacency. According to him, modernism, with or without benefit of Freud and Jung (let alone Marx), did not solve any fundamental problems for the human race.

Pessimism and the tragic spirit (which is ultimately affirmative) were at war in the works of O'Neill. In *The Iceman Cometh,* where the playwright seems to put a premium on desperation, and in some of his other work, for example, *A Moon for the Misbegotten,* he was prodigal with misery. But he was usually more inclined to be mordant than morbid, and his chief attitude was a determined reaction against the optimism of shallow people breezily at ease in Zion. "Sure I'll write about happiness," he declared in an interview in 1922, "if I can happen to meet with that luxury," and he went on to maintain that he found a compensating exaltation in writing tragedy. "A work of art," he said, "is always happy; all else is unhappy." But all these qualifications cannot quite remove an impression of incompleteness produced by much of his work. It is a tragic incompleteness, reflecting an incompleteness in the playwright himself.

It is hardly a secret that O'Neill's sense of desolation grew in part from the fact that he was an introspective man born and reared a Catholic who had lost his faith. He gave continual evidence of having had a traumatic youth, and the loss of religious faith was an important part of it; he makes much of the problem in *Dynamo* and *Days Without End.* His work reveals a keen sense of loss of connection—of connection with God, nature, society, family, father.

O'Neill's disaffection is no longer a secret. He set it down, dramatizing its source in the family situation with rough tenderness and candor when he wrote *Long Day's Journey into Night.* This play, written late in his career, is explicit about ambivalences projected and symbolized in his other work. He was a characteristically modern dramatist, a divided man who was acutely aware of the division not only in himself but in his fellow men. Like his exemplary modern playwright, Strindberg, O'Neill made division itself the subject of his plays and expressed it formally in his work with expressionistic devices, masks, and interior monologues.

Had O'Neill been a shallow man he might have settled for small satisfactions. Had he been an essentially irreligious man he might not have been concerned with the loss of faith. Had he been an unloving man he might have been content with the gregariousness that passes for love among low-voltage people. The tensions in his work are nearly always connected with his struggle against alienation. The secret of his dramatic intensity is to be found not in his theatricality but in his rebellion and anger, in an inability to resign himself to an arid view and way of life. He could not be at ease in a world without God, without love, and without trust in life.

The season of 1933-34 marked the end of O'Neill's dramatic division. He seemed to resolve his protracted conflict with the actual and symbolic fathers, a conflict directly represented in *Desire Under the Elms, Dynamo, Strange Interlude,* and *Mourning Becomes Electra.* In *Days Without End* the reconciliation is with God. In *Ah, Wilderness!,* the genial period comedy of O'Neill's boyhood, the reconciliation is with a worldly father, represented by the small-town editor Nat Miller who watches over his son's adolescence with amused tolerance. But the war with the fathers was resumed in the plays written subsequently, and the rift between O'Neill and the world appeared to have actually grown wider. He was found at odds with life once more in *The Iceman Cometh,* in which he contended that only illusions could make existence endurable. He celebrated its hopelessness with mixed sentimental and ironic overtones in *A Moon for the Misbegotten;* and he made disillusionment with parents and an elder brother the primal family trauma in *Long Day's Journey into Night.* Peace of the spirit had come briefly after great turbulence to his favorite author, August Strindberg; it is possible that O'Neill once expected such peace for himself, too. But it is evident that after he saw the world going from bad to worse in the Thirties he found justification for the worst construction he had put on human nature and the destiny of the species. The interview he gave to the press after the conclusion of World War Two supports this view.

Still, the source of the anguish in the late plays—as in the early ones—is personal, not political. If his plays have a larger reference than personal grief the credit belongs to his creative imagination. He had the true artist's power of imaginative projection necessary for the creation of significant drama. He also had the egocentricity of men of romantic sensibility who make the world a reflection of their own condition. He perceived the world primarily through his temperament and mood; division in himself became division in the rest of the world. When angry with the world he could have borrowed Othello's words about Desdemona:

> . . . when I love thee not,
> Chaos is come again.

His emotional power lies largely in this sense of significant torment. The loneliness of sailors in the *S. S. Glencairn* sea pieces, for example, becomes the loneliness of man in the universe; and the disorientation of Yank, the "hairy ape" who tries so desperately to "belong," is a symbol of man's severance from the world of nature. Yank, O'Neill declared somewhat awkwardly, is "the symbol of man who has lost his old harmony with nature, the harmony he used to have as an animal and has not yet acquired in a spiritual way." Unable to move forward toward complete humanity, Yank dies in his attempt to return to the animal state.

In a play filled with naturalistic dialogue as primitive as the mentality of Yank and his fellow stokers, O'Neill still had in mind only the larger meaning. "The subject," he said, "is the same one that always was and always will be the one subject for drama, and that is man and his struggle with his fate. The struggle used to be with the gods, but is now with himself, his own past, his attempt to belong." Anna Christie's father is continually conscious of the irony of fate and of a malevolence in the nature of things that the old sailor associates with the "old davil sea." And in succumbing to primal fears in the jungle, "Emperor Jones" re-enacts the whole drama of atavism, of humanity's inability to abolish the ghosts of the racial past.

Play after play reflects O'Neill's disinterest in literalness and dissatisfaction with the naturalism he scorned as "holding the family Kodak up to ill-nature" and favoring "the banality of surfaces." It was the deep experience and the large frame of reference that interested him. It is true enough that his efforts to employ symbolism and attain emotional resonance conflict noticeably with the low condition of most of his heroes and the commonplaceness of their dialogue. The familiar O'Neill characters such as Chris Christopherson, Yank, Orin, and Hickey are anything but Promethean figures. But they are frequently involved in situations that transcend their actual condition or environment. They rise in stature with their awareness of cosmic irony and of crass casualty in the universe. It is impossible to forget that O'Neill himself is speaking through them; it is *his* largeness of tragic feeling that constitutes their magnitude.

An amplitude of tragic perception appears even in so intimate a family drama as *Long Day's Journey into Night*. As family drama alone it is patently repetitive and labored; those who responded to it solely as a naturalistic slice-of-life were well entitled to their reservations. But there is more to *Long Day's Journey into Night*. The dramatic line of development in it includes O'Neill's introduction to a tragic view of life through youthful disenchantment. The family is the microcosm through which the artist gets his first hard look at the macrocosm. This first look is also romantic, recalling the doldrums of the lost generation of the eighteen-nineties; the young O'Neill broods on the lachrymose poetry of Ernest Dowson. But we know that the look grew harder in the course of O'Neill's career. The acute sense of human contradiction and division expressed in this play (and actually expressed in most of the plays that preceded it for more than two decades) is the final clue to O'Neill's course as a dramatist. The rift in the formative period of his life is reflected by the rifts in his playwriting. O'Neill's divided artistry has long been apparent and it will have to count importantly in any final appraisal. It involved discrepancies between vaulting emotion and lumbering execution, between intense action and prosy dialogue, between a passion for the austerities of high tragedy and an addiction to the schematic simplifications of commonplace psychopathology; and it produced the many fluctuations in dramatic form and style which made him alternatively a romantic, naturalistic, and expressionistic dramatist.

O'Neill became programmatically opposed to realism or naturalism, and (aside from favoring symbolism) resorted to the expressionist technique of fantastic distortion in such plays as *The Emperor Jones* and *The Hairy Ape*. Nevertheless, these and other means of stylization do not reveal him in the fullness of his power and apparently left him unsatisfied. He turned away from them, and some of his most powerful writing appears in the enriched naturalistic vein of *Desire Under the Elms*, *Mourning Becomes Electra*, *The Iceman Cometh*, *A Long Day's Journey into Night*, and *A Touch of the Poet*. O'Neill's dramatic writing is divided between imaginative flights and traffic with humanity on the gritty ground. Just as his feeling for sailors, derelicts, and commoners is generally preferable to his dealings with educated and highly placed characters, so is his realism to his fancies, his earthiness to his literary ambitions.

O'Neill's interest and power as a playwright were derived, in fact, from his dividedness. (The one exception is the sunny minor artistry of *Ah, Wilderness!*) The alienation apparent in his dramatic talent commands respect for a writer who had the courage of his discontent. This talent failed to carry him to the eminence of the indisputably great playwrights of the past, and it left room for very mixed reactions to his work. But alienation was the cross O'Neill had to bear, and he carried it further into the theater than any other modern playwright after Strindberg. No other dramatist of our century has thus far attained his dark impressiveness, and no degree of astute criticism has yet invalidated at least this much claim for his labors—the labors of a modern Sisyphus in Tartarus.

Chronology of Important Dates

1888   O'Neill born to Ellen Quinlan and James O'Neill, the celebrated actor-manager, October 16.

1902   Entered Betts Academy, a leading boy's school at Stamford, Connecticut.

1906-07   At Princeton.

1909   Married Kathleen Jenkins (divorced 1912); one son—Eugene O'Neill, Jr.
Went prospecting for gold in Honduras.
At sea for two years.
Lived in a waterfront dive, "Jimmy-the-Priest's," which became the locale for *Anna Christie* and *The Iceman Cometh*.

1912   Joined *New London Telegraph* in August as a reporter. Stayed four months. More interested in writing verse than gathering news.
Just before Christmas developed mild case of tuberculosis. Spent five months at the Gaylord Farm Sanatorium at Wallingford, Conn. Took to reading Strindberg and the Greek tragic poets.

1912-13   Convalescence from tuberculosis. During this period he wrote eleven one-act and two long plays. He tore up all but six of the one-acters.

1914   James O'Neill paid for the publication of five of these plays under the title of *Thirst*.

1914-15   Attended George Pierce Baker's "Workshop 47" at Harvard University.

1916   Moved to Provincetown, Mass.
Bound East for Cardiff (one-act play). Produced by the Provincetown Players at Wharf Theatre, Provincetown, Mass.
Thirst (one-act play).
Before Breakfast (a dramatic monologue, in one act). Produced by the Provincetown Players at the Playwrights' Theatre (popularly known as the Provincetown) in Greenwich Village, New York City, December 1.

1917   *Fog* (one-act play). Produced by the Provincetown Players, January 5.
The Sniper (one-act play. Produced by the Provincetown Players, February 16.
In the Zone (one-act play). Produced by the Washington Square Players, October 31.
The Long Voyage Home (one-act play). Produced by the Provincetown Players, November 2.
Ile (one-act play). Produced by the Provincetown Players, November 30.

1918 Married Agnes Boulton (divorced 1929); two children—Shane and Oona (Mrs. Charles Chaplin).
Moved to Cape Cod, occupying a former Coast Guard Station.
The Rope (one-act play). Produced by the Provincetown Players, April 26.
Where the Cross Is Made (one-act play). Produced by the Provincetown Players, November 22.
The Moon of the Caribbees (one-act play). Produced by the Provincetown Players, December 20.

1919 *The Dreamy Kid* (one-act play). Produced by the Provincetown Players, October 31.

1920 *Beyond the Horizon.* Produced by John D. Williams at the Morosco Theatre, February 2. First Pulitzer Prize.
Chris Christopherson (first version of *Anna Christie*). Produced by George C. Tyler in Atlantic City, March 8.
Exorcism (one-act play). Produced by the Provincetown Players, March 26.
The Emperor Jones. Produced by the Provincetown Players, November 3.
Diff'rent. Produced by the Provincetown Players, December 27.

1921 *Gold.* Produced by John D. Williams at the Frazee Theatre, June 1.
Anna Christie. Produced by Arthur Hopkins at the Vanderbilt Theatre, November 2. Second Pulitzer Prize.
The Straw. Produced by George C. Tyler at the Greenwich Village Theatre, November 10.

1922 *The First Man.* Produced at the Neighborhood Playhouse, March 4.
The Hairy Ape. Produced by the Provincetown Players, March 9.

1924 *Welded.* Produced by Macgowan, Jones, and O'Neill in association with the Selwyns at the 39th St. Theatre, March 17.
The Ancient Mariner (from the poem by Coleridge). Produced by the Provincetown Playhouse, Inc., April 6.
All God's Chillun Got Wings. Produced by the Provincetown Playhouse, Inc., May 15.
S. S. Glencairn (a sequence of the early sea-pieces). Produced at Provincetown, Mass., August 14. Revived on January 12, 1925 by Macgowan, Jones, and O'Neill in New York.
Desire Under the Elms. Produced by the Provincetown Players, Inc. at the Greenwich Village Theatre, November 11.

1925 *The Fountain.* Produced by Macgowan, Jones, and O'Neill in association with A. L. Jones and Morris Green at the Greenwich Village Theatre, December 10.

1926 *The Great God Brown.* Produced by Macgowan, Jones, and O'Neill at the Greenwich Village Theatre, January 23.
Honorary Litt.D from Yale University.

1928   *Marco Millions.* Produced by the Theatre Guild at the Guild Theatre, January 9.
        Strange Interlude. Produced by the Theatre Guild at the John Golden Theatre, January 30.
        Lazarus Laughed. Produced by the Pasadena Community Playhouse, Pasadena, Calif., April 9.

1929   *Dynamo.* Produced by the Theatre Guild at the Martin Beck Theatre, February 11.
        Married Carlotta Monterey, July 22.

1931   *Mourning Becomes Electra.* Produced by the Theatre Guild at the Guild Theatre, October 26.

1933   *Ah, Wilderness!* Produced by the Theatre Guild at the Guild Theatre, October 2.

1934   *Days Without End.* Produced by the Theatre Guild at the Guild Theatre, January 8.

1936   Nobel Prize for Literature.

1946   *The Iceman Cometh.* Produced by the Theatre Guild at the Martin Beck Theatre, September 2. (Revived under José Quintero's direction at the Circle-in-the-Square on May 8, 1958.)

1947   Stricken with Parkinson's Disease.
        A Moon for the Misbegotten. Produced by the Theatre Guild, February 20, but withdrawn after the tryout in Columbus, Ohio.

1953   Died November 27.

1955   *A Long Day's Journey into Night*, world premiere at the Royal Dramatic Theatre, Stockholm, February 10.

1956   Broadway opening of *A Long Day's Journey into Night*, November 7.

1957   Broadway opening of *A Moon for the Misbegotten*, May 2.

1957   Pulitzer Prize awarded posthumously for *A Long Day's Journey into Night*.

1958   World premiere of *A Touch of the Poet* at the Royal Dramatic Theatre, Stockholm, March 29. Broadway premiere October 12, 1958.

1962   World premiere of an adaptation of *More Stately Mansions* (left in rough draft by O'Neill) at the Royal Dramatic Theatre, Stockholm, October 9.

Notes on the Editor and Authors

JOHN GASSNER, Sterling Professor of Playwriting and Dramatic Literature at Yale University, is drama critic for the Educational Theatre Journal and other periodicals, and was formerly head of the Play Department of the Theatre Guild in New York. Mr. Gassner is the author of Masters of the Drama, Form and Idea in the Modern Theatre and Theatre at the Crossroads, and the editor of A Treasury of the Theatre and Best American Play series.

ERIC BENTLEY, Brander Matthews Professor of Dramatic Literature at Columbia University, was formerly drama critic for the New Republic, and is known for his translations and adaptations of the plays of Brecht, Pirandello, and others, as well as for The Playwright as Thinker, In Search of Theatre, and other books.

TRAVIS BOGARD, Professor of English and Dramatic Art and Chairman of Dramatic Art at the University of California, Berkeley, is the author of The Tragic Satire of John Webster and has written on other dramatists.

CYRUS DAY, Professor of English at the University of Delaware, is the editor of Songs of John Dryden and Songs of Thomas D'Urfey, and is a contributor to Modern Drama and other publications.

TOM F. DRIVER, Associate Professor of Christian Theology at Union Theological Seminary, New York, has been a drama critic for the Christian Century magazine since 1956, and for The Reporter. He is a member of the Editorial Board of Christianity and Crisis and author of The Sense of Greek and Shakespearean Drama.

RICHARD HAYES, drama critic for Commonweal magazine and contributor to other periodicals, received the Brandeis University Creative Arts Award in 1959.

HUGO VON HOFMANNSTHAL, who died in 1929, is the great Austrian poet and playwright whose collaboration with Richard Strauss resulted in Der Rosenkavalier and other well-known operas, and whose association with the theatrical producer Max Reinhardt at the Salzburg Festivals culminated in Jedermann.

JOHN HOWARD LAWSON, playwright and scenarist, author of The Theory and Technique of Playwriting, is best known for his expressionistic plays and social drama.

HELEN MUCHNIC is Professor of Russian Literature at Smith College. Author of An Introduction to Russian Literature, she is a frequent contributor to Comparative Literature and other publications.

EDGAR F. RACEY, JR., Assistant Professor of English at the University of Washington, is a contributor to Modern Drama and other publications. He has published studies on Ezra Pound and William Carlos Williams.

JOHN HENRY RALEIGH, Professor of English at the University of California, Berkeley, is the author of *Matthew Arnold and American Culture,* and is a contributor to *Partisan Review.*

EUGENE M. WAITH, Professor of English at Yale University, is the author of *The Pattern of Tragicomedy in Beaumont and Fletcher* and *The Herculean Hero,* and the editor of *Macbeth* for the Yale Shakespeare and *Bartholomew Fair* for the Yale Ben Jonson.

ROBERT F. WHITMAN, formerly at Princeton, teaches in the English department of the University of Pittsburgh. He has contributed to the *Quarterly Journal of Speech, PMLA,* and *Notes & Queries.*

STARK YOUNG, the distinguished critic, novelist, essayist, and translator, who died in May 1963, was drama critic for many years for the *New Republic.*

Selected Bibliography

O'NEILL'S PLAYS

O'Neill's first published collection of plays was *Thirst, and Other One-Act Plays,* a limited edition of 1,000 copies printed by The Gorham Press of Boston in 1914; and the first unlimited edition was *The Moon of the Caribbees, and Six Other Plays of the Sea,* published by Boni and Liveright (New York) in 1919. It was reissued by Boni and Liveright as a "Modern Library" edition, with an introduction by George Jean Nathan, in 1923, and subsequently under the title *The Long Voyage Home: Seven Plays of the Sea* (Modern Library, 1940). Later collections were the following:

The Complete Works of Eugene O'Neill. New York: Boni and Liveright, 1924-25. This edition was in two volumes and was limited to 1,200 copies (autographed).

The Works of Eugene O'Neill. New York: Boni and Liveright, 1925, in four volumes. (This edition lacked the plays of the sea.)

Nine Plays. Introduction by Joseph Wood Krutch. New York: Liveright, 1932. A one-volume compilation consisting of *The Emperor Jones, The Hairy Ape, All God's Chillun Got Wings, Desire Under the Elms, Marco Millions, The Great God Brown, Lazarus Laughed, Strange Interlude, Mourning Becomes Electra.* Issued as a Modern Library volume in 1932 and reprinted in 1941 and 1954.

The Plays of Eugene O'Neill. Wilderness Edition. New York: Scribner's, 1934-35, in twelve volumes, with illustrations and notes by the author; 770 autographed sets.

The Emperor Jones, Anna Christie, The Hairy Ape. Introduction by Lionel Trilling. New York: Modern Library, 1937.

The Plays of O'Neill. New York: Random House, 1941, in three volumes, containing all plays up to then except the plays in *Thirst, and Other One-Act Plays.* Reissued in 1951 with the addition of *The Iceman Cometh.*

The Lost Plays. New York: New Fathoms, 1950; reissued by Citadel Press, 1958. (Plays on which the copyright had been allowed to lapse as a result of O'Neill's indifference to these early one actors: *Abortion, The Movie Man, The Sniper, Servitude,* and *A Wife for a Life.*)

Three Plays. New York: Modern Library Paperbacks, n.d. This volume contains *Desire Under the Elms, Strange Interlude,* and *Mourning Becomes Electra.*

Uncollected later plays:
A Moon for the Misbegotten. New York: Random House, 1952.
A Long Day's Journey into Night. New Haven: Yale University Press, 1956.
A Touch of the Poet. New Haven: Yale University Press, 1957. Issued later as a paperback by the Yale University Press.
Hughie. (A long one-act play.) New Haven: Yale University Press, 1959.
More Stately Mansions. New Haven: Yale University Press, 1964.

An especially noteworthy publication of an individual play is *Mourning Becomes Electra*. New York: Horace Liveright, 1931. This limited edition includes O'Neill's "Notes and Extracts from a Fragmentary Work Diary"— the notes he made in preparation for writing the play. These valuable notes also appear in *European Theories of the Drama*, edited by Barrett H. Clark. New York: Crown Publishers, 1947.

Note: O'Neill published a number of poems and essays, and letters by him appear in various publications by his correspondents. The most important of the essays are the following:

Strindberg and Our Theatre. In the Provincetown Playbill No. 1 (1923-24), reprinted in the *New York Times*, January 6, 1924.

Memoranda on Masks. In the *American Spectator*, November 1932. This was followed by *Second Thoughts*, December 1932, and *American Spectator*, January 1933.

SELECTED BIOGRAPHY AND CRITICISM

Alexander, Doris. *The Tempering of Eugene O'Neill*. New York: Harcourt, Brace & World, 1962. A study of his theatrical background and early life.
———. "Eugene O'Neill as Social Critic," *American Quarterly*, VI (Winter 1954), 349-63.

Atkinson, Brooks. "The Iceman Cometh," in Atkinson's *Broadway Scrapbook*, New York, Theatre Arts, Inc., 1947, pp. 241-46.

Bentley, Eric. "A Moon for the Misbegotten," in *The Dramatic Event*. New York: Horizon Press, 1954, pp. 30-33.

Block, Anita. *The Changing World in Plays and Theatre*. Boston: Little, Brown, 1939, pp. 137-93.

Boulton, Agnes. *Part of a Long Story*. New York: Doubleday, 1958. Includes recollections of her life with O'Neill.

Bowen, Crosswell. *The Curse of the Misbegotten: A Tale of the House of O'Neill*. New York: McGraw-Hill, 1959.

Brown, John Mason. "American Tragedy," in *Still Seeing Things*. New York: McGraw-Hill, 1950, pp. 185-90.

———. "Christopher Marlowe to Eugene O'Neill," in *Letters from Greenroom Ghosts*. New York: Viking Press, 1934, pp. 69-116.

———. *Upstage: The American Theatre in Performance*. New York: W. W. Norton, 1930, pp. 60-77.

———. *Dramatis Personae*. New York: The Viking Press, 1963, pp. 39-66.

Cargill, Oscar. *Intellectual America*. New York: Macmillan, 1941, pp. 332-40, 685-720.

Clark, Barrett H. *Eugene O'Neill*. New York: Dover, 1947.

Clurman, Harold. *Lies Like Truth*. New York: Macmillan, 1958, pp. 24-33 and passim.

Dickinson, Thomas. *Playwrights of the New American Theatre*. New York: Macmillan, 1925, pp. 56-123.

Dobree, Bonamy. "The Plays of Eugene O'Neill," *Southern Review* II (Winter 1937), pp. 435-46.

Downer, Alan S. *Fifty Years of American Theatre*. Chicago: Henry Regnery, 1951, pp. 64-70, 92-97.

Edel, Leon. "Eugene O'Neill: The Face and the Mask," *University of Toronto Quarterly*, VII (October 1937), pp. 18-34.

Engel, Edwin A. *The Haunted Heroes of Eugene O'Neill*. Cambridge, Mass.: Harvard University Press, 1953.

Fagin, N. Bryllion. "Eugene O'Neill," *Antioch Review*, XIV (Spring 1954), pp. 14-26.

Falk, Doris. *Eugene O'Neill and the Tragic Vision: An Interpretative Study of the Plays*. New Brunswick: Rutgers University Press, 1958.

Fergusson, Francis. "Eugene O'Neill," *Hound and Horn*, III (January-March 1930), pp. 145-60.

Flexner, Eleanor. *American Playwrights: 1918-1938*. New York: Simon and Schuster, 1938, pp. 130-97.

Gagey, Edmond McAdoo. *Revolution in American Drama*. New York: Columbia University Press, 1947, pp. 39-70.

Gassner, John. *Masters of the Drama*. New York: Dover Publications (third enlarged edition), 1954, pp. 629-61, 735-36.

———. *The Theatre in Our Times*. New York: Crown, 1954, pp. 257-66 and passim.

———. *Theatre at the Crossroads*. New York: Holt, Rinehart and Winston, 1960, pp. 66-76 and passim.

Geddes, Virgil. *The Melodramadness of Eugene O'Neill*. Brookfield, Conn.: The Brookfield Players, 1934, 44 pages.

Gelb, Arthur and Barbara. *O'Neill*. New York: Harper & Row, 1960, 1962. The complete biography of O'Neill, which may be considered definitive.

Goldberg, Isaac. *The Theatre of George Jean Nathan*. New York: Simon and Schuster, 1926, pp. 14-65.

Isaacs, Edith J. R. "Meet Eugene O'Neill," reprinted from *Theatre Arts* (October 1946) in *Theatre Arts Anthology*. New York: Theatre Arts Books, 1950, pp. 168-76.

Krutch, Joseph Wood. *American Drama Since 1918*. New York: Random House, 1939 (revised edition—New York: George Braziller, 1957), pp. 77-133.

————. *"Modernism" in the Modern Drama*. Ithaca, New York: Cornell University Press, 1953, pp. 117-20, 122-24, and passim.

Lamm, Martin. *Modern Drama*. New York: Philosophical Library, 1953, pp. 315-33.

Langner, Lawrence. *The Magic Curtain*. New York: Dutton, 1951, pp. 275-87 and passim.

Lawson, John Howard. *Theory and Technique of Playwriting*. New York: Putnam's, 1936, pp. 129-41 and passim.

McCarthy, Mary. *Sights and Spectacles*. New York: Farrar, Straus and Company, 1956, pp. 81-88.

Moses, Montrose. *The American Dramatist*. Boston: Little, Brown, 1925, pp. 415-39.

Muller, Herbert J. *The Spirit of Tragedy*. New York: Knopf, 1956, pp. 311-19.

Nathan, George Jean. *The Intimate Notebooks of George Jean Nathan*. New York: Knopf, 1932, pp. 21-38.

Norwood, Gilbert. "The Art of Eugene O'Neill," *Dalhousie Review* XXI (July 1941), pp. 143-57.

Shipley, Joseph. *The Art of Eugene O'Neill*. Seattle: University of Washington Chapbooks, 1928.

Sievers, W. David. *Freud on Broadway*. New York: Hermitage House, 1955, pp. 97-133.

Skinner, Richard Dana. *Eugene O'Neill: A Poet's Quest*. New York: Longmans, Green, 1935.

————. *Our Changing Theatre*. New York: Dial, 1931, pp. 76-96.

Winther, Sophus Keith. *Eugene O'Neill: A Critical Study*. New York: Random House, 1934.

Young, Stark. *Immortal Shadows*. New York: Scribner's, 1948, pp. 61-66, 132-39, 271-74. In Hill and Wang "Dramabook" paperback, pp. 57-62, 121-29, 247-50.

Attention may be called to other collections of essays on O'Neill: an O'Neill issue of *Modern Drama* (Vol. III, No. 3, December 1960), and the following comprehensive volume:

O'Neill and His Plays, edited by Oscar Cargill, N. Bryllion Fagin, and William J. Fisher. New York: New York Universtity Press, 1961

TWENTIETH CENTURY VIEWS

American Authors

TWENTIETH CENTURY VIEWS

European Authors